Ethics for Police Translators and Interpreters

Advances in Police Theory and Practice Series
Series Editor: Dilip K. Das

Ethics for Police Translators and Interpreters
Sedat Mulayim and Miranda Lai

Delivering Police Services Effectively
Garth den Heyer

Civilian Oversight of Police: Advancing Accountability in Law Enforcement
Tim Prenzler and Garth den Heyer

Collaborative Policing: Police, Academics, Professionals, and Communities Working Together for Education, Training, and Program Implementation
Peter C. Kratcoski and Maximilian Edelbacher

Corruption, Fraud, Organized Crime, and the Shadow Economy
Maximilian Edelbacher, Peter C. Kratcoski, and Bojan Dobovšek

Policing in Israel: Studying Crime Control, Community Policing, and Counterterrorism
Tal Jonathan-Zamir, David Weisburd, and Badi Hasisi

Policing Terrorism: Research Studies into Police Counterterrorism Investigations
David Lowe

Policing in Hong Kong: History and Reform
Kam C. Wong

Cold Cases: Evaluation Models with Follow-up Strategies for Investigators, Second Edition
James M. Adcock and Sarah L. Stein

Crime Linkage: Theory, Research, and Practice
Jessica Woodhams and Craig Bennell

Police Investigative Interviews and Interpreting: Context, Challenges, and Strategies
Sedat Mulayim, Miranda Lai, and Caroline Norma

Policing White Collar Crime: Characteristics of White Collar Criminals
Petter Gottschalk

Honor-Based Violence: Policing and Prevention
Karl Anton Roberts, Gerry Campbell, and Glen Lloyd

Policing and the Mentally Ill: International Perspectives
Duncan Chappell

Security Governance, Policing, and Local Capacity
Jan Froestad with Clifford D. Shearing

Police Performance Appraisals: A Comparative Perspective
Serdar Kenan Gul and Paul O'Connell

Los Angeles Police Department Meltdown: The Fall of the Professional-Reform Model of Policing
James Lasley

Financial Crimes: A Global Threat
Maximilian Edelbacher, Peter Kratcoski, and Michael Theil

Police Integrity Management in Australia: Global Lessons for Combating Police Misconduct
Louise Porter and Tim Prenzler

The Crime Numbers Game: Management by Manipulation
John A. Eterno and Eli B. Silverman

The International Trafficking of Human Organs: A Multidisciplinary Perspective
Leonard Territo and Rande Matteson

Police Reform in China
Kam C. Wong

Mission-Based Policing
John P. Crank, Dawn M. Irlbeck, Rebecca K. Murray, and Mark Sundermeier

The New Khaki: The Evolving Nature of Policing in India
Arvind Verma

Cold Cases: An Evaluation Model with Follow-up Strategies for Investigators
James M. Adcock and Sarah L. Stein

Policing Organized Crime: Intelligence Strategy Implementation
Petter Gottschalk

Security in Post-Conflict Africa: The Role of Nonstate Policing
Bruce Baker

Community Policing and Peacekeeping
Peter Grabosky

Community Policing: International Patterns and Comparative Perspectives
Dominique Wisler and Ihekwoaba D. Onwudiwe

Police Corruption: Preventing Misconduct and Maintaining Integrity
Tim Prenzler

Ethics for Police Translators and Interpreters

Sedat Mulayim
RMIT University
Melbourne, Australia

Miranda Lai
RMIT University
Melbourne, Australia

CRC Press is an imprint of the
Taylor & Francis Group, an **informa** business

CRC Press
Taylor & Francis Group
6000 Broken Sound Parkway NW, Suite 300
Boca Raton, FL 33487-2742

© 2017 by Taylor & Francis Group, LLC
CRC Press is an imprint of Taylor & Francis Group, an Informa business

No claim to original U.S. Government works

Printed on acid-free paper
Version Date: 20161019

International Standard Book Number-13: 978-1-4987-4650-2 (Hardback)

This book contains information obtained from authentic and highly regarded sources. Reasonable efforts have been made to publish reliable data and information, but the author and publisher cannot assume responsibility for the validity of all materials or the consequences of their use. The authors and publishers have attempted to trace the copyright holders of all material reproduced in this publication and apologize to copyright holders if permission to publish in this form has not been obtained. If any copyright material has not been acknowledged please write and let us know so we may rectify in any future reprint.

Except as permitted under U.S. Copyright Law, no part of this book may be reprinted, reproduced, transmitted, or utilized in any form by any electronic, mechanical, or other means, now known or hereafter invented, including photocopying, microfilming, and recording, or in any information storage or retrieval system, without written permission from the publishers.

For permission to photocopy or use material electronically from this work, please access www.copyright.com (http://www.copyright.com/) or contact the Copyright Clearance Center, Inc. (CCC), 222 Rosewood Drive, Danvers, MA 01923, 978-750-8400. CCC is a not-for-profit organization that provides licenses and registration for a variety of users. For organizations that have been granted a photocopy license by the CCC, a separate system of payment has been arranged.

Trademark Notice: Product or corporate names may be trademarks or registered trademarks, and are used only for identification and explanation without intent to infringe.

Library of Congress Cataloging-in-Publication Data

Names: Mulayim, Sedat, author. | Lai, Miranda, author.
Title: Ethics for police translators and interpreters / Sedat Mulayim, Mir.
Description: Boca Raton : Taylor & Francis Group, 2017. | Series: Advances in police theory and practice | Includes bibliographical references and index.
Identifiers: LCCN 2016022340 | ISBN 9781498746502
Subjects: LCSH: Interviewing in law enforcement. | Translating and interpreting--Moral and ethical aspects.
Classification: LCC HV8073.3 .M8498 2017 | DDC 174/.93632--dc23
LC record available at https://lccn.loc.gov/2016022340

Visit the Taylor & Francis Web site at
http://www.taylorandfrancis.com

and the CRC Press Web site at
http://www.crcpress.com

I dedicate this book to my dear parents, Ali and Behiye Mulayim, who raised me and my dear siblings against all odds in Turkey and my lovely family of my own in Australia – my dear wife and one and only love Arzu; my handsome, intelligent, extraordinary son Ali; and my gorgeous, calm, intelligent daughter Aylin.

Sedat Mulayim

I dedicate this book to my late mother, who has always offered me protection and guidance from high above.

Miranda Lai

Contents

Series Preface	xiii
Foreword	xvii
Prologue	xix
Acknowledgements	xxiii
Introduction	xxv
Authors	xxxvii

1 Common Ethical Theories and Approaches — 1

Introduction	1
Traditional Ethical Theories	1
Normative Ethical Theories	3
Utilitarianism	4
Deontology	6
Virtue Theory	7
Eastern Approaches to Ethical Questions	8
Contemporary Ethical Approaches	10
Applied Ethics	10
Postmodern Ethics	11
Ethics of Justice and Ethics of Care	12
Summary	13

2 What Is a Profession? — 15

Introduction	15
What Is a Profession?	16
Characteristic 1: Serving the Public Good	20
Characteristic 2: Possessing Special Knowledge and Training	22
Characteristic 3: Other People May Be Vulnerable during the Practice of the Profession	25
Trust and the Professional	27
Summary	30

3 The Profession of Interpreting and Translating — 31

Introduction	31
What Do Interpreters and Translators Do?	31

	Applying Fullinwider's Schema to Interpreters and Translators	35
	First, the Performance for the Public Good	36
	Second, Possessing Special Knowledge and Training	40
	Police Interview 1	43
	Police Interview 2	44
	Police Interview 3	44
	Lastly, Other People May Be Vulnerable as a Result of the Practice of the Professional	47
	Summary	49
4	**Professional Ethics**	**51**
	Introduction	51
	Codes of Ethics	51
	Shortcomings of Codes of Ethics	54
	Codes of Conduct	58
	Common Areas of Concern	59
	Impartiality	59
	Conflict of Interest	61
	Privacy and Confidentiality	61
	Summary	63
5	**Professional Ethics for Police Interpreters and Translators**	**65**
	Introduction	65
	The Value of the Primary or Preexisting Relationship	69
	Primary or Preexisting Relationship between Police and Suspects/Witnesses	71
	When Language Assistance Is Needed	72
	To Intervene or Not to Intervene	77
	Other Areas of Concern in Police Settings	80
	Competence	80
	Filtering, Omitting or Summarising Content	82
	Interpreter Giving Instructions or Prodding Speakers	87
	Giving Advice, Opinion or Information	88
	Inaccuracies and Distortions	93
	Impartiality	96
	Conflict of Interest	101
	Privacy and Confidentiality	103
	Summary	105

6 Compliance with Codes of Ethics: A Wicked Problem   107

Introduction   107
The Value of Moral Self-Understanding in Compliance   112
The Need for an Oath/Affirmation for Police Interpreters
and Translators   119
Use of Personality Measures in Screening for Suitability   122
Summary   125

7 Epilogue   127

Attributes of a Professional Police Interpreter and a Translator   132

References   135

Index   149

Series Preface

While the literature on police and allied subjects is growing exponentially, its impact on day-to-day policing remains small. The two worlds of research and practice of policing remain disconnected even though cooperation between the two is growing. A major reason is that the two groups speak in different languages. The research work is published in hard-to-access journals and presented in a manner that is difficult to comprehend for a lay person. On the other hand, the police practitioners tend not to mix with researchers and remain secretive about their work. Consequently, there is little dialogue between the two and almost no attempt to learn from one another. Dialogue across the globe, amongst researchers and practitioners situated in different continents, is of course even more limited.

I attempted to address this problem by starting the International Police Executive Symposium (IPES, www.ipes.info), where a common platform has brought the two together. IPES is now in its seventeenth year. The annual meetings that constitute most major annual events of the organisation have been hosted in all parts of the world. Several publications have come out of these deliberations and a new collaborative community of scholars and police officers has been created whose membership runs into several hundreds.

Another attempt was to begin a new journal, aptly called *Police Practice and Research: An International Journal* (*PPR*), that has opened the gate to practitioners to share their work and experiences. The journal has attempted to focus on issues that help bring the two on a single platform. *PPR* completed twelve years of publication in 2011. It is certainly evidence of growing collaboration between police research and practice that PPR, which began with four issues a year, expanded into five issues in its fourth year and, now, it is issued six times a year.

Clearly, these attempts, despite their success, remain limited. Conferences and journal publications do help create a body of knowledge and an association of police activists but cannot address substantial issues in depth. The limitations of time and space preclude larger discussions and more authoritative expositions that can provide stronger and broader linkages between the two worlds.

It is this realisation of the increasing dialogue between police research and practice that has encouraged many of us – my close colleagues and I connected closely with IPES and *PPR* across the world – to conceive and implement a new attempt in this direction. I am now embarking on a book series, *Advances in Police Theory and Practice*, that seeks to attract writers from all parts of the world. Further, the attempt is to find practitioner contributors. The objective is to make the series a serious contribution to our knowledge of the police as well as to improve police practices. The focus is not only on work that describes the best and successful police practices but also one that challenges current paradigms and breaks new ground to prepare police for the twenty-first century. The series seeks comparative analysis that highlights achievements in distant parts of the world as well as one that encourages an in-depth examination of specific problems confronting a particular police force.

An increasingly globalised world and mass migration of people across borders and continents has seen an unprecedented increase in the need for interpreting and translating services in policing, law enforcement and the administration of justice in general. These services are the critical link between two parties when they need to communicate but are unable to do so because of language barriers. What police interpreters and translators should or should not do within their professional role boundaries, or whether they are violating or crossing these boundaries, have significant implications. There is no or very little readily accessible information in these two areas for those seeking to clarify the role and its boundaries.

It is from these (two) angles that this book by Sedat Mulayim and Miranda Lai has been written to fill that information/knowledge gap. The book highlights the significance of pursuing a role-based ethical decision-making approach that can be applied in a whole range of policing and criminal justice settings, rather than a restrictive rule-based model. This book seeks to highlight the importance of practitioners in interpreting and translating in developing first a clear understanding of (their own) moral standards and then their application of this understanding to their professional role as a basis for decision making to resolve ethical dilemmas and to improve compliance. To do this, the book draws from traditional ethical approaches and concepts as well as extensive literature on professional ethics in policing and other mainstream professions including traditional learned professions. This book is an important contribution to this series.

It is hoped that through this series it will be possible to accelerate the process of building knowledge about policing and help bridge the gap between the two worlds – the world of police research and police practice. This is an invitation to police scholars and practitioners across the world to come and join in this venture.

Dilip K. Das, PhD
*Founding President,
International Police Executive Symposium, IPES, www.ipes.info*

*Founding Editor-in-Chief, Police Practice and Research:
An International Journal,
www.tandf.co.uk/journals*

Foreword

Police organisations are set up to enforce criminal law and protect the public from crime. One of the important activities undertaken by the police, when investigating crime, is to conduct interviews with victims, witnesses or suspects to elicit further information and to add to evidence. To most members of the public, being interviewed by the police can be a daunting experience, if not intimidating, not so much because of the image of the fluorescent light and a few officers and psychologists watching behind the one-way window perpetuated by Hollywood movies, but the strict formal procedures and highly unusual discourse. When the person being interviewed does not speak the same language in which the interview is conducted or has a hearing impairment, the services of professional interpreters and translators are called for. The addition of such a third party into the dialogue inevitably makes things more complicated and creates additional dynamics that need to be managed by all parties involved. This is especially important in police activities, which may involve interpreters and translators in highly sensitive operational contexts.

Any professional service is expected to be guided by a code of ethics. This is also true for interpreters and translators. This book not only provides a good introduction to the common themes in ethics in general, but also fills a significant gap in clarifying the role interpreters and translators play from an ethical perspective specifically in the police activities in which they are engaged. This book will therefore be a useful resource for professional interpreters and translators as well as law enforcement officers who may increasingly need interpreting and translating services in many parts of the world where societies are becoming more culturally and linguistically heterogeneous.

Although the subject matter of this book is focused on police settings, the conceptual framework proposed for ethical decision making, based on service to two parties and respecting their primary relationship, can be equally useful in other settings such as sensitive counselling sessions and formal interviews. I hope the addition of this professional resource will lead to greater interest by practitioners, researchers and academics in this highly specialised field. I congratulate the authors on this worthy endeavour.

Ray Bull
Professor of Forensic Psychology,
University of Leicester, UK

Prologue

> ....Regardless of how it is designed or presented, a code of professional ethics needs to serve to support moral understanding by connecting a profession to a moral purpose, thereby helping professionals to see their practices as 'performance for public good'.
>
> **Robert Fullinwider, 1996, p. 73**

Interpreters and translators provide a critical service where there is a language barrier between two parties who need to communicate. The interpreting and translating profession is complicated by the fact that it always takes place within another professional activity, which, in the context of this book, is policing. While many police activities are undertaken behind the scenes, many more involve contact with the public in investigations or community policing initiatives. In the United States, more than forty million citizens age sixteen or older had face-to-face contact with police in 2012 (Elliot & Pollock, 2014, p. 231). It is inevitable that in countries such as the United States where there are significant numbers of migrants as well as people who are deaf or hearing impaired, some members of the public will come into contact with police while lacking sufficient language proficiency to deal with the police. Communication in these situations is often assisted by interpreters and translators, especially in formal procedures such as interviews.

As in any other professional activity, interpreters and translators are expected to comply with codes of ethics and conduct such as impartiality and confidentiality. The fact that interpreters and translators always work within the confines of another profession brings about additional issues and ethical considerations, for example, violation of role boundaries, a situation that may not be as common in the usual work contexts of other professions. Therefore, a significant part of this book is about clarifying what the role boundaries of interpreters and translators are, or should be, and how this may impact on their decisions in a range of ethical and conduct issues.

Edmund D. Pellegrino (1991), M.D. and past director of Georgetown University Center for the Advanced Study of Ethics, posits that when people in need of help seek some expert advice or service from a professional, a relationship of trust begins immediately. In an interpreter- or translator-assisted encounter, the two parties – the police officer and the suspect/witness/victim – *trust* that the interpreter or translator will provide a competent and impartial communication service, because they make decisions based on what was interpreted or translated. We argue that fidelity of an interpreter and translator should, first and foremost, be to this trust, and any exercise of professional discretion in ethical decision making must first be guided by this trust.

Many interpreter and translator professional associations as well as organisations that employ interpreters and translators have regularly developed codes of ethics – often in bullet-point form. These codes do a great job in promoting the good standards professional interpreters and translators must practise and reminding them of undesirable acts they must avoid. A review of some codes of ethics and professional standards, primarily for the interpreting and translating profession, highlights two major shortcomings: a lack of emphasis on the interests of the service users or society at large, and a lack of the provision of an overarching principle to guide ethical decision making and the exercise of discretion in many situations that could not possibly be included in bullet-point codes. This book aims to fill this gap by proposing a role-based ethical approach, rather than a rule-based model, focusing on the needs and expectations of the beneficiaries of interpreting and translating services. We call this service-oriented interpreting and translating, within the field of policing.

Established professions from medicine and law to engineering, teaching and policing have extensive literature and scholarship on ethical issues and debates in their respective fields. This does not appear to be the case for interpreters and translators in that most scholarship appears to focus on technical and linguistic aspects of the profession, rather than on what makes those activities a profession as far as society is concerned. Abbott (1998) points to the task that must be undertaken, asserting 'to say a profession exists is to make one' (p. 81). Ethicist Robert Fullinwider (1996) holds that a profession that seeks to be recognised and accepted by society as a profession must first connect the profession to a moral purpose. This is done, according to Fullinwider, by demonstrating the need the profession directly serves for public good in its code of ethics. An understanding of the moral force behind a profession, in this case interpreting and translating within policing, can act as an overarching tool in defining the professional role boundaries, ethical decision making and promoting voluntary compliance with ethical and conduct standards.

Through an extensive cross-disciplinary literature review and analysis of case studies, we hope to provide an ethical construct to help interpreters and translators working in police settings in their ethical decision making based on professional role boundaries. This will also help to empower the interpreters and translators as a profession that directly serves a need of society. We also believe the discussions in this book will be of benefit to police officers and other law enforcement agents who work with interpreters and translators when undertaking critical tasks such as interviewing suspects or taking a statement from witnesses.

The authors believe in using plain English and a clear expression to facilitate understanding by a wider diverse readership. The issues covered in this book are not intended to be culture or language specific. Examples provided illustrate areas of concern commonly encountered across a wide range of languages in police settings.

Sedat Mulayim
Miranda Lai

Acknowledgements

The inspiration and guidance of Professor Dilip K. Das is greatly appreciated. Mavis Clifford's encouragement and tireless work in proofreading the manuscript a number of times is also acknowledged.

Introduction

> Ethics...is the study which arises from the human capacity to choose among values. That capacity is one of the distinct characteristics of human beings. Indeed, there is no human life at all, let alone a worthwhile one, without ethics!
>
> **Preston, 2014, p. 7**

Ethical questions arise from many activities in our daily private and public lives. You make an ethical choice when you place a recyclable bottle into the rubbish bin but not in the recycling bin next to it, when you tell friends about the gambling or drinking problem of a common friend or when you call in sick to take a day off when you are perfectly healthy. People affected by your ethical decisions may be other family members, close friends, clients, a stranger or the broader society. Ethical dilemmas can also include animals and nature in general. Is it okay to continue to use monkeys in scientific tests when advanced computer technology can assist with simulations and testing? Is it okay to go and watch animals forced to do tricks in a circus? Is it acceptable to waste large amounts of perfectly edible food and clean drinking water in one part of the world, when people in another part of the same world subsist on a handful of rice a day, if they are lucky?

Ethical issues can relate to organisations. These can include your employer, a public service such as the police force or a group within society. In fact, any human interaction, whether it is face to face or through the use of communication media, may give rise to some ethical issues that require a person to consider the options available and make a decision. It is not unusual to see at least one or two news stories covering incidents involving ethical issues in the media every week, if not every day. It may be about a politician or a public servant in a responsible position using his or her authority for personal gain or misusing taxpayers' money, a company executive involved in insider trading or claims of discrimination and bias in the selection or promotion process. In a recent case in Australia, the parliamentary speaker was accused of misusing $5000 of taxpayers' money by hiring a helicopter to travel from Melbourne to Geelong, 50 minutes by car, for a fundraiser for her own political party. Although she claimed everything was within the guidelines and proper, she said she agreed it was 'poor judgement'. She initially repaid the money but refused to apologise, but later apologised and finally resigned. The media scrutiny of this case revealed some other members of the parliament with similar questionable expenses. A senior minister said the problem with the system was that it relied 'too much on people' and had to be fixed. This incident demonstrated that despite written, detailed guidelines and regulations painstakingly prepared by public servants and audited by the relevant authorities within the system, ethical issues can still arise due to 'poor judgment', as not all circumstances and situations can possibly be covered in such guidelines. It also shows that ethical issues are often complex and rarely is there a clear solution. It is often not a matter of 'yes' or 'no'; rather, they are matters that are more grey than black and white (Strandberg, 2007). This is sometimes referred to as the 'it depends' option (Koehler, 2015). What this situation tells us is that, at some point, a person will need to use *discretion* in evaluating possible options and making a judgement call. The word '*discretion*', according to the *Oxford English Dictionary*, is 'freedom to choose what should be done in a particular situation'. How professionals can best use this freedom and how we can effectively influence professionals in making desirable choices are two important questions this book focuses on.

Some ethical issues may be clear cut and most people will agree on what needs to be done or avoided, such as a professional having an inappropriate relationship with a client or a government minister making a decision that will impact favourably on his or her personal wealth. Some other issues may sound trivial, such as the case of two council workers in Victoria, Australia, who were sacked for accepting free steak sandwiches from a sporting club for filling a couple of potholes in the club car park using leftover asphalt worth $2. The workers claim they served some public good, arguing '…no I don't think I did [the wrong thing], because I believe that we are a community service and that doing a little bit of hot mix that was there I believe is doing the right thing by the community' (Lauder, 2009). But the council begged to differ and argued, 'the few dollars of bitumen and a steak sandwich can melt into a lot of other things and by not doing anything at the time, the Council would have actually allowed a message to go out to the staff that this doesn't really matter'.

Some other issues may involve both ethics and criminal offences, such as bribery allegations involving government departments or representatives of foreign governments or their agencies. One recent example is the corruption charges involving Fédération Internationale de Football Association (FIFA) officials for allegedly misusing their power and making deals, in return for money, to favour one country over another in choosing countries to host the soccer world cup. Then there are the perennial ethical debates on issues such as euthanasia, abortion, use of animals in research and capital punishment, which attract a great deal of public attention. Take euthanasia, for example. Opponents will say killing a person, no matter how much he or she is suffering from a disease, is wrong, whereas proponents will say ending the life of someone is justified to end his or her suffering.

How one should behave in such situations and how his or her decisions can best be guided has been the focus of Ethics, a discipline that has been the subject of considerable debate for centuries, be it in the writings of Greek philosophers such as Plato, Socrates and Aristotle; in the holy books of the major religions; or in the moral traditions of Eastern religions and philosophy. Secular thinkers such as Immanuel Kant (1724–1804), Jeremy Bentham (1748–1832) and John Stuart Mill (1806–1873) contributed immensely to the philosophical debates in normative ethics, leading to the later development in postmodern schools of thought, and to the more contemporary branch of applied ethics.

This book starts by providing an introduction to the main ethical approaches, as they continue to provide philosophical underpinnings and inform many current approaches and debates about how one should make ethical decisions and how one explains and justifies such decisions. Consciously or unconsciously, individuals in society frequently tend to gravitate towards principles of ethics in deciding their actions in their private, professional and societal relationships; and this helps societies to function as harmoniously and productively as possible. Ethics and considerations of it are, therefore, ubiquitous in all aspects of our lives, private and public.

The conceptual construct of *profession* is the bedrock for *professional ethics*. Chapter 2 of this book, therefore, discusses what it means to be a profession, in particular, using American ethicist Robert Fullinwider's (1996) schema to identify the *defining interest* of a profession in society. Fullinwider contends that *the essential need a profession serves for public good* is the first step in professionalisation. He further argues that promoting *moral self-understanding* by a particular profession and the moral purpose a profession serves in society must be the first objectives of a code of ethics for any profession. An understanding of the *moral purpose* of a profession also serves as an overarching tool for informed ethical decision making in a range of ethical dilemmas. This is important for improving compliance with codes, as it can remind professionals of *why* they should be adhering to the standards listed in their codes.

For Hughes (2013), a profession serves a need in society not just by stating its employment field or setting or technical aspects of the professional activity, but also by making a commitment or pledge to the clients or people who benefit from its service. This means that, in our case, if you identify yourself as a professional interpreter or translator serving the communication needs between a police officer and a witness, you essentially make a commitment to these people that you have the specialised skills and knowledge to provide the language assistance needed and adhere to the ethical standards that attach to that role. This is what the two parties who need language assistance expect of you and trust you to do.

Trust plays a big role in professional practice. Pellegrino (1991) points out that when people in need of help seek some expert advice or service from a professional, *a relationship of trust* begins immediately. Although he examines this in the context of the doctor–patient relationship, the implications of such a relationship of trust is similar in most professions where people place trust in the person who possesses special skills and knowledge to find a solution to their particular problems. In this process, they assume that the professional would act with the client's best interest at heart.

For interpreters and translators, the *defining interest* and the *moral purpose* of the profession must be to serve, competently and impartially, the communication needs of two parties who need to communicate in a 'forced encounter' such as a police interview but do not share a common language. Using Pellegrino's conception, when people seek communication help so they can go about their business, they *trust* the interpreter and translator to have special skills and knowledge and to use those skills and knowledge competently and impartially to assist them with communication, not to harm them. This trust bestowed by service users must be respected by interpreters and translators. And it should be the primary consideration in their decision making to guide their eventual ethical conduct.

The communication setting in which interpreters and translators work, without exception, involves at least two parties needing language assistance in that the language barrier is an impediment for both parties, not just the one who is not proficient in the official or common language (Mulayim, Lai & Norma, 2015). In other words, these two parties have a primary or preexisting relationship in the sense that such a relationship is already there before the involvement of the interpreter or translator (Gentile, Ozolins & Vasilakakos, 1996). For example, a patient sees a doctor to seek medical advice about a persistent and severe headache. The patient expects and trusts that the doctor can help him or her with the specialised skills and knowledge the doctor possesses. Similarly, a victim or witness will be spoken to by a police officer, trusting that the officer can help him or her. This relationship between a professional and a client or a person needing his or her help is often *fiduciary* in nature. The *Merriam–Webster Dictionary* defines a *fiduciary* relationship as 'the relation existing when one person justifiably reposes confidence, faith, and reliance in one whose aid, advice, or protection is sought in some matter'. Basically, a fiduciary relationship is about confidence in someone whose specialised skills and knowledge a person needs. Similarly, according to the *Australian Law Dictionary* (2010), a fiduciary relationship is 'one in which a person is obligated, to a greater or lesser degree, to subordinate his or her own interests to the interests of another person… the vulnerability of one person in relation to another, or the existence of a reasonable expectation…'.

When an interpreter is needed in this relationship, then the two parties, in our case, a police officer and a victim/witness/suspect, trust that the interpreter will assist them both to communicate. This means a new, often fiduciary, relationship has emerged between the parties and the interpreter. Interpreters and translators may intervene in this relationship, inadvertently or deliberately, through the things they say or do. For example, acts such as filtering information, distorting meaning to help someone or failing to maintain confidentiality can have significant implications, potentially changing the original, primary or preexisting relationship between the parties. These dynamics and their impact on interpreted police interviews are discussed using case studies in Chapter 5.

It is worth drawing attention to the differences between professional ethics and personal ethics, as they can be confusing. Coady and Bloch (1996) observe that 'what is in the eye of the storm are not the ethics of private individuals so much as the ethical behaviour of groups, whether these groups are professions, businesses, government or non-government organisations' (p. 1), highlighting the fact that the focus in professional ethics is about what a profession should or should not be doing as a whole, not as private persons under a professional title. For example, it is not uncommon to hear a doctor refusing to perform an abortion based on his or her personal belief and regarding it wrong to terminate pregnancy under any circumstances – a topic attracting heated public debate. People may or may not agree with the doctor's standpoint, as long as it remains in private. The public debate starts when the doctor makes a professional decision based on his or her personal views, not as his or her professional identity requires.

Ethical considerations in private life and professional practice have different implications and consequences. This book is not about personal ethics but rather about the application of ethics in specialised areas of professions (Beauchamp & Childress, 2009). In Chapter 4, the authors explore what can and should guide professional translators and interpreters in making ethical decisions and exercising discretion in the course of practising their professions so they can minimise instances of poor judgment and uphold the respect for their profession.

Codes of ethics are set up to guide a group of people who make up a profession in a society and they may even apply across national borders, such as the Hippocratic Oath for doctors. But still, individual members of that profession interpret their standards based on the generally accepted norms or ethical standards of a particular society. Some professions, such as medicine and law, historically referred to as primary or learned professions, have developed fairly comprehensive bodies of literature on what ethics is and how it applies to their professional practice, while others, translating and interpreting being one of them, appear to treat it as a set of rules supplemented by bullet-point explanations, lacking a substantial body of literature or overarching principles or norms that the practitioners can refer to.

Some professions appear to delineate a code of ethics to express the profession's 'underlying values' (Longstaff, 1994, p. 242), while leaving the more rule-bound instructions for appropriate behaviour to a separate set of codes of conduct. Some have one but not the other, or they cover the two areas within the one code. Longstaff (1994), observing the differences between codes of ethics and codes of conduct, remarks that 'the less specific a code of ethics is, the more significant the document' (p. 242). He argues that a code of ethics demands more than mere compliance and 'it calls forth an exercise in understanding that is linked to a requirement that people exercise judgment and accept responsibility for the decisions that they make' (p. 242). This necessarily leads to the reflection of making a moral judgment, about which Rachels (1991) asserts that it

> ... must be supported by good reasons. If someone tells you that a certain action would be wrong, for example, you may ask why it would be wrong, and if there is no satisfactory answer, you may reject that advice as unfounded. In this way, moral judgments are different from mere expressions of personal preference... moral judgments require backing by reasons, and in the absence of such reasons, they are merely arbitrary. (p. 438)

A school principal would tell students, 'We must not disrupt the class', and then would add something like, 'We all need to respect other students' rights to learn in a positive learning environment and the rights of the teachers to teach'. In other words, the principal explains the moral reason behind the rule. This should work the same way in professional ethics. For example, the National Council on Interpreting in Health Care (NCIHC, USA) Code of Ethics for Interpreters in Medical Settings states that 'the interpreter limits his or her professional activity to interpreting within an encounter' (NCIHC, 2004a, p. 8). This is a standard that hardly anyone would argue against. But unless the reasons *why* an interpreter should limit his or her activity are clearly stated in the professional code, it may impede the effective promotion of a key standard such as this and impact negatively on voluntary compliance. Similarly, when we say, 'An interpreter or translator must be accurate', the first standard in almost all codes of ethics for interpreters and translators, we should also back it up with an explanation of why they have to be accurate. The moral force behind the profession of translating and interpreting needs to be clearly stated in any professional code, right at the outset, so practitioners can use it to guide their discretion and justify why they need to act in a certain way. In other words, an effective code of ethics should not just dictate what needs to be done, but also state the reasons *why* it has to be done that way. Laster and Taylor (1994) argue that 'the codes are frequently presented as sets of rules, which deny the need to debate and question ethical principles' (p. 206). For example, The International Association of Conference Interpreters (AIIC) Code of Ethics starts with

Introduction

I. Purpose and Scope

Article 1

1. This Code of Professional Ethics (hereinafter called the 'Code') lays down the standards of integrity, professionalism and confidentiality, which all members of the Association shall be bound to respect in their work as conference interpreters.
2. Candidates and precandidates shall also undertake to adhere to the provisions of this Code.
3. The Disciplinary and Disputes Committee, acting in accordance with the provisions of the Statutes, shall impose penalties for any breach of the rules of the profession as defined in this Code. (AIIC, 2012)

The Code does not mention at all what the defining interest – the direct need the members of AIIC serve for the good of society – is. In fact, in this code's entirety it hardly refers to the users or beneficiaries of the services of the association. This seeming deficiency appears to be prevalent in most codes of ethics for interpreters and translators.

The approach in this book is at times critical of the bullet-point codes of ethics, some accompanied by separate codes of conduct, that we come across in many professions, including interpreting and translating, from the point of view of achieving their supposed objectives and informing society who they are and what they do. This should not be interpreted as an all-out attack on bullet-point, rule-based codes of ethics. There is no doubt that they work well to remind practitioners of the issues and standards a particular profession considers essential in a concise form. They also play a key part in reassuring members of the public that they will be served appropriately by the members of that particular profession. In this sense, a formal code of ethical practice is viewed to be a key stage in professionalisation (Leggatt, 2010). However, if they are to move beyond technical conceptions of their profession and guide ethical decision making in a wide range of situations as real-life practice necessarily entails, practitioners in a profession must understand clearly the role they play in society and the boundaries for this role. Miller, Blackler and Alexandra (2006) highlight the importance of the profession-specific virtues to be developed and the vices to be avoided, stating that '…taking on a particular role has important implications for the way role-players should think about what they do and, indeed, for what sort of personal qualities they should develop' (p. 9). They add that the first factor in determining a role is the end it serves – similar to the defining interest as Fullinwider (1996) proposes. For example, a comedian's aim is to entertain, and a doctor's aim is to cure (Miller et al., 2006).

Preston (2014) defines professional ethics as 'the ethics of role', referring to professional role. This, in turn, highlights the relevance of examining in detail what is understood by the term 'profession' and its significance, for the purposes of ethics, of the social role a profession plays in a society. The insights of these scholars point to the potential of role-based ethics as opposed to the limitations of rule-bound codes.

In Chapter 5, the authors dissect the primary or preexisting relationship interpreters and translators work in, and discuss situations where interpreters and translators may intentionally or inadvertently intervene. Such intervention can have significant adverse effects, especially in criminal justice settings, which covers police and courts. This is why there is a tendency, or even preference, in legal settings to view interpreters and translators as a 'linguistic conduit', strictly limiting their role to linguistic transfer and nothing else. The law is regarded as a 'profession of words' (Mellinkoff, 1963, p. 140), and there has long been a mistrust of interpreters amongst the legal profession. Legal professionals are primarily concerned that interpreters may usurp the judicial function of 'interpreting' the law (Morris, 1999, pp. 25–26) during the process of transferring something spoken in another language into the language they can understand, and vice versa. The legal profession wants a truthful and complete account of what is said and how it is said, rather than an 'interpretation' of it by the interpreter. In other words, they want to hear the words straight from the horse's mouth, so to speak, or as much as practicably achievable, from the interpreter, so that they have total control of deducing, inducing, inferring, extrapolating or hypothesising from what they hear to do their job properly, rather than receiving a version of it that has already been somehow deduced, induced, inferred, extrapolated or hypothesised by the interpreter.

This is the 'conduit' model often demanded by those in the legal profession, reflecting its precise need for an unadulterated version of utterances given by the person they are dealing with. This imposition of 'conduit' role on interpreters and translators has been much criticised by predominantly translating and interpreting scholars, arguing that it depicts interpreters and translators as mere machines.

Laster and Taylor (1994) remind us, on the other hand, that the power interpreters or translators hold is often not recognised enough in the 'conduit' model, which depicts them as mere mechanical transmitters, and 'there is much to be gained from treating the interpreter in legal proceedings as a real person with power' (p. 176). They, therefore, propose the conceptualisation of a 'communication facilitator' (p. 126), which places more emphasis on interpreters' (and translators') 'more active and discretionary role' (Laster & Taylor, 1995, n.p.) in engaging in the 'cerebral, non-verbal and cultural dimensions of human interaction' (n.p). In an interpreted event, there is at least one party at any given time who does not understand what the other

Introduction   xxxiii

parties are saying (Bot, 2005), and the interpreter is often the only person who has access to the meanings of utterances made by the speakers in the primary relationship. Concurring Bot's observation, the authors contend that the power interpreters and translators hold comes from the position of trust they hold in the communicative event bestowed by the primary speakers, not from the other things they can do beyond language assistance, for example, advocacy or culture brokerage. This book examines the power interpreters and translators can wield in various police activities, both for the benefit of interpreters and translators in guiding their ethical decision making and also for the police officers they work with.

Ethical issues have always been, and continue to be, regarded as serious matters by society. This book aims to propose new ways of guiding ethical decision making by police interpreters and translators, rather than creating a new set of bullet-point standards. The objective is to 'minimise instances of poor judgment' in ethical decision making by developing an awareness of the service to the public provided by the interpreting and translating profession, and an appreciation of the trust bestowed by service users that renders the users vulnerable. This is because 'errors of judgment' cannot be eliminated totally, as they are, in most cases, largely subjective and depend on many factors such as the circumstances of a particular situation, personality, upbringing, cultural background and knowledge of the individuals making the decision.

Errors of judgment appear to be not so rare. A quick look at an Australian job-seeking website reveals that half of the top ten reasons for termination of employment are related to ethics, ahead of reasons such as unsatisfactory performance or changes to business (Doyle, n.d.). Breaches of ethics in workplaces can be misconduct, such as using company property for personal gain, or matters calling for disciplinary actions such as accepting gifts or bribes, or a conflict of interest such as awarding a contract to a relative without declaring the relation in the first place. They can also range from incidents on the lighter end of the scale such as using the office colour copier to print holiday photos or using a company car or phone for personal reasons, to the more serious scandals of embezzlement involving people at the top. As compliance, or rather noncompliance, occupies a significant part of ethical debates and features as something that many professions are grappling with, Chapter 6 is dedicated to a discussion of this very issue. An overarching framework to guide ethical decision making by interpreters and translators in a wide range of situations is proposed.

What Is Ethical Behaviour?

Although frequently seen in public discourse, ethics appears to be one of those widely debated yet often confusing notions. The Greek word *ethikos* meaning 'moral custom' is the origin of the word 'Ethics'. The *Longman Dictionary of Contemporary English* provides the following definition for ethics: 'moral rules or principles of behaviour for deciding what is right and wrong'.

Preston (2014) defines ethics as 'the study which arises from the human capacity to choose among values' (p. 7). It is concerned with 'how individuals ought to behave and suggests ways of improvement' (p. 16). Banks (2013) explains that 'essentially, ethics, in prescribing certain standards of conduct, gives us a way of making choices in situations where we are unsure how to act' (p. 5).

Ethical behaviour is, then, behaviour that 'corresponds to the accepted and idealised principles that express what is considered right and wrong conduct' (NCIHC, 2004b, p. 6). The process of choosing what ethical behaviour to follow appears to be as complicated as the ethical behaviour itself. Parsons (2001) proposes the following steps:

1. Identifying the problem
2. Defining the problem
3. Identifying a solution
4. Choosing a solution
5. Reviewing the process
6. Implementing and evaluating the decision
7. Continuing reflection

Parsons (2001) also cautions that this should not be viewed as a linear process, but one that 'weaves back and forth across the steps' (p. 185), which again requires use of discretion.

Similarly, according to Sternberg (2015, p. 219), behaving ethically involves a challenging and fairly complex process, which requires an individual to

1. Recognise that there is an event to which to react
2. Define the event as having an ethical dimension
3. Decide that the ethical dimension is of sufficient significance to merit an ethics-guided response
4. Take responsibility for generating an ethical solution to the problem
5. Figure out what abstract ethical rule(s) might apply to the problem
6. Decide how these abstract ethical rules actually apply to the problem so as to suggest a concrete solution
7. Prepare for possible repercussions of having acted in what one considers an ethical manner
8. Act

Introduction

Whether, in practice, each of these eight steps is handled as a distinct stage or a few steps are combined together, is difficult to observe. What is obvious, however, is that each step involves making a separate decision requiring use of discretion, which means things may go wrong in subsequent steps if a wrong decision is made. Things may then get more complicated. As we discussed earlier in this introduction, the fact that ethical decisions, or lack of them, are a source of ongoing public debate shows that it is not a simple matter of choosing between right and wrong in a long list of rules or options. Brazilian anthrophilosopher Valdemar W. Setzer (Samovar, Porter, McDaniel & Roy, 2015) believes this is because ethics involves not just thinking but also feelings. And often human beings are poised between equally desirable, yet ultimately incompatible courses of action when it comes to ethical conduct. The mere idea of 'ethics' in terms of indicating how one should behave carries with it a multiplicity of contexts and situations that can make it quite difficult to decide on what the best course is. There might be a debate to be had as to which set of standards or conditions might be better than another, or which criteria are more valid for the purpose of defining ethical conduct. But in the end, individuals have to decide for themselves. Further complications arise from the fact that ethics has been defined by various authors according to their understanding and experience in life. Some definitions are even influenced by the cultural and social norms of the environment in which one lives. Ethics or ethical standards are ultimately defined by the society, culture, norms, lifestyle and background of various people in varying aspects of life. What seems ethical in one society or to one person might not be ethical or acceptable to others. This is captured by the concept of *cultural relativism*, which describes how different societies or groups may end up with differing or even clashing beliefs and opinions on similar issues in our lives (Banks, 2013).

The practice of gift giving is a good example. In some cultures and traditions, offering and accepting gifts is an almost ritualistic practice. The value of the gift may symbolise the level of respect and the value of the relationship. It is not only *what* you give, it is also *why*, *how* and *when* you give it. While in some other cultures gifts are given to show you care, in others they are given to show you submit to their authority or supremacy. Gift giving in the West is turning into a complex issue. Dr. Ellen Langer, a Harvard psychology professor who has studied how gifts strengthen social ties, says that to give a really good gift, 'you must ask yourself: what do I want the gift to convey, what are the various ways to convey it, and how might I be misunderstood' (Around the World Etiquette for Gift Giving, n.d.).

Given the complexity of gift giving and different approaches in different cultures and traditions, one can ask 'can't we come up with a universal standard to apply to all?' This approach is reflected in the concept of 'Absolutism', which questions diversity of opinions and approaches to ethical behaviour and dictates that there are universal (absolute) moral truths that are above all and apply to anyone who claims to be are moral (Banks, 2013). Absolutism or universality will face challenges, however, as people will question who has the authority to set those rules and on what basis.

Mizzoni (2010) claims, that 'as rational beings, humans can control their feelings and actions, and can choose what kinds of habits they will develop' (p. 36). This then brings up the questions with which the study of ethics is concerned – how do we influence people's decision-making habits? How do we achieve compliance with codes of ethics? In light of the common areas of ethical concerns outlined in Chapter 5 for interpreters and translators working in police settings, classified under competence, impartiality, conflict of interest and confidentiality, we attempt to address how best to improve voluntary compliance in translating and interpreting in Chapter 6, before we wrap up the book by drawing conclusions in Chapter 7.

Summary

Ethics and ethical behaviour have always attracted the attention of philosophers, religious figures, academics and ordinary members of the public. They have occupied and will continue to occupy a great deal of public debate. Any human interaction may give rise to some ethical dilemmas and will require use of discretion in making a decision about how to handle the situation. Ethics is about how this decision-making process can be influenced so people make the 'right' decisions in their private, professional and societal lives, which, in turn, helps societies to function as harmoniously and productively as possible. Ethics and considerations of it are therefore ubiquitous in all aspects of our lives, in private and in public.

This book focuses on professional ethics, rather than broad debates about how one should live and behave in society. Professional ethics is essentially based on the role a profession plays in serving a need in society. This book is about the role of interpreters and translators when they operate in police and law enforcement contexts and the implications for professional ethics. The authors discuss how moral self-understanding of the professional role can act as an overarching principle in guiding ethical decision making. The fiduciary relationship that emerges during the course of providing a professional service and the trust bestowed on the interpreter or translator by the service users should serve as a guide for ethical decisions.

To unpack where this trust in a fiduciary relationship comes from and how professionals operate ethically to uphold such trust, it is both useful and appropriate to introduce traditional ethics theories and thinking that underpin current ethical approaches and debates. The classic theories form the bedrock of ethics for a wide range of professions, including police and law enforcement, and translators and interpreters, which are the focus of this book.

Authors

Dr. Sedat Mulayim was the former discipline head of the translating and interpreting programs at Royal Melbourne Institute of Technology (RMIT University), Melbourne, Australia. He sadly passed away in 2016 after a battle with cancer. He had a master of arts (translation studies) by research, and, during his illness, he completed his PhD research and received his doctorate degree in public service translation and interpreting. His research interest included police interpreting, global security issues in multilingual settings, ethics for interpreters and translators, and public service translating and interpreting.

He was a certified interpreter in the Turkish language, and he had more than 20 years of experience in interpreting in police interviews and courts. He developed and delivered training programs for interpreters in legal and police settings in Australia and overseas. He also produced resources for other professionals on how to work with interpreters.

Miranda Lai is currently a lecturer and trainer in interpreting and translating at Royal Melbourne Institute of Technology (RMIT University), Melbourne, Australia. She is undertaking her PhD research into PEACE (Preparation and planning, Engage and explain, Account, Closure, and Evaluate) police interviewing mediated by interpreters. She has developed and delivered training programs for interpreters in Australia and overseas. She is a certified interpreter and translator in the Chinese language and has many years of practice experience. Her research interests include investigative interviewing in multilingual settings, ethics for interpreters and translators and public service translation and interpreting.

Common Ethical Theories and Approaches

1

> Moral issues... are sources of deep disagreement. It is the hope of moral philosophy that we can illuminate the bases of these disagreements, and by assessing the principles on which disagreements ultimately rest, to resolve them.
>
> **Christopher Bennett, 2010, p. xiv**

Introduction

Interest in ethics and ethical behaviour has always been strong. Bennett (2010) posits that this is mainly because in a society, people feel a need or are even compelled to explain or defend their decisions to others, especially those that may have significant consequences. He further adds that 'Ethics is the study of what actions really can be defended under scrutiny' (p. xiv). This aspect has been the motivation for searching for theories or approaches that will help members of society to decide on ethical matters – decisions they will be able to defend if questioned. This chapter presents some of the commonly known traditional and current theories and approaches in the West. A brief introduction is also provided to some of the common approaches in the Eastern traditions, with a view to making the background information more diverse and allowing readers to make some comparisons.

Traditional Ethical Theories

The traditional approach to the study of ethics is essentially concerned with the question of how best to justify people's decisions or actions when they are faced with a whole range of dilemmas in everyday life. It broadly falls under three classifications: *meta-ethics*, *normative ethics* and *applied ethics* (Banks, 2013).

Meta-ethics deals with the broader abstract debate about whether morality exists, by exploring the following questions: 'Do we need to be ethical, and why?', 'Do we need morals, and why?', 'Who is to decide what moral is?' or 'What does "good" mean?' (Banks, 2013, p. 2).

Normative ethics deals with the reasoned construction of moral principles, and at its highest level determines what the fundamental principle of morality is (Kuusela, 2011). It then attempts to provide frameworks that can be used as a tool to guide our decisions in various practical dilemmas, which underscores the significance of reasoning. Banks (2013) highlights the relevance of normative ethics in the criminal justice system:

> Normative ethics is fundamental to ethical decision making in the criminal justice system. A central notion in normative ethics is that one's conduct must take into account moral issues; that is one should act morally, using reason to decide the proper way of conducting oneself. (p. 5)

Applied ethics, on the other hand, is 'the art or science of reflecting on moral dilemmas and moral problems in different social contexts' (Collste, 2012, p. 18). These social contexts can range from business, politics and medicine, to particular problems, such as abortion (Childress, 1986) or the use of animals in experiments.

We highlighted in the Introduction to this book that these ethical approaches can relate to any situation in which a moral judgement needs to be made. They are not specifically framed for professional practice settings. Even if they were, as some of these approaches are centuries old, some of the applications in today's very different world of professional practice would be hard to justify. Although this book is concerned primarily with professional ethics, an overview of these approaches is warranted for interpreters and translators and law enforcement officers in the context of this book, as traditional ethical theories have shaped many values and expectations in society (Houser, Wilczenski & Ham, 2006), regardless of whether in private or professional contexts. If we try to locate professional ethics in the traditional ethics studies, it falls under the domain of applied ethics in that it serves as a response to moral problems facing professionals in their work (Collste, 2012).

Before we delve into the traditional ethical approaches, it is worthwhile pointing out that the terms 'ethics' and 'morality' are often used interchangeably by laypersons. They are different concepts, although they do share overlapping spheres (Muraskin, 2001). Both ethics and morality deal with human relationships – how human beings treat each other to promote mutual welfare, growth, creativity and meaning – as they strive for good over bad, and right over wrong (Muraskin, 2001; Thiroux & Krasemann, 2007). According to Muraskin (2001), morality is 'conduct that is related to integrity' (p. 2), and it is 'a practice of these [what is considered right and good] principles on a regular basis, culminating in a moral life' (p. 2). Thompson, Melia, Boyd and Horsburgh's (2006) interpretation of morals and morality, however, refers to the domain of personal values and the rules of behaviour regulating social interactions. From a different perspective,

Common Ethical Theories and Approaches

Alexandra and Miller (2010, p. 1) contend that morality is about minimum standards of behaviour and attitude. For example, do not kill the innocent, do not tell lies, do not steal. These are minimum standards of behaviour, or moral principles most people would agree on. Ethics, on the other hand, goes further than minimum standards; it is a wider notion that involves ideals and aspirations to be attained. Such a distinction echoes Weiss's (1942) view that 'a man is moral if he conforms to the established practice and customs of the group in which he is. He is ethical if he voluntarily obliges himself to live in the light of an ideal good' (p. 381).

In addition, when referring to ethics and ethical debates in our private and public lives within society, unavoidably terms such as 'ethical dilemmas' and 'ethical issues' used by laypeople come up frequently. It is helpful to explain that an ethical dilemma 'is the responsibility of an individual and requires a decision to be made "by the person"' (Banks, 2013, p. 12), whereas an ethical issue usually relates to 'public policy involving ethical questions' (p. 12) such as capital punishment or the availability of euthanasia, and issues involving consideration of morality. An ethical issue does not require most individuals to make immediate decisions. But it does not mean that individuals are helpless to influence these debates on social issues (p. 12), and sometimes, individuals' views on these ethical issues may change with time; for example, someone may change his or her mind regarding euthanasia because of a personal life experience involving loved ones suffering from a difficult medical condition.

Normative Ethical Theories

Theories that set out to equip people with a means of working out how to act in a given situation or dilemma involving morality in private and public contexts is part of what is called 'normative ethics'. *Normative ethics* are generally classified based on whether they consider the consequences of an action in making an ethical decision (*Consequentialism*) or not (*Non-Consequentialism*) (Banks, 2014). Normative ethics regards all acts as having three things that might be relevant to the consideration of morality: first, the person who performs the act – the agent; second, the act itself; and third, the consequences of the act. As a result, three types of normative ethical theory have emerged – virtue ethics (corresponding to the agent of the act, that is, the person), deontology (corresponding to the act itself, therefore non-consequentialist) and consequentialism (corresponding to the consequences of the act) (Moral Philosophy, n.d.).

Consequentialist ethics, represented by utilitarianism, does not consider the actions taken or whether the actions are right or wrong in themselves; it only looks at the end result – the consequence(s). In contrast, *deontological ethics* is a non-consequentialist approach, which concentrates on the act we perform, regarding certain types of act as being intrinsically good or bad. In other words, an ethical decision or action must be taken out of duty, not out of discretion; otherwise it is meaningless (Moral Philosophy, n.d.). *Virtue ethics*, as opposed to the previous two, focuses on the moral character of the agent, rejecting the previous consequentialist and non-consequentialist approaches, and proposes that ethical standards come from a combination of human nature and society. *Virtue ethics* advocates that we should strive to exhibit desirable character traits such as courage, generosity, compassion and so on in our actions (Moral Philosophy, n.d.).

Let us now examine each of these approaches of normative ethics in more detail, which will be helpful to anchor abstract philosophical ideas in tangible and practical terms for our later discussions of professional ethics.

Utilitarianism

Perhaps the most widely known Consequentialist approach is *Utilitarianism*, which can be found in many of the decisions and practices utilised in everyday life (Houser et al., 2006). The term comes from the Latin *utilis*, meaning 'useful', and is an ethical philosophical doctrine according to which an action can be judged as 'good' or 'right' if it is going to increase human pleasure or happiness. It is most notably represented by the works of philosopher and theorist Jeremy Bentham. In his *An Introduction to the Principles of Morals and Legislation* (1789), Bentham described *utility* as that which minimises the pain and maximises the pleasure. Thus, good actions will be those producing pleasure both for the individual and the group, while, on the other hand, bad actions are those that reduce or prevent pleasure. This principle is called the 'utility principle'. Utility then becomes a tool to quantify the pleasure produced by an action. Consequently, when facing a moral dilemma, our duty is to carry out an action that has consequences that can be measured in terms of the greatest possible amount of good rather than evil for the most people.

Mizzoni (2010) explains utilitarian thinking to be the way we care about the consequences of our actions on others.

> We consider whether our action will contribute to their good feelings; we consider whether our actions will contribute to their suffering. In other words, we think about the usefulness, or utility, of a particular action on our feelings and others' feelings. (p. 89)

The guiding principle of utilitarianism is that 'one ought always to do whatever will have the most utility for all concerned' (Mizzoni, 2010, p. 89). Considerations about the morality of the act have no relevance. For example, according to this theory, capital punishment for a drug trafficker or a serial killer can be justified, as it would be for the benefit of more people in their

Common Ethical Theories and Approaches 5

society. Again, according to a strict interpretation of this approach, even the murder of someone who has done evil deeds can be considered 'right' if it results in the greatest net utility for a group or community. These examples point to the focus on the end results, that is, the consequences of an action, in deciding whether it is the right thing to do or not.

Elliot and Pollock (2014) point out the shortcomings of Utilitarian thinking, arguing 'Utilitarian logic relies on the erroneous belief that one can predict the outcome of a given course of action, a belief wholly void of empirical support' (p. 247). If a person strictly applies the utility principle in everything he or she does, then his or her own well-being or the well-being of his or her family may need to be sacrificed at the expense of making others happier. This nondiscriminant approach to handling matters in our lives may not be as ideal and may lead to problems. One common example is that of a disruptive student in a classroom and how this should be handled. One action can be to remove this child from the classroom for the benefit of others in the room and justify this decision ethically by arguing that this action brings 'the greatest happiness to the greatest number of people', the maxim of this approach. Such ethical justification would not give much consideration to whether this student should be helped in the school so that he or she could be integrated into the school community.

Consider another well-known example proposed by Colby, Gibbs, Kohlberg, Speicher-Dubin and Candee (1979), which demonstrates how a utilitarian approach itself may lead to justification of different outcomes:

> In Europe, a woman was near death from a special kind of cancer. There was one drug that the doctors thought might save her. It was a form of radium that a druggist in the same town had recently discovered. The drug was expensive to make, but the druggist was charging ten times what the drug cost him to make. He paid $200 for the radium and charged $2,000 for a small dose of the drug. The sick woman's husband, Heinz, went to everyone he knew to borrow the money, but he could only get together about $1,000, which is half of what it cost. He told the druggist that his wife was dying, and asked him to sell it cheaper or let him pay later. But the druggist said, 'No, I discovered the drug and I'm going to make money from it'. So Heinz got desperate and considered breaking into the man's store to steal the drug for his wife. (p. 1)

In this scenario, a strict application of utilitarian principle 'greatest amount of happiness for the greatest number of people' (Bentham, 1976/1988) with a focus on the consequences of an action, rather than the action itself, would mean that the act of stealing would have to be considered ethical, as more people would be happy (Heinz and his wife) as a result of the theft. However, the act of stealing is illegal in their society and if one focuses on the action, not on its consequences, then in this case the act of stealing would have been unethical and also illegal, regardless of whether it saves his wife or not.

Deontology

Deontological or non-consequentialist ethics argues the opposite of the consequentialist philosophy that we have outlined in the previous section. Deontology originates from the Greek word *deon*, meaning 'duty', and *logos*, meaning literally, 'word', but we extend that to mean the science or the study of. It is largely based on the ideas of German philosopher Immanuel Kant (1724–1804), who laid out the theory of 'duty' as a moral force in *Groundwork for the Metaphysics of Morals* (Kant, 1785/1998). His goal was to establish a moral system that did not rely on the use of discretion of people but on strict duties that have been agreed on by everyone and are not subject to individual interpretations.

This approach, then, requires the creation of universal moral laws that everyone strictly follows and applies consistently (Alexandra & Miller, 2009). According to this theory, ethical action means fulfilling one's duties. Kant proposed the principle of *categorical imperative*, which requires one to act according to the following imperatives:

1. Act so that you can will the maxim of your action to become a universal law.
2. Act so as never to treat another rational being merely as a means. (Kolb, 2008, p. 1436)

One of the examples provided by Kant himself to describe the process of making a decision is whether breaking a promise is the right thing to do:

1. First determine what maxim (rule) you would be following (e.g. I can break a promise because I feel like it).
2. Second, ask yourself, would I want this universally applied across the whole of society?

If you find that you would not want to see everyone break their promises, then you should not break your promises either. If you decide that everyone should act this way all the time, that is, people should never break their promises, then your action is moral.

The main criticism for this approach is that it does not allow for circumstances (Mizzoni, 2010). In this approach, there is no room for 'ifs or buts' or 'how abouts'. For example, even if a person is terminally ill and is suffering, euthanasia would never, in deontological ethics, be an option, as it is our duty to prevent the death of someone at all costs.

Mizzoni (2010, p. 153) gives the story of Stanley 'Tookie' Williams to demonstrate how utilitarian ethics and deontological ethics can lead to different actions in the same case. The story is: Stanley 'Tookie' Williams was the co-founder of the Crips gang and the state sentenced him to death for being involved in several murders. While he was on death row, Williams started writing educational anti-gang books for young people and those books seemed to have an impact on children's lives. When the time came for his execution, some people asserted that because he killed four people in the past, and he knew it was wrong, he therefore deserved death. This is the deontological approach. Others argued that because he was writing books that potentially helped to save more lives than the four he ended, he should not be executed. This is the utilitarian approach.

Virtue Theory

A major approach that does not give much consideration to the consequences of actions or actions themselves is Virtue Theory. This approach does not fall under either consequentialist or non-consequentialist theories. It is best represented in the question, 'How best is it to live?' posed by Greek philosophers such as Plato and Aristotle (Ryan, 2001, p. 25). They answer the question by explaining ethical actions through the combination of human character, practical judgement and orientation towards human well-being. Virtue ethics is therefore concerned with virtues and moral character. Many philosophers believe that morality consists of following precisely defined rules of conduct, such as 'don't kill' or 'don't steal'. Virtue ethics places less emphasis on the structured learning of rules and examining consequences. The emphasis is on developing oneself as a good person overall by acquiring the essential virtues. The assumption is if you are a good person overall, your ethical decisions will also be good, unlike deontological ethics, where the imperative is to do what is right (Banks, 2014, p. 290). Aristotle lists the following essential virtues:

Benevolence	Industriousness
Civility	Justice
Conscientiousness	Loyalty
Cooperativeness	Moderation
Courage	Reasonableness
Courteousness	Self-confidence
Dependability	Self-control
Fairness	Self-discipline
Friendliness	Self-reliance
Generosity	Tactfulness
Honesty	Tolerance (Rachels, 1999, p. 178)

According to Aristotle (Banks, 2014, p. 290), moral virtues are manifested in habits and these can be acquired only through practice and consistency. You are not born with them. If someone, for example, practises tolerance in dealing with people at work persistently and displays tolerance consistently in various situations and at different times, then he or she can be said to have the virtue of tolerance. Virtue Theory, often criticised for being too idealistic to offer any real help with practical dilemmas, appears to have made a comeback. Modern ethics philosophers appear to have drawn on some of the virtue concepts, albeit asking a slightly different question: 'What should I do?', shifting their attention from the self to the action, in attempting to solve moral and ethical dilemmas in today's world. Hence, ethics should be more than how to act in certain dilemmas. It should be about how we should live our lives. The two questions to consider in trying to solve and assess moral and ethical dilemmas are: 'How should I be?' and 'What should I do?' (Ryan, 2001, p. 29). According to this approach, good people with good virtues (habits) are good practitioners!

Critics will argue that this approach offers no real guidance in the everyday situations of ethical dilemmas. Ryan (2001) recognises that 'Virtue ethics correctly points out that most of the time we do not face difficult ethical quandaries and that a preoccupation with techniques for solving those quandaries is misguided' (p. 29). He also points to the fact that there will be situations in which one will need a technique or tool to decide what to do, which will mean that we need to consider obligations and consequences, not just virtues. Benn (1998) argues that one of the fundamental shortcomings of the Virtue approach is that 'we cannot eliminate the idea of right and wrong conduct, replace it with virtue concepts, to do with good and bad character' (p. 169). However, in its current application, Benn (1998, p. 171) contends that virtue theory exists in the idea of integrity – a virtue – which appears in many current codes of ethics.

Eastern Approaches to Ethical Questions

Ethical approaches originating from the Far East have guided millions of people in their ethical decision making in the past and continue to do so today. A brief introduction to some of the main philosophical concepts and approaches may help professionals working in increasingly diverse and challenging settings to make informed decisions as well as to understand the decisions and actions of others who have adopted their approaches from these theories.

The four main Eastern theories and philosophical approaches most commonly referred to are Confucianism, Taoism, Hinduism and Buddhism (Shanahan & Wang, 2003; Houser et al., 2006). Overall, these approaches tend to highlight the need to find a balance between available options, rather than committing to a set rule, although they seem to point to different virtues in doing so.

Common Ethical Theories and Approaches

Confucianism, originating from the ideas and experiences of Kong Fuzi (Master Kong), around about 551–479 BCE, is similar to the philosophical approaches of Greek philosophers, centring on the importance of developing good virtues as a good human being, but places more emphasis on obligations to others (Houser et al., 2006). Smith (1991) lists the major concepts of Confucianism as *Li* and *Ren*. *Li* refers to *standards of acceptable social behaviour* manifested through manners, rituals and etiquette; it is acquired primarily through observation of exemplary behaviour. It emphasises 'seeking *the mean (chun yung) or the middle way* or balance of extremes' (Smith, 1991, p. 58) in making a decision. *Ren*, on the other hand, highlights respect towards others, being good and benevolent. And it requires one to make an effort to make decisions or act in a way that is essentially based on respect for others.

Taoism, also from China and also dating from 500 BCE, emerged, some authors argue, in response to a critical view of the Confucian approach to intervention in the natural development of human nature (Kohn, 2001). Based on the teachings of Laozi, the main concepts in Taoism include *Tao* (desirable way or path), *yin–yang* (balancing opposites such as weaker–stronger, negative and positive), *the harmony of opposites* and *relativity* (relativity is discovery through examining the opposite and the significance of context in making judgments), and *wu wei* (non-action, not doing anything that will disrupt the normal or natural course of events) (Houser et al., 2006, p. 61). One of the most relevant approaches of Taoism to ethics is in the idea that 'there are no absolutes, but everything is relative including morals and ethics' (p. 62) and the control of the 'seven perversions of emotions, joy, happiness, anger, sadness, love, hate and desires' in making decisions (p. 63).

Buddhism is a religion and philosophy in the East, and increasingly in the West. It emerged from the teachings and life experiences of Gautama (Buddha – the enlightened one) in around 563–483 BCE. Buddha identified humanity's fundamental realities as suffering (human life involves pain), impermanence (the transitory and ever changing nature of humans) and no-self (unselfishness) (Houser et al., 2006, p. 73). The Buddhist goal is to reach *Nirvana* (salvation) by following the *Noble Eightfold Path*, consisting of *Wisdom* (Right Understanding, Right Thought), *Morality* (Right Speech, Right action, Right livelihood) and *Meditation* (Right effort, Right mindfulness, Right Concentration). Following this path is the means to acquiring 'the knowledge of *the middle way*, and thus to *avoid extremes* in order to escape the continuous cycle of birth, suffering and death' (p. 75). One of the most relevant steps in the *Noble Eightfold Path* of Buddhism for professional ethical practice is probably in 'Right livelihood, a worthwhile job or way of life, which avoids causing harm or injustice to other beings' (p. 75). This is similar to the concept that underpins medical ethics and increasingly is found in many other modern professions in the form of *help and do not harm*.

Hinduism, dating back to 2500 BCE, is another Eastern tradition concerned with the quest for a moral life and the principles by which that goal is attained. Hindu ethics prescribes behaviour for a spiritual life (Houser et al., 2006, p. 66). This is where it differs from secular ethical concepts such as Utilitarianism, which aims at obtaining the greatest good for society (p. 67). Ethical decision making in Hinduism requires one to determine the most pressing *dharma* (virtue, duty and righteousness) in each context and make a moral judgement about what to do under those circumstances (p. 68). Hindu ethics is subjective and personal, with the goal to purify the mind of greed and selfishness to attain perfection. The emphasis on the role of personality over the action to be taken is similar to the approach in virtue ethics, which dates back to Aristotle (Simpson, 1997). Hindu concepts such as serving others and kindness and tolerance in all human relations have relevance for professional ethics even in modern times.

Contemporary Ethical Approaches

The traditional theories outlined in the preceding sections continue to inform many current debates and theories of ethics to do with our lives, both in private and public spheres. This section briefly introduces the more recent developments in ethical approaches and some of the more notable contemporary theories.

Applied Ethics

As opposed to normative ethics, which is concerned with broad philosophical issues, applied ethics, according to Collste's (2012) delineation, is an academic discipline analysing moral problems in different social arenas. James Childress (1986), one of the most influential philosophers in the field of applied ethics, defined applied ethics as the application of ethics to special arenas of human activity, such as business, politics and medicine. In Kuusela's (2011) view, applied ethics is concerned with the analysis of specific, controversial moral issues such as abortion, animal rights or euthanasia. In recent years applied ethical issues have been subdivided into convenient groups such as medical ethics, business ethics, environmental ethics and sexual ethics. Beauchamp and Childress (2001, p. 12) proposed four principles for biomedical ethics to highlight the values behind ethical rules:

- Respect for autonomy (respecting the decision-making capacities of autonomous persons)
- Nonmaleficence (avoiding the causation of harm)

Common Ethical Theories and Approaches

- Beneficence (providing benefits and balancing benefits against risks and costs)
- Justice (distributing benefits, risks and costs fairly)

These four values, which represent commitments by the professionals, have also been inspirational in other fields. Most service-oriented professions will highlight respect for their clients, providing a professional service that will be of benefit to the clients and be fair and just in service delivery. Professional ethics, the focus of this book, as it is mainly concerned with the response to moral problems facing professionals in their work, also falls under applied ethics. This is discussed in detail in Chapter 4.

Postmodern Ethics

While the three traditional ethical approaches are well known and frequently utilised in ethical debates, Polish sociologist Zygmunt Bauman argued that the challenges resulting from the use of advanced technology and employment structures increased insecurity and uncertainty in postmodern times. These insecurities mean there will be ethical dilemmas that traditional theories cannot resolve (MacVean & Neyroud, 2012). Examples of the new challenges in postmodern times are actions or decisions by teams or committees where it is hard to pinpoint where the moral responsibility lies, or for example, decisions and actions in attacks by drones where the decision maker, implementer and consequences are separated by time and space.

The underlying concepts of Bauman's 'postmodern ethics' include the following:

- People are neither 'good' nor 'bad'; they are morally ambivalent. No single, logically coherent code will fit this.
- Moral phenomena are inherently nonrational and do not fit utility or rules that presume one right choice.
- Most moral choices are ambiguous and any 'moral' approach taken to extremes will produce an immoral result.
- Morality is not universal; one single imposed moral code is immoral.
- Morality is irrational. This irrationality can be demonstrated in the conflict between personal autonomy and the community. (MacVean & Neyroud, 2012, p. 10)

Some of the practical approaches discussed in Bauman's ideas and the criticism of traditional approaches are also shared in applied ethics.

Ethics of Justice and Ethics of Care

A more recent development in the field of normative ethics arose in the second half of the twentieth century, among which the ethics of justice and the ethics of care have been prominent. Both have been adopted and debated particularly in the 'helping professions' such as medicine, nursing, social work and teaching.

The ethics of justice refers to 'an ethical perspective in terms of which ethical decisions are made on the basis of universal principles and rules, and in an impartial and verifiable manner with a view to ensuring the fair and equitable treatment of all people' (Botes, 2000, p. 1072); the ethics of care, on the other hand, 'constitutes an ethical approach in terms of which involvement, harmonious relations and the needs of others play an important part in ethical decision making in each ethical situation' (p. 1072). West (1997) argues the ethics of care should be the moral guiding principle in the judicial system to balance the need to dispense justice and compassion. According to Brook (1987, p. 370), the principal aim of the ethics of justice is to ensure fair and equitable treatment of all people. By making verifiable and reliable decisions based on universal rules and principles, the agents who subscribe to the ethics of justice constantly endeavour to let justice prevail by making decisions (Brabeck, 1993, p. 35). To enable objective decision making about ethics, the individual acts in the capacity of an autonomous, objective and impartial agent (Edwards, 1996, p. 80). Conversely, the person who subscribes to the ethics of care fulfils the needs of the people in the ethical situation and in this way maintains harmonious relations (Gilligan, Ward & Taylor, 1994, p. xxi). Care, therefore, implies that ethical decisions are taken in an attempt to fulfil the needs of others and to maintain harmonious relations. In the context of each unique ethical situation, the agent is involved and empathetic towards every other role-player.

The 'justice' and 'care' ethical approaches should not be interpreted as one being more humane or appropriate than the other. Rather, these are used as a means to conceptualise tendencies in moral reasoning in society (Klingberg-Allvin, Tam, Nga, Ransjo-Arvidson & Johansson, 2007, p. 43). From concept analysis, Botes (2000, p. 1072) identifies the following four attributes of the ethics of justice:

1. Fairness and equality
2. Verifiable and reliable decision making based on universal rules and principles
3. Autonomy, objectivity and impartiality
4. Positivistic rationality

Common Ethical Theories and Approaches

And the defining attributes of the ethics of care are (Botes, 2000):

1. Care
2. Involvement, empathy and maintaining harmonious relations
3. Holistic, contextual and need-centred nature
4. Extended communicative rationality

Considering these two sets of polarised attributes, if the helping professions were to use only one of these two approaches in their ethical decision making, most likely certain ethical dilemmas would not be resolved. When making ethical decisions, blindly obeying the rules and regulations in an attempt to achieve fairness and equity is as dangerous as relying solely on one's emotions and urges in providing care. A better solution is to apply rules coupled with care, thus effecting a complementary application of the ethics of justice and the ethics of care (Loewy, 1996, p. 32; Edwards, 1996, p. 154). Flanagan and Jackson (1987, p. 626) echo this approach by concluding that there is no logical reason preventing anyone from using both sets of ethics in the process of ethical decision making related to ethical conundrums.

Summary

How one should decide what is the best thing to do in a range of ethical dilemmas has been the concern of ethics, a discipline that has occupied human thought and debates for centuries. This chapter introduced traditional theories of ethics as well as current approaches that continue to inform debates on ethical decisions. The chapter started with normative ethics, which seeks to equip people with a means of working out how to act in a given situation or dilemma involving morality in private and public contexts. *Normative ethics* are generally classified based on whether they consider the consequences of an action in making an ethical decision (*Consequentialism*) or not (*Non-Consequentialism*). Three types of normative ethical theory have emerged: utilitarian (consequentialist), deontological (non-consequentialist) and virtue ethics.

Ethics is obviously not just a Western concern. In many parts of the world, people make decisions in the society in which they live and justify these decisions. After an introduction to the traditional theories, an overview of some of the well-known Eastern traditions and beliefs was provided, offering a glimpse of how Eastern principles have informed and guided ethical decision making by people in Asia since ancient times.

The chapter then moves on to an introduction to the more recent approaches. *Applied ethics* is concerned with particular social arenas such as business, politics and medicine and with particular issues such as abortions or the use of animals in experiments; *postmodern ethics*, on the other hand, questions some of the traditional approaches. The chapter finishes with an introduction to the *ethics of justice* and the *ethics of care*; the former focuses on the fair and equitable treatment of all people, and the latter on the maintenance of harmonious relations while fulfilling people's needs. How to achieve a balance between the two has been the centre of inquiry for proponents of these approaches.

What Is a Profession?

2

...professionals process to know better than others the nature of certain matters, and to know better than their clients what ails them or their affairs.
Everett Hughes, in Wueste, 1994, p. 7

Introduction

The previous chapter presented an overview of some of the traditional Western ethical theories and approaches such as utilitarianism, deontology and virtue theory. These theories have not only informed but also continue to inform, in modern times, ethical behaviour and considerations in private and public spheres. We also briefly introduced some more current approaches such as the *ethics of justice* and the *ethics of care*, the supporters of which advocate the need to strike a balance between the need to treat others with fairness and equity on the one hand, and with empathy and compassion on the other.

These theories and approaches have informed and guided the development of professional ethics. Most prominent professions in society such as medicine, law, psychology and policing have examined how these theories may apply, or if they apply at all, in various ethical dilemmas in their respective professions. For example, can a doctor justify assisting someone who is suffering from a condition that cannot be helped and would rather die, using a utilitarian approach? Or should the patient be treated until his last moment, regardless of how futile it is, using a deontological approach? Or can a police officer use a child as an informant, because this will be of benefit for a larger section of the society? It is, therefore, without question that an understanding of these underpinning theories is highly desirable for all professions.

As this book focuses on professional ethics for interpreters and translators working in a very important field – policing and law enforcement – this chapter starts with a discussion of the essential question of what is meant by 'profession' and how it should be defined. We consider this critical because any study of professional ethics must first start with the identification of the role played by a particular profession in the society in which it operates. Ultimately, the question of whether something is appropriate or not in any professional practice will have to be judged by its relevance to the professional's role in a particular situation. This is also important for police interpreters and translators, as many activities in policing increasingly involve people with language barriers, resulting in the need for language assistance. In many formal activities, such as a police interview, this language assistance needs to be provided by an interpreter or a translator.

What Is a Profession?

A quick review of literature shows there are as many definitions of what a profession is as there are professions. Dictionaries provide a number of definitions of the word.

The *Cambridge Dictionary* defines profession as 'the type of work that needs special training or a particular skill, often one that is respected because it involves a high level of education'.

The *Collins Dictionary* defines it as 'an occupation requiring special training in the liberal arts or sciences, especially one of the three learned professions, law, theology or medicine'.

These definitions highlight one key quality in a profession – that it refers to specialised training and skills. Webb and Webb (1917) concur that 'a profession can be defined as a vocation founded upon specialised and extensive educational training' (as cited in MacVean & Neyroud, 2012, p. 19). Such a definition seems unable to explain why a car mechanic, who also has to go through extensive training and apprenticeship and, as a result, possesses specialised knowledge about cars is unlikely to be regarded as a professional in the traditional sense (Sokolowski, 1991, p. 26). Sokolowski suggests that one reason may be that when we go to a car mechanic, all we entrust to this person is the car. However, when we approach a professional, we subject something more than a possession to the professional's expertise – we hand over the steering of our life to this professional, because we are unable to do this by ourselves in this particular matter. Therefore, in this sense, we hand over not just one of our things, but also our choices and activities themselves (p. 27). In other words, the professional deals not merely with our possessions *but with us*. In this sense, Barber (1963) provides more guidance on when an occupation is to be considered a profession by pointing out four necessary features:

1. General and systematic knowledge
2. Orientation towards community interest and well-being
3. Self-monitoring through internalised codes of ethics
4. Rewards that symbolise accomplishments in work that are sought as ends in themselves

What Is a Profession?   17

O'Day (2000) lists only three professions – medicine, law and clergy – as existing in the Middle Ages. Since then, however, professions have undergone and continue to be faced with significant changes in the composition of their practitioners, their activities and the way they are practiced and regulated both by self-regulation by the industry and through acts/regulations. Most importantly, they face changes in the way they are questioned and are held more and more accountable by the people they serve. Professions continue to hold a special and privileged place in society, partly owing to 'the quasi-monopolies they have over core services, often sustained through exclusive licensing' (Freidson, 1986, p. 1991). The three 'learned' professions listed previously maintained a monopoly on professional status and privileges associated with this monopoly for centuries (O'Day, 2000). However, modern times have witnessed many occupations becoming sufficiently specialised to claim professional status and hold a certain monopoly (Scanlon, 2011, p. 2), which, to some, is what partly constitutes a profession (MacVean & Neyroud, 2012). Patten (2003) contends that public perception is probably the most important characteristic of a profession and quotes Lord Justice DuParq in *Carr vs. IRC*:

> It seems to me to be very dangerous to try to define the word 'profession'. I think that everybody would agree that before one can say a man is carrying on a profession, one must see that he has some special skill or ability or some special qualification derived from training or experience. Even then one has to be very careful, because there are many people whose work demands great skill and ability and long experience and many qualifications who would not be said by anybody to be carrying on a profession. Ultimately one has to ask this question: Would the ordinary man, the ordinary reasonable man… say now, in the time in which we live, of any particular occupation, that it is properly described as a profession? Times have changed. There are professions today which nobody would have considered to be professions in times past. Our forefathers restricted the professions to a very small number; the work of the surgeon used to be carried out by a barber, whom nobody would have considered a professional man. The profession of chartered accountant has grown up in comparatively recent times, and other trades, or vocations…may in future years acquire the status of professionals. (p. 2)

Various authors have attempted to list different characteristics of a profession. Cheetham and Chivers (2005) believe that a profession

- Confers status within society
- Organises itself into some sort of professional body
- Is learned – that is, requires prolonged and specialised training and education
- Is altruistic (orientated towards service rather than profit)

- Offers autonomy within the job role
- Is informed by an ethical code of some kind
- Is noncommercial
- Has collective influence within society
- Is self-regulatory
- Is collegial
- Is client-focused (p. 20)

Similarly, Lord Benson (1992) provides a comprehensive nine-point definition of a profession, giving prominence to the necessity of a governing body that suppresses members' selfish private interests, sets conditions of entry and standards of education and takes disciplinary actions when called for. For the members, Lord Benson stresses the quality of being independent in thought and outlook, as well as being willing to speak their minds without fear or favour. For the public they serve, he highlights the need for protection rather than exploitation.

Preston (2014) identifies the following criteria for the label of profession: 'a certain status in the community, a university level professional preparation, a professional association and code of ethics; recognition of a trust on behalf of clients seeking specific services' (p. 158). Preston points to the service orientation of professions, and the trust required between a professional and a client. We, first, need to understand how 'a certain status (for a profession) in the community' develops. What makes society think that a certain activity is a professional activity in the same way as it considers the traditional learned professions of medicine and law?

Andrew Abbott (1988) claims 'a profession is not "objectively" definable precisely because of its power and importance in our culture' (p. 318) and at best, he says, professions can be loosely defined as 'exclusive occupational groups applying somewhat abstract knowledge to particular cases' (p. 318).

A similar view is expressed by Langford (1978): 'It is an important part of the idea of a profession that its members, although acting as principals, nevertheless act, in their professional capacities, in the interests of others' (p. 15). Langford further asserts that core professional services provided to others, such as doctors treating people or teachers educating children, distinguish members of a profession from others. Continuing the theme of emphasising service to society, Lieberman (1956) lists the following characteristics of a profession:

1. A unique and essential social service
2. An emphasis on intellectual techniques in performing its service

3. A long period of specialised training
4. Autonomy for the individual practitioners and the occupational group as a whole
5. Acceptance of personal responsibility for actions performed within the scope of individual autonomy
6. An emphasis on the service rendered rather than the economic benefit to the practitioner
7. A self-governing organisation of practitioners
8. A code of ethics

A member of a profession is referred to as a professional. According to Cruess, Johnston and Cruess (2004), professionals profess their commitment to competence, integrity and morality, altruism and the promotion of the public good within their expert domain; furthermore, professionals are accountable to those served and to society. Although the various aforementioned definitions describe the universal features of professions, it is when it comes to how a profession is practised by individuals that variations appear. For example, in the case of police officers, MacVean and Neyroud (2012, p. 41) quote Reiner's (1978) four types of policing styles, based on how each individual dealt with the same or similar situations:

- The Uniform Carrier – this officer is lazy, disillusioned and cynical.
- The New Centurion – this officer believes that the role of the police is crime-fighting and maintaining the thin blue line between order and lawlessness.
- The Professional – this is a career-minded police officer who has a good knowledge of the police role and function.
- The Bobby – this officer is able to apply a range of policing techniques to situations that are effective and achieve the right outcomes.

The preceding is a good example to show that one of the biggest issues with consistency of practice lie with the individual practitioners. However, with wider consensus on the central characteristics of a profession, variations in behaviour among practitioners could be minimised.

In this book we use the following framework proposed by Robert Fullinwider (1996) to examine the essential characteristics of a profession, the profession of translating and interpreting in particular. Fullinwider holds that a profession has certain characteristics that distinguish it from other activities and earns the respect of society in general and makes it more than an occupation or an activity for money. He further asserts that a recognition of these characteristics by all professing an allegiance to that profession also underpins ethical decision making in that particular profession. Fullinwider (1996, p. 75) proposes that for an activity to be accepted as a profession, it must meet the following three central characteristics:

- Serving the public good
- Possessing special knowledge and training
- Understanding that other people may be vulnerable during the practice of the professional

Although Fullinwider's proposals are focused mainly on examining professions in which professionals and service-users work one-to-one, and often alone, such as in doctor–patient or lawyer–client settings, Fullinwider further proposes that these three characteristics can be used as a tool to determine if any activity can be viewed as a profession by society, rather than merely an occupation. These characteristics can also be used to examine the activity of interpreting and translating.

We will first look at each of the three characteristics in detail. This will be followed by a discussion of the same essential characteristics for interpreting and translating.

Characteristic 1: Serving the Public Good

The reason professionals exist in the first place is that members of the public need a service that they cannot fulfil themselves. By serving the need of individuals, professionals thus serve the good of the public. Such service provided by a profession for the good of society is regarded by Fullinwider (1996) as the *defining interest* of that profession, and therefore the *moral force* behind that profession. Once identified and agreed on by the members of a profession, this *moral force* becomes key to decision making in a range of ethical dilemmas for the profession. It is also essential for compliance, as it informs the members of the profession not just what they must do but also *why* they must do so. As a result, the defining interests of a profession must be promoted prominently by their relevant code of ethics. Fullinwider posits this is how a profession can connect itself to a moral purpose.

How do we, then, determine the defining interest of a profession and the public good it serves? The following schema proposed by Fullinwider (1996) serves as a useful tool for such reflection:

The profession of _____ serves the _____ needs of persons. (p. 74)

In essence, the professional needs to directly serve an important interest or need of other persons in society. This is important, as it means that unless an activity serves the public good, its claim for professional status will be weak. As Freidson (2001) contends, a profession is also 'an ideology serving a

What Is a Profession?

transcendent value and asserting greater devotion to doing good work than to economic reward' (p. 180). In the same vein, Fullinwider (1996) gives an example using the legal profession, arguing that a definition such as 'lawyers are professionals who make money by selling legal advice' (p. 84) would not be accurate, as it fails to identify what really makes lawyers professionals and the moral aims of the profession, as someone selling bad legal advice or selling advice to someone who does not need it cannot be regarded as a professional. He argues lawyers are professionals first because they directly serve a need of society in meeting individuals' needs for legal advice, not because they make money by selling legal advice.

With respect to policing, in 1829, Sir Robert Peel, the then Home Secretary of England, set up the Metropolitan Police Force in London. The original tenets of policing he proposed have not changed much since:

- The prevention of crime
- Detection of offenders if a crime is committed
- Protection of life and property
- The preservation of public tranquillity (Grieve, Harfiled & MacVean, 2007, pp. 19–20)

These functions still ring true in today's policing context. For example, the European Code of Police Ethics (Banks, 2014) lists the purposes of the police in society as

- To maintain public tranquillity and law and order in society
- To protect and respect the individual's fundamental rights and freedoms
- To prevent and combat crime
- To detect crime
- To provide assistance and service functions to the public (p. 358)

Moreover, in contemporary terms, Miller, Blackler and Alexandra (2006) identify the public need served by the police as 'the preservation of order and the enforcement of law' (p. 10). This need is not determined by a group of police officers but emerges and develops over time in a society. George Brouwer (2007), director of the Office of Police Integrity, Victoria, Australia, also states that 'Police are responsible for preventing and detecting crime; preserving peace and safety; and enforcing and upholding the law in a manner which has regard to the public good and rights of the individual' (p. 3). The aim to serve the public good is unquestionably prominent in the UN Police code of ethics, which states that 'Law enforcement officials shall at all times fulfil the duty imposed on them by law, by serving the community and by protecting all persons against illegal acts, consistent with the high degree of responsibility required by their profession' (United Nations, 2004, p. 2).

None of us lives in a vacuum. Our sense of safety and security is 'irreducibly social' (Loader & Walker, 2001, p. 26) and it is deeply entrenched in the relationships we share with those who live in the same society. In a way, policing is 'an exercise in symbolic demarking of what is immoral, wrong and outside the boundaries of acceptable conduct. It represents the state, morality and standards of civility and decency by which we judge ourselves' (Manning, 1997, p. 319). Waldron (1993) views such public good from a sociological perspective, asserting that it is 'something which is said to be valuable for human society without its value being adequately characterisable in terms of its worth to any or all of the members of the society considered one by one' (Waldron, 1993, p. 358), and 'no account of their *worth* to anyone can be given except by concentrating on what they are worth to everyone together' (Waldron, 1993, pp. 358–359; emphasis in original).

Characteristic 2: Possessing Special Knowledge and Training

Serving the public good necessitates the possession of specialised skills and knowledge and extensive training. Sociologist Everett C. Hughes (as cited in Wueste, 1994) maintains that 'professions provide esoteric services' (p. 6) and posits that every act of a professional is assumed to be based on esoteric knowledge that has been systematically formulated and applied to the problem at hand. For a professional, 'how knowledge is attained, maintained, passed down and certified' (Beaton, 2010, p. 9) is important; it is even more important to consider how that knowledge is put into practice – in other words, 'how professionals use their knowledge has a great deal to do with real professionalism and its proliferation' (p. 9). Abbott (1988) highlights the importance of specialised knowledge in defining a profession, asserting that 'while many professions battle over turf, only professions that expand their cognitive dominion by using abstract knowledge to annex new areas, define them as their own proper work' (p. 8). Kaplan and Owings (2015) further contend that the abstract knowledge over which the profession claims a monopoly must be recognised by the public, not just the professionals themselves, by saying 'a profession can keep its authority if the public accepts its claims of expertise and if the profession's internal structure of well-defined and agreed-upon knowledge and skills support it' (p. 28).

It should be pointed out that what a professional does is often more than technical or mechanical tasks such as filling out a template that can be done by a technician, or a routine procedure such as processing paperwork that can be undertaken by someone without requiring significant decision making. Being a professional involves making autonomous decisions in undertaking the key professional activities. The autonomy in professional decision making involves two essential abilities, according to Fullinwider (1996):

- The ability to judge a client's needs
- The ability to deal with problems for which no routine or mechanical solutions exist, by selecting appropriate means to meet the client's needs (p. 76)

Professional practice is essentially a claim that a member of that profession is creative in judging a client's needs and selecting the means to meet the identified needs. These two tasks require using discretion and making decisions in a process that considers and tests and finally excludes other possible needs or means. A professional often undertakes this process alone without a colleague or mentor immediately around. For example, a doctor listens to a patient who is complaining of a sore throat, headache, stuffed nose, painful muscles and chills; checks out other indicators and eliminates other potential causes; and then gives the diagnosis: 'You appear to have the flu. You need to rest well. Drink enough fluids. You can take a painkiller to control fever, aches and pains'.

Often professionals work in isolation. In making autonomous decisions, the professional exercises a higher degree of independent action than other providers of service and has to bear the responsibility and liability that come with this. Some of these decisions may not have serious consequences but some other decisions may be a matter of life and death. For example, in one case in Victoria, Australia, two paramedics declared a crash victim dead, despite recording that he was still breathing although faintly, and packed up and left, to allow the other services to remove the body and the debris. The members of the fire brigade at the scene then realised the man was not dead and called another ambulance. The crash victim has since made a full recovery. The criteria about declaring a person dead, according to the CEO of the Ambulance Service, include: 'you must be pulseless; you must be cold; fixed, dilated pupils; non-breathing' (*ABC*, 2012). However, in the aforementioned case, the medics made a professional, autonomous decision using their special knowledge and training which, on this occasion, appear to have failed them. Miller et al. (2006) hold that 'professional autonomy implies legal liability' (p. 208). This means professionals may potentially be accused of negligence. It is probably fair to say that one of the most feared incidents in the career of a professional is a charge of negligence alleged by a client. They can be extremely traumatic and emotionally draining for the professional involved, and the loss of reputation and the fear of penalties or punishment is a great concern (Pierscionek, 2008, p. 142). Negligence is an area of tort law that comes under the general body of the law known as the law of obligations. Tort is the French word for a 'wrong' and it deals with the civil law of wrongdoing that is not serious enough to instigate criminal proceedings but should be dealt with by some form of compensation to the party on the receiving end of the wrongdoing (p. 142). The development of tort law is grounded in common law – the law made by the courts based on precedence – and therefore may change with time, as opposed to the law made by acts of parliament, which will not change unless repealed (p. 142). Charges of negligence must fulfil three conditions:

1. There has to be a duty of care owed by one party to another.
2. The duty of care must have been breached.
3. Harm must have been suffered as a result of that breach of duty of care. (p. 143)

Law enforcement is another profession that involves constant exercise of discretion in carrying out its daily duties. Elliot and Pollock (2014) point out that a police officer, which they call peace officer, '...is the only domestic agent of government with the power to take life, based solely on their *discretion*' (p. 234). Two weeks before Christmas 2008, two Victoria Police (Australia) officers shot dead a troubled fifteen-year-old boy at a suburban skate park. The boy walked towards one of the officers, threateningly wielding two large knives and refused to surrender. The other officer said it was at this moment he realised he might have to shoot the fifteen-year-old, 'because there was nothing else that I could do and I had to protect Dodsy [his partner]'. His partner reflected five years later that: 'I go over it every day. I don't have to be asleep to have this particular nightmare. I still can't think of what else we could have done to make him back down'. Although a Victorian coroner, after a long inquest, said the case 'shocked and bewildered' the Victorian community, he also rejected the notion that the officers' response was disproportionate and found that at least one of their lives was in immediate danger. This case serves as an example of the long-lasting impact both on officers and society at large of having to make a professional judgement in a split second (*ABC*, 2014; Silvester, 2014).

With respect to policing, the skills for effective work are identified as not only having knowledge of the law and of relative cognate areas of criminology, but also contextual, specific knowledge in other areas such as finance, psychology and medicine (Miller et al., 2006). To achieve the service goals for the public, contemporary police training, on top of domain-specific knowledge in criminology, law, mental health, national security, traffic management and so forth, has moved to focus more on developing skills such as self-directed learning, problem solving, decision making, critical thinking and personal communication (Birzer & Tannehill, 2001; Cleveland & Saville, 2007; Marenin, 2004; McCoy, 2006). Police use this knowledge and skills in making professional, autonomous decisions, in a

What Is a Profession?

range of peaceful or hostile settings and in a range of emotions and feelings. Miller et al. (2006) hold that police officers experience more demands and challenges in the course of their work, and they experience emotions and feelings of 'fear, anger, suspicion, excitement and boredom to a far greater extent than people in other occupations' (Miller et al., 2006, p. 11). They also highlight a unique feature of policing, that police must provide their service irrespective of conditions or circumstances. For example, in a hostile environment, the police do not have the option of walking away or refusing to undertake their professional duty, which may be a possibility in many other professions.

Characteristic 3: Other People May Be Vulnerable during the Practice of the Profession

Carr-Saunders and Wilson (1993) observe that 'a professional brings asymmetrical knowledge to the service of his client, and thereby exercises power over his client. Therein lie the duties and obligations of a professional to his client' (p. 499). According to Fullinwider (1996), two other sources also contribute to the power and result in client vulnerability:

1. 'Clients often must disclose to them private information ordinarily not shared with strangers or even with intimates'.
2. 'Clients sometimes put their funds and assets under the control of the professionals'. (p. 77)

At the receiving end of the asymmetrical relationship with professionals, those people who are served by professionals trust that they have their clients' best interests at heart, rather than their own. Professionals, therefore, need to balance their power with their care for the public good, as discussed earlier. Miller et al. (2006) identify the public need served by the police as the preservation of order and the enforcement of law. To do this, the police are granted powers, and rights and privileges, such as depriving a person of freedom of movement, carrying a gun, accessing personal details or records or listening to private communications such as phone intercepts. Powell (2002) suggests that 'the greater the communication and social barriers, the more vulnerable the interviewee is to providing information that is misleading, unreliable and self-incriminating' (p. 44). As noted by Bull (2010), there is no internationally agreed definition of 'vulnerable' with regard to witnesses. The Tasmania Law Reform Institute (2006) identified the following as 'groups that may require special protection during an arrest' (p. 32):

a. Children and young people
b. Aborigines and Torres Strait Islanders

c. Mentally ill or mentally disordered persons, and persons with developmental disabilities
d. Persons from non-English-speaking backgrounds (NESB)
e. Other persons, who by reason of some disability, are unable to communicate properly with the police (such as the visually or aurally impaired, persons who cannot speak, and so on) (Bartels, 2011)

MacVean and Neyroud (2012) contend that the police, unlike members of traditional service-oriented professions such as doctors or lawyers, do not serve a need of a client as such, but the need of the broader public directly. Therefore, they argue, although people become vulnerable because the police have powers and can use deadly force, this vulnerability is not similar to the vulnerability that is experienced in activities of traditional professions. However, vulnerability is a direct consequence of allowing someone to make decisions and take actions that affect a person who is in need of something. It can be argued that the society itself views the police as occupying a role of trust and relies on them being accountable and responsible in enforcing the law and preserving peace. This relationship, then, creates vulnerability in the same way other professions do.

MacVean and Neyroud (2012) suggest that 'this relationship may be understood as a kind of contract under which the professional assumes certain duties towards the client' (p. 10). They explain that although this is often not a legal contract as such, clients usually have expectations from the professional they are meeting with, and this forms a moral contract, based on trust. Such trust underpins any professional service and ought to be a major consideration in professional ethics. The significance of trust, therefore, warrants further discussion.

Fullinwider's schema does not spell out the value of trust in the moral force behind a profession, although it is implied. Without such elements as the pursuit of moral excellence (Reid, n.d.) when distinguishing professions from trades, it is hard to argue how one's skillful, honest and hard-working local plumber is not, by definition, a professional. Crafts and trades do not fit into the professional mode because they are commercial and profit-driven. Unlike a profession, they are not by definition altruistic or ethical (Beaton, 2010). Professionals have a mandate: that is to protect the interests of those they serve and of the society itself (Beaton, 2010). Beaton describes the value of trust in professionalism as being:

...not only a skills set in a given occupation; it is an ineffable something that the person exudes in manner, dress, speech and standards of practice that is palpably powerful: standards like honesty, due diligence, perseverance, willingness to listen and learn, creative thinking within a framework of training, and other qualities most people would be hard put to describe but which they expect in the professionals with whom they engage. Another word for these standards is 'virtues' and the hard-to-describe something exuded is 'trustworthiness': the sum total of these virtues. (p. 5)

Beaton (2010) further states that 'The power that asymmetric knowledge gives one person over another must oblige the practitioner to act in the client's best interests' (p. 9). For example, when an anaesthetist tells a patient 'I am going to put you to sleep so you will not feel the incision and you will wake up in about 2 hours' time', the patient trusts his life at the hands of the anaesthetist. That is why trust is considered the most essential component of professionalism, around which all the other hallmarks of professionalism revolve.

Trust and the Professional

Trustworthiness is an issue and a promise precisely insofar as it is essentially a response to someone's appeal: the one, professing the ability to help, responds to the other, standing in need of and asking for help.

Zaner, 1991, p. 57

Trust, according to the *Oxford Dictionary*, is a 'firm belief in the reliability, truth or ability of someone or something'. Trust underpins all relationships, from the mother–baby bond to family, marriage and even business partnerships.

As we discussed earlier, the specialised skills, the knowledge and associated privileges possessed by professionals put them in a position in which people who need those skills and knowledge may be vulnerable if those skills and knowledge are not used properly. The clients need to be able to trust that the professional will not abuse this vulnerability. Baier (1986) defines trust as 'reliance on others' competence and willingness to look after, rather than harm, the things one cares about which are entrusted to their care' (p. 259), drawing attention to the fact that the competence in skills and knowledge that makes them professional can potentially be used to cause harm or loss, instead of providing assistance. Pellegrino (1991) explains that 'Trust is ineradicable in human relationships. …Trust is most problematic when we are in states of special dependence – in illness, old age or infancy, or when we are in need of healing, justice, spiritual help or learning' (p. 69). This is mostly due to the fact that people in need of those skills do not have much control over how those skills and knowledge are used, and so trust emerges as a key aspect of the relationship between a professional and a client. Barber (1983) lists three characteristics in a professional activity, which leads to a need for trust by the users of the professional service:

1. Possession of powerful knowledge by the professional
2. The autonomy necessary to their practice
3. Their fiduciary obligation to individuals and society (p. 9)

People rely on the integrity of professionals in a way unprecedented in other occupations, because the services offered by a professional are intangible, unlike a chair or TV sold by a manufacturer or a shop (Spada, 2009). The purchaser of services has to take them on trust. Pellegrino (1991) explains that when people seek some expert advice or service from a professional, a relationship of trust immediately starts. Sokolowski (1991) observes that 'The client trusts the professional and entrusts himself or herself – not just his or her possessions – to the professional' (p. 31). Such a relationship between professional and client is a fiduciary relationship. He further contends that 'the difference between a profession and an art [in the sense of a vocation or occupation]...lies in the fiduciary relationship that is built into the profession but not into the art' (p. 31). Pellegrino (1991) gives the doctor–patient relationship as an example, 'to seek professional help is to trust that physicians possess the capacity to help and heal' (p. 72). He adds that in professions in which the professional and the person they are serving are in direct contact, trust rests with the person, rather than the system or process and includes the personalities, feelings and emotions of the parties, unlike, say, trusting a building company that built an office tower, where trust is placed in the processes and systems that have been put in place to ensure the building is well built. In any close and direct professional and client relationship, clients share some of their most confidential, intimate, personal and sensitive details with a stranger who is a professional, with the expectation that the professional will use his or her special skills and knowledge to serve them 'with circumspection – neither intruding nor presuming too much nor undertaking too little' (p. 73). When it comes to translators, Bokor (1994) is of the view that

> One of these peculiarities is the elusive nature of the product we [translators] sell, which is not the sheets of paper …we actually deliver to our customers, but the skill acquired through years of language and subject matter studies and practice, as well as the time and effort expended to produce an expert translation. Selling these skills and their result (the translation) to customers who often cannot correctly evaluate them requires a unique degree of trust in the translator–client relationship and a mechanism to prevent and … resolve conflicts. (p. 99)

According to Rotter (1967) interpersonal trust is 'an expectancy held by an individual or a group that the word, verbal or written statement of another individual or group can be relied upon' (p. 651). Therefore, trustworthiness is a highly valued quality in professionals. We often come across national or international ratings of the most trustworthy professions. For example, a German research organisation, GFK Verein, conducted a survey in 2014 that included around 28,000 interviews carried out in 25 selected countries in Europe, North and South America, in the Asia/Pacific region and in Africa. The findings reveal that the professional groups that are trusted the most are firefighters, followed by doctors, nurses, pharmacists and other medical professionals and teachers, while politicians appear to be at the bottom of the list, along with insurance agents. Some high-profile professions such as lawyers and priests and pastors have a mixed rating in the middle. The police appear to have been ranked as high as firefighters and doctors in Canada, Australia, the United Kingdom, the United States and some west European countries (about 80%); however, the public do not appear to have a good experience with the police in some other parts of the world (48% in Turkey, where it is the second to last profession in the ladder just above politicians; 50% in India and a very low 25% in Kenya) (GFK Verein, 2014).

Two interrelated terms – professional trust and respectful regard – are worth highlighting here, as they play a significant part in influencing the views of society about a particular profession. *Professional trust* is a commitment to those who benefit from the professional service that they can rely on decisions and opinions provided by a professional and they will not be exploited or taken advantage of. Zaner (1991) describes it as 'the essential promise that trust is warranted and always an issue to be made good on in the course of the encounter' (p. 57). Routman (2014) contends that 'personal trust precedes professional trust and is its foundation' (p. 22) and cautions that 'once trust is broken, it is extremely difficult to re-establish' (p. 24). Professional trust, once achieved, results in *Respectful Regard*, which reflects how highly beneficiaries of a professional service and the broader public value and respect the services, opinions and judgement afforded by the professional. Hughes (as cited in Wueste, 1994, p. 7) identifies the rule in delivering a professional service as *credat emptor*, or let the buyer or beneficiary trust by saying that 'the "buyer" in the professional relation is to give credence to or to trust is significant' (p. 7). If one wants to be recognised as belonging to a profession, then members of that profession must win respectful regard of the public first. Anyone who professes to be a member of a profession has, consequently, an ongoing duty to uphold and maintain such respectful regard. The Professional Trust and Respectful Regard are key objectives in any definition of a profession whose aim should be to provide unstinting professional trust and to do everything in its power to earn Respectful Regard. The first step in achieving professional trust and respectful regard is to explain to the public the need a profession directly serves for society and how this is done. These two aspects are discussed in detail in Chapter 3.

Summary

A discussion of professional ethics must first start with a definition of what a profession is. However, defining a profession is a challenging task, as there does not appear to be a universal consensus. Many other professions now enjoy a certain level of monopoly in particular fields, enjoyed in the past only by the traditional learned professions of medicine, clergy and law. The most distinguishing features that define a particular activity as a profession are special skills and knowledge and training. Increasingly, the social aspects of a profession and the service it provides for the public are highlighted.

The chapter highlights Robert Fullinwider's (1996) schema, which believes that a profession must first identify the defining interest it serves in society and that defining interest will serve as the moral force behind a profession. His schema will be used as a framework to discuss the interpreting and translating profession in Chapter 3.

In any close and direct professional and client relationship in which a client needs the services of a professional, the client shares some of his most confidential, intimate, personal and sensitive details with a stranger who is a professional. This makes them vulnerable. The clients trust that the professionals will use their special skills and knowledge to serve them, not harm them. Gaining *professional trust* and *respectful regard* are two key objectives of any profession, as they are critical to society's recognition of a profession.

The Profession of Interpreting and Translating

3

To say a profession exists is to make one.
Andrew Abbott, 1988, p. 81

Introduction

In Chapter 2, we discussed what makes an activity a profession, not just an occupation, and the social nature of professions. We looked at the distinguishing features of professions, especially with respect to policing – the main context of this book. In this chapter, we examine interpreting and translating as a professional activity through the lens of Fullinwider's (1996) schema. Dael and Metselaar (2001) assert that everyone who works has an occupation but not necessarily a profession and they contend that 'acquiring a professional status is closely related to the tasks carried out by the individual workers' (p. 188). They are of the view that professions claim monopoly over certain tasks, which they call jurisdiction, and this is a key step in the professionalisation of an occupational activity. This brings us to the question: What tasks define the translating and interpreting profession?

What Do Interpreters and Translators Do?

In layperson's terms, interlingual communication, interpreting (oral) and translating (written) are activities whereby words in one language are expressed in another language. Although there is much commonality between these two forms of interlingual operations, there are also a number of significant differences. Shuttleworth and Cowie (1997) explain that some of the major differences relate to the communication skills required (oral vs. written), timing (interpreting is often instant whereas translation allows more time) and preparation (interpreters must prepare in advance for an assignment whereas translators can refer to references and resources during the task). Although much of the discussions in this book apply equally to both activities, we shall in the following section shift the focus more to interpreting, as it is the form that is called for more frequently in police settings.

Gerver (1971, p. viii; cited in Pöchhacker, 2007, p. 16) defines interpreting as 'a fairly complex form of human information processing involving the reception, storage, transformation and transmission of verbal information', which highlights its nature of performing multiple cognitive tasks concurrently. Interpreting is practised in a number of modes, depending on whether it is done at the same time as the speaker (simultaneously) or after the speaker (consecutively) (Gile, 2009).

Interpreters have been described in many different ways, from 'a phonograph…a transmission belt…a bilingual transmitter' in the legal realm (Morris, 1999, p. 8), to an 'electric transformer' (Wells, 1991, as cited in Gibbons, 2007, p. 247) and a 'conduit of communication' (Laster, 1990, p. 18; Laster & Taylor, 1994, p. 112; Russell, 2002, p. 117), as well as a 'cipher', a 'medium of communication' and a 'language machine' (Roberts-Smith, 2009, p. 14). They are also described in metaphorical terms as a 'black box' (Westermeyer, 1990, p. 747) or a 'cultural mediator' (Katan, 1999, p. 12, as cited in Leanza, 2007, p. 14). A less flattering description of court interpreters is afforded by Morris (1999) as 'a piece of gum on the bottom of a shoe – ignored for all practical purposes, but almost impossible to remove' (p. 7). For example, in the health setting, another common area where interpreters and translators are required often, interpreters and translators are increasingly expected to fill a number of other roles. The professional standards outlined by the National Council on Interpreting in Health Care (NCIHC) and California Health Interpreting Association (CHIA) (Ozolins, 2015) include

- Message converter
- Message clarifier
- Cultural clarifier
- Patient advocate (p. 322)

The ways in which interpreters are described seem to differ according to the extent to which the commentator believes interpreters should be an integral part of the communication interaction. Furthermore, it must also be mentioned that in the different contexts under which interpreters and translators work, for example, education, medical or legal, different expectations or norms are placed on what their role should be. As a result, interpreters are described as either 'black boxes' or 'cultural mediators' depending on the extent to which an interventionist approach to their professional work is recognised.

At one end of the spectrum, Canadian academic Roda Roberts (2002) recommends that the role of the interpreter is to

> …explain cultural differences and misunderstandings and to make explicit what may be behind the responses or decisions of the person who does not speak the official language, in order to ensure that the latter receives full and equal access to public services. (p. 159)

The Profession of Interpreting and Translating

As well, Wadensjö (1998) points out that in interpreted interactions, 'the meaning conveyed in and by talk is partly a joint product' (p. 8) and the interpreter takes on the role not only of language translator but also that of an active builder and processor of speech, inevitably influencing the speech itself. Sergio Viaggio is similarly proactive in his recommendation that interpreters should 'first and foremost ascertain what counts as relevance (for the speaker, for the speaker's addressees and mutually)' (2000, p. 229). He describes relevance as the 'propositional content conveyed by the speaker's utterance(s)' in terms of the listener, and notes that this relevance 'can only be assessed on the basis of and in the light of the pragmatic intentions behind it' (p. 231). So, according to Viaggio, 'in order to understand him, and not simply what he is saying officially, you must look behind his official discourse' (p. 231).

In the context of legal interpreting, a middle-ground view is perhaps taken by González, Vásquez and Mikkelson (1991, pp. 16–17), who accept the idea of 'dynamic equivalence' developed by Nida and Taber in 1974, but note that, in the courtroom environment, equivalence must be carried one step further, 'in that the form and style of the message are regarded as equally important elements of meaning' (González et al., 1991). They contend that the interpreter must mediate between these two extremes: the verbatim requirement of the legal record and the need to convey a meaningful message in the Target Language (TL). These requirements – to account for every word of the Source Language (SL) message without compromising the syntactic and semantic structure of the TL – are seemingly mutually exclusive. However, the dichotomy is resolved by focusing on conceptual units that must be conserved, not word-by-word, but concept-by-concept. To be true to the global SL message, paralinguistic elements such as hesitations, false starts, hedges and repetitions must be conserved in a verbatim style and inserted in the corresponding points of the TL message (p. 17). The authors' position on interpreting and translating undertaken in legal and police contexts is well reflected by Dan Barnes, a retired Chief of Language Services at the US Department of State, who described the role of interpreters as a *pane of glass* through which light passes without alteration or distortion – an analogy describing a role that allows for the communication of ideas without modification, adjustment or misrepresentation (Schweda-Nicholson, 1994, p. 82). This is the role the authors identify with, which will be promoted in police settings and discussed in detail in the following chapters.

One major shortcoming in features of interpreting and translating briefly discussed earlier and in the relevant literature in general is that much attention appears to focus primarily on the core activity of transferring meaning from one language into another. Questions appear to focus on issues such as, How should interpreting or translating be done? Should it be free or literal?

Should it be author/speaker–oriented or reader/listener–oriented? Hale (2007) summarises this debate, with respect to translation:

> Throughout the history of translation studies, there have been strong arguments proposing different degrees of 'faithfulness' to the original text, and by inference different definitions of the meaning of 'fidelity'. These range from the need to be as literal as possible to the original at one extreme, to the virtual disregard of the source text at the other. Grades of these two extremes appear in between. (p. 5)

There appears to be much less interest in debating or researching interpreting and translating as a 'profession'. As Abbott (1988) puts it, 'to say a profession exists is to make one' (p. 81). This means the characteristics of this professional activity and role boundaries must be clearly defined and explained to the members of society at large as well as the service users. For example, legal professionals have 'a vast legal and jurisprudential literature on the duties of lawyers to their clients, the court and the legal system' (Laster & Taylor, 1994, p. 111), not just debates about how to defend cases and so forth.

Early references to the need for competent, independent interpreters in Australia's comparatively short history can be found in the mid-1800s, when Australia received people from all around the world during the Gold Rush. Inevitably, people who were not proficient in English, the language of the government and the criminal justice system, came into contact with public services including police and courts. The following newspaper report is from the *South Australian Register* (Adelaide, SA: 1839–1900) of Thursday 9 October 1851. If the date and language were changed, it could well be any news piece in one of today's suburban papers in Melbourne.

> We hardly think justice was done to our German fellow-colonists in the vote of yesterday with reference to a German Interpreter. The argumentation by which the vote was supported was not less remarkable for its weakness than for a degree of inconsistency, as measured by the proceedings of the previous day. In voting additional salary to the two Judges, great stress was laid on the necessity of securing the pure administration of justice, regardless of mere motives of economy. A sworn Interpreter between German and English litigants, as well as between the Bench and German witnesses in criminal cases, is admitted on all hands out of the Council to be necessary; and yet a concession so necessary to the attainment of the ends of justice has been refused on the score of economy. It was futile on the part of the Advocate-General to allege that no complaint was made that an Interpreter was wanted in civil cases, when repeated instances have shown that an Interpreter was absolutely required. The learned Advocate defended his opposition by a still weaker argument in assuming that an Interpreter could be called on to give evidence in the same manner as a witness, forgetting that the attendance of a witness can be compelled, while that of an Interpreter must always be voluntary; and

we wonder that the obvious fact did not occur to the Advocate-General that where an Interpreter is employed by one of the litigants, his evidence is likely to be subject to undue bias in regard to the views or the interests of the party who has employed him. What the German community has claimed as a right, and what the English have felt was necessary to the impartial course of justice, is, that *a sworn Interpreter should be appointed, whose position and character secure him from all suspicion of colouring, suppressing or distorting the evidence he has to translate. These desirable qualifications cannot be secured in a chance Interpreter*, and we hope the German community will still agitate the matter, and appeal to His Excellency to place a sum on the Estimates for the purpose, so as to give the Council an opportunity of reconsidering the matter. (Emphasis added)

This story describes a need felt by members of the community for a professional in legal settings, whose services for communication between two or more parties can be trusted. Let's examine this professional role in the rest of the chapter through Robert Fullinwider's (1996) schema.

Applying Fullinwider's Schema to Interpreters and Translators

As discussed earlier, the social role played by a profession in society not only defines that profession but also has significant implications for its ethical practices. This social role played by the translating and interpreting profession often does not receive the attention it deserves. Codes for interpreters such as those developed by the International Association of Conference Interpreters (AIIC) for its members do not appear to mention the role of their profession in society. Interestingly, interpreters and translators appear to be one of the few professions that have to resort to 'definition by negation' by specifying what they *do not* do, for example, they do not offer cultural advice, and they do not advocate for clients and so forth. As is evidenced by Hale's (2007) analysis of seventeen interpreting and translating codes around the world, few professional codes actually define the role of interpreters (and translators), but almost all codes state what the role of the interpreter is not. This probably serves to accentuate the codes' position to the users of interpreters and translators and the intention to quell users' commonly held misconceptions about translators and interpreters. Hale's (2007) interpretation of this phenomenon is: 'the codes seem to be attempting to rectify the practice of many [translating and interpreting] practitioners who are mostly ad hoc and untrained' (p. 124).

In this section we analyse the profession of translating and interpreting using Fullinwider's (1996) schema to identify the social function of this profession, that is, the *moral force* behind it, so that it can be promoted to society as a profession like others such as doctors and lawyers long accepted by traditional definition. This can subsequently serve as a guide in ethical decision making for practitioners in their daily work. It must be explicitly pointed out, though, that the translators and interpreters this book refers to are those who are engaged to provide competent and impartial interpreting and translating service. Those who assist in other capacities, for example, as a volunteer, as part of their job function (such as a bilingual worker) or simply as a helping hand to a work colleague who is dealing with a client, and are not trained or called for in the capacity of a professional service provider for language assistance, are not included in the discussion in this book.

First, the Performance for the Public Good

Typically any description of translating and interpreting either by laypersons or in translation and interpreting studies focuses heavily on the mechanics of interpreting and translating, without much regard to where these activities sit in relation to the communication for which they are facilitating. To appreciate the public good served by interpreters and translators, the critical role they play as a communication channel must be recognised. This recognition cannot occur unless one has an appreciation of what communication is about. The *Oxford English Dictionary* defines communication as 'the imparting, conveying or exchange of ideas, knowledge and information'. Canale (2013) describes communication as 'the exchange and negotiation of information between at least two individuals through the use of verbal and non-verbal symbols, oral and written/visual modes, and production and comprehension processes' (p. 4) and explains that communication has the following characteristics:

1. It is a form of social interaction, and is therefore normally required and used in social interaction.
2. It involves a high degree of unpredictability and creativity in form and message.
3. It takes place in discourse and sociocultural contexts that provide constraints on appropriate language use and also clues as to correct interpretations of utterances.
4. It is carried out under limiting psychological and other conditions such as memory constraints, fatigue and distractions.
5. It always has a purpose (e.g. to establish social relations, to persuade or to promise).
6. It involves authentic, as opposed to textbook-contrived language.
7. It is judged as successful or not on the basis of actual outcomes. (p. 3)

In modern communication theory, every act of communication is considered to have three dimensions: Speaker (or author), Message and Audience.

The Profession of Interpreting and Translating

The success of the communication is measured by the response or reaction of the audience, which is called feedback (Steinberg, 2007). For example, the speaker will tell a joke and if the audience laughs, the communication attempt will be considered successful.

Wilbur Schramm (1954, in Steinberg, 2007) illustrates the basic activities in a communication event in the diagram shown in Figure 3.1. In this model, communication is not a one-way process; both participants play the role of 'sender' and 'receiver' by undertaking the essential tasks of decoding (understanding), eliciting the intended meaning (interpreting) and encoding (expressing) the message.

Obviously communication is not as straightforward as this models suggests. Claude Shannon (1948), known as the father of the modern communication theory, recognises the challenge in communication by stating: 'The fundamental problem of communication is that of reproducing at one point either exactly or approximately a message selected at another point' (p. 379). This remains a challenge in any form of communication, including ones facilitated by interpreting and translating (i.e., the 'message' at the top of Figure 3.1 and the 'message' returned by the receiver at the bottom are in different languages). From the point of view of the receiver in Figure 3.1, there may be factors that impact on the understanding (decoding) of the intended message that reach the receiver; there may also be others factors that affect the receiver when it comes to expressing (encoding) a response in return. Shannon refers to these factors as 'noise', which can be environmental, physiological impairment, semantic, syntactical, cultural and psychological. Schramm (1954) believes that, for effective communication, the participants must share 'a common language, common backgrounds and a common culture' (as cited in Steinberg, 2007, p. 56), and argues that if these essential elements are missing, then 'noise (such as internal prejudices) may

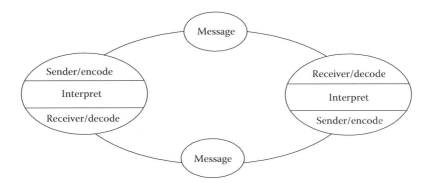

Figure 3.1 Schramm's model of communication. (From Steinberg, S., *An Introduction to Communications Studies*, Cape Town, South Africa: Juta & Co., 2007.)

be introduced and cause misunderstanding or different interpretations of the message by the participants' (p. 55).

Often the main factor in successful communication is attributed to the channel, as both the sender of the message and the receiver would need to share one. One of the most common channels of communication is language, referred to by Chomsky (1998) as 'par excellence' (p. 21). Canale's and Schramms's concepts and steps about communication outlined in the preceding text mostly relate to monolingual settings. When people in society need to communicate in a range of everyday settings but do not share a language, something extra is needed to overcome the language barrier for the communication process to take place. This service is often provided by interpreters and translators, who act as a channel. But because two languages are involved, the interpreter/translator undertakes a decoding, recoding and transmission process within the process Shannon described. Needless to say, dealing with any 'noise' (Shannon, 1948; Schramm, 1954 in Steinberg, 2007) is a task that also needs to be handled by the interpreter or translator. This process, which occurs only once in a monolingual communication setting, takes places twice in any bilingual communication facilitated by an interpreter or a translator. In other words, translators and interpreters create a *nested loop* – a loop within a loop (see Figure 3.2) – by undertaking these cognitive processes in their transfer process a second time. In the case of interpreters, they do this instantly. For example, in a police interview in which the police officer is trying to gather information from a witness to a store robbery,

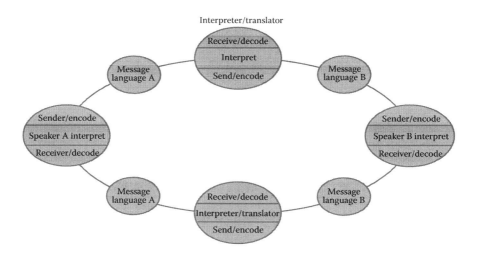

Figure 3.2 Interpreted communication model based on Schramm's.

Police: Are there any other views that you had of the robbers?
Interpreter: [to police officer] View as in eyesight?
Police: [to interpreter] Yes.
Interpreter: [in LOTE to witness] Are there any other views that you had of the robbers? (Lai, 2016)

The interviewing police officer in this situation is Speaker A, who poses a question. The interpreter receives message in English, decodes it and finds the issue of polysemy arises in discerning the meaning of 'view' as in 'eyesight' or a certain 'point of view', resulting in the need to go back to the police officer to clarify the meaning of 'view', before the question can be encoded in Langue B (i.e., LOTE) to be put to the interviewee, that is, Speaker B.

The sort of communication service described in the preceding text is provided by interpreters and translators in various settings such as government services for education, healthcare, human services and legal and law enforcement, as well as others in such areas as business, international trade and diplomacy. Regardless of the type or manner of engagement or who covers the cost, interpreters and translators directly meet the needs of both parties, whether individuals or organisations, for a competent and impartial means of communication where a common language is lacking. They thus serve the good of society by solving the fundamental problem in communication described by Shannon (1948): 'reproducing at one point either exactly or approximately a message selected at another point' (p. 371). To do so, they have the skills and knowledge to overcome the challenges created as a result of a lack of a common language, common understanding or common culture, which Schramm (1954, in Steinberg, 2007) argues are essential for effective communication. It is therefore appropriate to regard translating and interpreting as a service-oriented profession like other traditionally defined professions. As we highlighted earlier, professionals use their specialised skills and knowledge to meet the clients' needs, rather than their wants.

Using Fullinwider's (1996) schema for this exercise, identifying the *defining interest* for translators and interpreters can then be proposed as follows:

The profession of translating and interpreting serves *the competent and impartial communication* needs of persons *who do not share a language*.

The need for a competent, impartial and confidential service is the main reason that professional translators and interpreters are engaged in many formal settings. Society needs these qualities in many professional services from medicine and law to social work or teaching. An interpreter or translator is often needed to provide a competent and impartial service, even though the parties involved may be able to find other means of communicating. For example, even if a relative of one of the parties may be able to provide language assistance for an instruction or a simple interview or if a police officer who speaks another language can translate a threat letter or an abusive email equally correctly, for the purpose at hand, this interaction would still lack the protection of professional ethics. The need for impartiality or confidentiality would not be met. Or it may be the case that a third person, who is independent, is brought in, but then competence may be an issue and the protection of professional service may be lacking.

In court settings, the provision of an interpreting service has been viewed as necessary to put the speaker of another language on the same linguistic footing with other participants who speak the language of the court (Mikkelson, 1998, p. 22; Hale, 2004, p. 9; Shlesinger & Pöchhacker, 2010, p. 2). In police and law enforcement settings, the service provided by interpreters and translators, whether by independent professional interpreters or by staff interpreters, enables police officers to do their job and provides members of the public with a means of expressing what they have to say either as victims, witnesses or suspects. Thus, it is a service critical for natural justice and hence for the public good. Niska (1990, as cited in Schweda-Nicholson, 1994, p. 82) explains the conduit role of an interpreter in this situation as based on the fact that 'the principle of information transfer is... to conceal, to add or to change nothing'. This is essentially what the judge ruled in *Gaio vs. The Queen* (1961) in the Australian High Court, where a patrol officer interviewed the suspect via an interpreter and the suspect's evidence given in court about the interview was challenged as hearsay. The High Court held that this evidence was admissible, because 'the process was analogous to talking through a machine which interpreted from one language to another' (Roberts-Smith, 2009, p. 14). This comment is often misunderstood. When the High Court likened an interpreter to a language machine, it was not referring to the linguistic, cultural or social aspects of interpreting, but to the jurisprudential theory of the interpreter's role as a matter of legal admissibility (p. 14).

The decision for *Gaio vs. The Queen* (1961) also defines the boundary for the professional activities of interpreting and translating in this setting. In other words, the interpreter's involvement should simply be restricted to assisting with communication between the parties in the communicative event, such that the message expressed at one end is produced as closely as possible at the other end.

Second, Possessing Special Knowledge and Training

> Equality before the law, for the Non English Speaking Background [NESB] person means that he or she must be placed on the same linguistic footing as an English-speaking person within the system.
>
> **Laster & Taylor, 1994, p. 209**

For a person not proficient in English (in the Australian context) to be equal before the law, as explicated by Laster and Taylor earlier, requires

The Profession of Interpreting and Translating

certain skills and knowledge possessed and applied by a professional interpreter or translator. Napier (2005), reports the most desirable skills and competencies in an interpreter as nominated by the leading authors in the field, such as

- Language competencies
- Interpersonal skills
- Public speaking skills
- Advocacy skills
- Listening skills
- Visual processing skills
- Cognitive information processing skills
- Effective short- and long-term memory
- Cultural awareness
- Analytical skills
- Contextual knowledge
- World knowledge
- Specialist knowledge
- Professionalism (p. 3)

The diversity of skills and competencies listed here is a good indication of the inherently complex nature of the job contexts interpreters and translators find themselves in. The fundamental reason for this complexity is aptly captured by Edward Sapir (1956):

No two languages are ever sufficiently similar to be considered as representing the same social reality. The worlds in which different societies live are distinct worlds, not merely the same world with different labels attached. (p. 69)

Languages are shaped by a range of factors, including different cultures, social experiences, religions and beliefs and geographical locations, all of which impact on communication as Laster and Taylor (1994) observe: 'Effective communication in all languages is based upon shared cultural assumptions which allow listeners to comprehend the full import of what is being conveyed verbally and non-verbally' (p. 115). Languages and cultures have unique features that may not always have a one-to-one equivalent in other languages (Mulayim, Lai & Norma, 2015). Furthermore, people from different geographical locations and regions lexicalise ideas and actions differently depending on their needs or conditions. This then results in major differences in vocabulary, grammatical structures, registers, styles and non-verbal features of speech. Although some languages that are geographically and socially close may share many similar linguistic features, it would still not be a matter of a mechanical or technical replacement of words from one language with ones from another to achieve effective communication, especially in high-stakes settings such as policing. Communication, however, can be effectively achieved by a competent person through a range of transfer tools. Jakobson (1959) holds that 'all cognitive experience and its classification are conveyable in any existing language. Whenever there is deficiency, terminology may be qualified and amplified by loanwords or loan-translations, neologisms or semantic shifts and, finally, by circumlocutions' (p. 234). Transfer is, obviously, not limited to managing lexical gaps. In a police interview setting, all verbal and nonverbal features of speech are relevant and would need to be conveyed as much as possible through a range of means available. In legal settings, this is not just expected but often demanded.

This is the need a professional interpreter or translator possessing the ability and knowledge can meet where no routine or mechanical solutions exist. For example, in Indonesian there is no distinction among a rope, a wire and a string. Therefore when an Indonesian victim says he or she was tied with a rope/wire/string, the interpreter may have to clarify with the person before the statement can be rendered correctly. Another example is the word 'know'. A number of languages (inter alia French, German, Italian, Indonesian, Mandarin, Portuguese, Spanish) have two words for know – know a fact and know a person – whereas in Arabic, English and Vietnamese, for example, only one word covers both ideas. Apart from lexical differences among languages, there are also grammatical features that reflect different worldviews that may be difficult to transfer. Some readers may remember a scene in the Hollywood movie *Die Hard*, where the leader of the bad guys says into his radio, to the troops on the next floor down, 'Kommt. Sofort'. The subtitles accurately translate this as 'Come. Immediately'. But what the German conveys, by using the plural imperative form Kommt instead of the singular form Komm, is that he wants more than one bad guy to come, alerting them that there is trouble – Detective McLean (Bruce Willis) – which will need more people to fix. In English, of course, which has only one form, 'come', for both singular and plural, it is difficult to convey such subtlety (D. Deck, personal communication, 20 July, 2015). These are just some examples of the usual challenges facing this profession when interpreting and translating between two languages and cultures, which some people are unable to fully fathom or appreciate.

Interpreters and translators make autonomous decisions, using their special skills and knowledge, to convey what is said or written in one language into another. As explained previously, there cannot be, at least with the current technology, a routine or automated way of doing this reliably enough. Machine translation tools such as Google Translate, translation apps and audio-recorded tools in multiple languages in devices such as automatic teller machines or lifts are helpful but by no means able to replace the

The Profession of Interpreting and Translating

service provided by a human interpreter or translator in many high-stakes settings such as police interviews or cross-examinations in court where it is not just what people say, but also how they say it that is significant. In addition to conveying the meaning, other features such as the speaker's attitude and intention, including sarcasm, scepticism, approval and disapproval, also need to be expressed as much as is practicably possible. Roy (2000) highlights a complicating feature in any conversation, 'speakers present their ideas using different linguistic structures and also by following different automatic and unconscious conventions for using those structures' (p. 5).

Another factor that makes a routine or automated means of interlingual transfer challenging, if not impossible, to achieve via technology is that people hardly ever use language in strict adherence to rules of grammar, syntax or coherence. Drew (1990) explains:

> One of the reasons linguists, including Chomsky, have traditionally been sceptical of the value of investigating naturally occurring speech, instead favouring single, well-formed but fabricated sentences as the primary unit of analysis, is that what people actually say often does not conform with the rules of proper syntax. What comes out of their mouths is a syntactic mess. And for the traditional linguists the mess, the false starts, the unfinished clause or sentence, the hesitancies, the repetition of words are all, by the standards of linguistic competence, imperfections. They are the corrupt details of language use. (p. 40)

Indeed when one looks at a truthfully transcribed version of conversation between a police officer and an interviewee, for instance, it frequently requires a process of deciphering owing to such features as false starts, repetitions, using common lexical items inaccurately or with uncommon meanings, changing topics and wrong use of punctuation. The following examples from police interviews illustrate this point.

Police Interview 1
A suspect being questioned about a sprinkler system he claims he set up to water ferns but when he could not afford to purchase ferns, he planted cannabis.

Police: Was that set up (.) predominantly to (.) ah to ah… to water these// ah
Suspect: mm…no
Police: No?
Suspect: No. There was going to be ferns and that in there… and I put those in there because we couldn't afford ferns. and (.) stuff like that, so,

Police:	But you ah can afford to (.) grow… the marijuana plants…
Suspect:	Doesn't cost anything.
Police:	Right… now… do you use any fertilisers... or anything in … the soil... at all?
Suspect:	Nah...nup

(Heydon, 2005, p. 128)

Police Interview 2

Police:	Has any threat, promise or offer of advantage held out to you to take part in this interview?
Suspect:	What's that one?
Police:	Has any threat, promise or offer of advantage held out to you to take part in this interview?
Suspect:	Has any threat, promise…[whispering]
Police:	Has any threat, promise or offer of advantage held out to you to take part in this interview?
Suspect:	Have I been bribed to be here, is that what you mean?
Police:	Exactly what it says, has there been threat; have you been threatened in any way?
Suspect:	No, no.
Police:	Have you been promised by anything or with anything to take part in this interview?
Suspect:	No.
Police:	Do you understand what a promise is?
Suspect:	A promise is a promise!

(Hall, 2008, p. 86)

Police Interview 3

Police:	Right w'l y' how co- can you start Friday what di- what started on Friday
Suspect:	Well what started Friday was Friday morning when I received a phone call n that was around ten yeah ten to ten thirty cause it was not far after the news so I picked it up answered and they said Joh-ah Johnny... Johnny I said yeah speaking they said right if you go anywhere near the shop or anywhere near the house you're going to get your legs broken and that was it just hanged up.

(Heydon, 2005, p. 81)

The sorts of common 'imperfections', 'syntactic mess' and 'corrupt details' (Drew, 1990, p. 40) shown in this dialogue are also among the common sources of 'noise' (Shannon, 1948; Schramm, 1954 in Steinberg, 2007) if we were to use the terminology of communication theory. These issues in language can be a result of the level of literacy or education, or emotional state of the speaker or author (of a text) or may be deliberate and intentional – an occurrence not uncommon in police interviews. Some of the semantic or syntactic imperfections can also result from other factors that are beyond the control of the speaker or author, such as developmental or physiological, age or medical conditions such as aphasia (Gentile, Ozolins & Vasilakakos, 1996).

Aphasia (NHS, n.d.), for example, is a condition that affects the brain and leads to problems using language correctly when speaking or writing. It is usually caused by stroke, sudden brain injury, brain tumour or dementia. Sometimes people may not be aware of it. Aphasia is often classified as 'expressive' or 'receptive' aphasia, depending on whether there are difficulties with understanding or expressing language, or both. People with expressive aphasia may have some of the following signs and symptoms:

- Slow and halting speech
- Struggling to get certain words out, such as the names of objects, places or people
- Content of speech stripped down to simple elements and containing basic nouns and verbs, for example, 'want drink' or 'go town today'
- Spelling or grammatical errors
- Using the wrong word, such as saying 'chair' instead of 'table'
- Difficulty constructing a sentence
- Being able to write or speak fluently, using long sentences, but often including nonsense words or speech lacks meaning (NHS, n.d.)

In contrast, people with receptive aphasia may have some of the following signs and symptoms:

- Difficulty understanding what people say
- Difficulty understanding written words
- Misinterpreting the meaning of words, gestures, pictures or drawings
- Giving responses that may not make sense if they've misunderstood questions or comments
- Not being aware of their difficulties with understanding (NHS, n.d.)

These imperfections in language use, no matter what causes them, are not confined to monolingual settings. They also occur in interpreted interviews equally frequently, and they are exactly the sorts of issues an interpreter has to not just understand, but also to convey from one language into another, often *instantly*, as in a police interview or speech pathology assessment, where an interpreter does not have the time or resources to sit down, check dictionaries or online resources or consult colleagues. This is not just limited to police or criminal justice settings. The following example is from Australia's former prime minister Kevin Rudd, who was known for his unusual choice of language at times, in a press conference with German chancellor Angela Merkel. Mr Rudd said it was unlikely any progress would emerge from the Major Economies Forum 'by way of detailed programmatic specificity'. This had to be interpreted instantly by a German interpreter for Chancellor Merkel and members of the press, which, understandably, had the interpreter scrambling for a meaning (Preedy, 2009).

The task of dealing with such speech features instantly requires specialised skills and knowledge and often there is no routine or technical means of carrying out these tasks. We have already noted that specialised skills and knowledge refer to two key abilities – the ability to identify the needs of clients and the ability to find a means to meet those needs. This is not so different from the interpreting and translating process. Interpreting and translating can be conceptually simplified as a *transfer* process involving two core abilities: 'comprehension' of message expressed in one language and 'expression' of the same as closely as possible in another (Mulayim et al., 2016). Gile (2009) identifies two essential factors in comprehension, even in a seemingly simple utterance: linguistic knowledge and extralinguistic knowledge. He cautions, however, that 'comprehension is not a binary variable that takes on one of two values, namely "comprehension" and "non-comprehension"' (p. 82), noting that comprehension is hardly ever definite, as it depends on many variables at any given time. One of the significant variables, and challenges, in comprehension, according to Gile, is that 'speeches are not heard in advance and...the unexpected is to be expected' (p. 86). Once the interpreter decides he or she has comprehended the meaning conveyed by the speaker, he or she then uses the linguistic resources of the other language to convey the meaning. Imagine a police interview in which the suspect does not speak the language the interview needs to be conducted in. In this setting each piece of text or an utterance produced by one person in one language represents a 'need', be it a word or paragraph, in that the speaker needs the other party to understand that text or utterance, as it was intended. The interpreter in this case is the person who can meet this need by conveying the message into the other language.

This step of converting utterances and paralinguistic features into ideas is difficult to observe directly, as it occurs in the mind and is represented in words or paralinguistic features in the other language in a bilingual communication setting. This is the inherent difficulty in researching transfer process, which still remains one of the least researched areas in translation and interpreting studies. The specialised skills and knowledge go beyond simple bilingualism. Those who do this are not just concerned with conveying the linguistic as well as the paralinguistic elements of meaning, but are also expected to maintain 'a common language, a common background and a common culture' (Schramm, 1954, as cited in Steinberg, 2007, p. 56) – the essential conditions for effective communication. These esoteric skills and knowledge enable interpreters and translators to decipher the 'imperfections', 'syntactic mess', 'corrupt details' (Drew, 1990, p. 40) and 'noise' (Shannon, 1948, p. 379) to identify the intended meaning and then convey all of this into the other language. As Canale (2013) points out, one of the features of everyday communication is that it involves authentic, as opposed to textbook-contrived language. Interpreters and translators use what Wueste (1994) calls 'abstract professional knowledge' (p. 8) to provide a competent and impartial channel for the communication needs of participants who do not share a common language and rely on their service.

Lastly, Other People May Be Vulnerable as a Result of the Practice of the Professional

People needing a professional service may be vulnerable because of the knowledge and power asymmetry that exists between them and the professional. Both parties will be acting and/or making decisions on the assumption that everything they say or that the other party says is based on good faith. This is particularly significant when the party that receives the professional service has no choice but to believe that the other party has its best interests at heart, pointing to the *trust* bestowed on the professional. Trust is embedded in the professional relationship (Pellegrino, 1991; Sokolowski, 1991). This trusting relationship still applies when the two parties do not speak the same language, and require the service of an interpreter or translator.

In her survey investigating experiences of Deaf people with interpreters, Napier (2005) found that Deaf clients overwhelmingly identified linguistic ability and trustworthiness as two key attributes they valued in an interpreter. It is fair to assume the professionals who were providing these services to the Deaf people would value the same attributes. For example, when interpreting between a professional such as a medical doctor or lawyer and a non-English-speaking person, an interpreter is interpreting not just for the non-English-speaking person, but for the professional as well. The professional passes his or her professional skills and knowledge through the interpreter, and the medical advice or legal advice he or she provides relies on the accuracy and integrity of the interpreting performance. Interpreters and translators occupy a notionally central position in this situation. Anderson (1976/2002) regards the interpreter occupying a position in the middle, sometimes physically and always metaphorically and enjoying 'the advantage of power inherent in all positions which control scarce resources' (p. 218). Zaner (1991) highlights the ethical obligation this power brings on the professional: 'Not only must the power be used competently and concernfully, but it must never be misused or abused' (p. 54).

The parties who rely on an interpreter or translator essentially abandon control of the circumstances or outcomes during a transaction (e.g. a police interview), and this dependence on the interpreter or translator accentuates the parties' loss of autonomy in dealing with their own business, having to bestow their *trust* on the person who provides language assistance in the belief that what they say and mean is faithfully captured and transferred to the other party. This inevitably results in these parties being placed in a vulnerable position. Such a relationship between an interpreter or a translator and the benefit from their services can be described as a fiduciary relationship. Latimer and Maume (2015) define 'fiduciary' as 'duties of fidelity and faithfulness which are given to one person, (the fiduciary), to be exercised for the benefit of another' (p. 88). They explain that it is 'a relationship of trust and confidence' and 'a relationship of reliance including reasonable expectations – where one person may rely or may be entitled to rely on the other because of their relationship of trust and confidence' (p. 89). This is the case when people rely on the interpreter and translator to provide accurate and impartial language assistance. The rule for a professional interpreter and translator is, as Hughes (as cited in Wueste, 1994) puts it, *credat emptor*, to gain the credence or trust of the beneficiaries of his or her service.

As discussed in the earlier chapters, in an interpreted event, at any given time, there is at least one person who does not understand what is being said (Bot, 2005). That means the parties have access only to the part of the conversation in the language they can speak. The interpreter is the only one who can communicate with both parties. In this sense the fiduciary relationship includes both parties who benefit from the language assistance. A police officer may, theoretically, be as vulnerable as a suspect or witness who does not speak the language of the interview as he or she also relies on the interpreter/translator to do his or job properly. This reliance creates a certain level of vulnerability. The professional's vulnerability is further exacerbated by the latitude the interpreter or translator wields in the process of his or her professional operation. The other professional, the police officer, has to deliver his or her own professional service, business or transaction, for which he or she is ultimately accountable and sometimes liable, by trusting the service provided by the interpreter or translator. Interpreters and translators, in this sense, wield great power that others in the encounter do not have. The interpreter has the initial power to deduce, induce, infer, extrapolate or hypothesise from the utterances he or she hears from either party. These operations on the utterances of which only he or she comprehends influence the utterances he or she produces for the opposite party, which then influence any operations that opposite party needs to perform.

The analysis so far of what interpreters and translators do, using the schema proposed by Fullinwider (1996), clearly demonstrates that interpreting and translating is a profession, not an occupation. Serving a need using 'esoteric' (Hughes, as cited in Wueste, 1994, p. 6) skills and knowledge may also increase the likelihood of vulnerability of both parties in the transaction. This will inevitably lead to ethical dilemmas that must be appropriately dealt with by the professional translators and interpreters. This is covered in professional ethics, which is discussed in Chapters 4 and 5.

Summary

This chapter examined what interpreters and translators do as a professional activity to form the basis for the discussion of professional ethics. Ethicist Robert Fullinwider (1996) asserts that a profession serves a need of individuals, thus serving the good of society. He refers to this as the *defining interest* of a profession, which is also the *moral force* behind that profession. Interpreters and translators serve as a *competent and impartial* channel for the communication needs of individuals, thus serving the good of the public. Fullinwider (1996) offers two more characteristics that an activity must have to be defined as a profession: the use of specialised skills and knowledge, which cannot be replaced by technical means; and the fact that people may be vulnerable while receiving that professional service.

Interpreters and translators have a range of highly specialised skills and knowledge to enable them to comprehend what is said or written in one language and to convey it into another. People benefiting from such service are potentially vulnerable, as they rely on the interpretation or translation to make decisions. For example, in a police interview, both the police officer and the suspect rely on what they hear from the interpreter and trust that the interpreter is competent and impartial. This basic reliance creates vulnerability. Interpreting and translating, when viewed using the maxim proposed by Fullinwider (1996), are professions, not merely occupations. Any professional activity leads to ethical dilemmas because of the use of specialised skills and knowledge and the vulnerability of clients/beneficiaries in this process.

Professional Ethics

4

Because knowledge is power, true professionals adhere to ethics when dealing with clients in order to harness that power for the good.
George Beaton, 2010, p. 10

Introduction

Chapters 2 and 3 discussed in general the characteristics and features that make an occupational activity a profession and focused on interpreting and translating in particular. The special skills and knowledge possessed by professionals give them a certain level of power over their clients. This power can potentially be abused to the disadvantage of the clients, creating a need to regulate these special skills and knowledge and to reassure users of these services. This is usually done through setting minimum standards for a particular profession. This chapter, therefore, examines the significance of these standards for a profession. A code of ethics for a specific profession normally covers the core activities unique to the profession, whereas a code of conduct can include the more generic issues that are applicable in many professional fields. Although not all professions delineate clearly their codes of ethics and conduct this way, and some may have one covering both areas, we opt for discussing the two separately in this chapter for the purpose of clarity.

Codes of Ethics

Users of various professional services in society expect to be protected by professional ethics. This is not just for traditional professions such as doctors and lawyers but also many other service providers such as psychologists, nurses, engineers, accountants and public services. Freckelton (1996) cautions that 'A professional grouping risks being characterised as unethical if it does not now espouse a set of principles enshrined in a code of ethics' (p. 131). The demand for Professional Codes of Ethics has been especially loud since the 1980s, when it started to become an expectation of society. It has become almost fashionable that any service industry, not just a select group of high-profile professions, has to have a code of ethics or code of conduct.

Professions have responded to the expectations of society by developing codes of ethics and/or codes of conduct; some have both, while others have one but not the other. Generally a code of ethics covers the core values and guiding principles of a profession with respect to its core professional activity, whereas a code of conduct spells out in more detail the practical issues in a professional practice. According to Laster and Taylor (1994), the significance of a code of ethics lies in its proclamation of the legitimacy of a profession: '...ethics are devices for promoting consistency in conduct and good business practice among members. By being seen to discipline its members, a profession reassures clients and the public of its legitimacy' (p. 204). A later section in this chapter goes into more detail about codes of conduct. Suffice it to say that having codes of ethics and/or conduct for a profession is to reassure their clients and service users that they will be served appropriately and as a result, some claim, this will also attract new clients in a competitive market. It is not uncommon to see codes of ethics and/or codes of conduct displayed in prominent places in physical workplaces or on websites to profess precisely the importance an organisation or profession attaches to such proclamations.

Codes of ethics have also changed over time in response to changing employment patterns. Traditionally, professionals would work as sole practitioners (most still do). However, increasingly in modern employment conditions, many traditional professions, for example, medicine and the law, are practised within an organisation such as a hospital or a law firm. A doctor may work for the army or a lawyer may work for a university. These conditions have also had an impact on the codes of ethics of the workplace. Many professionals working either as sole practitioners or as a staff member of an organisation continue to deliver their core professional service in one-to-one settings, in direct contact with their clients or services users. This setting is the main concern of professional ethics.

One of the earliest examples of a Code of Ethics is the Hippocratic Oath for medical doctors. At the core of this *professional code* is the principle that a doctor's core value is *to heal and do no harm*, which refers clearly to what medical doctors can do with the specialist skills and knowledge they have (Zaner, 1991, p. 46). However, medical doctors are also expected to comply with many other rules typically found in codes of conduct arising out of the legal and legislative requirements of society such as conflict of interest, privacy and confidentiality, all of which are relevant to a greater or lesser extent to all other professions. The 1948 Declaration of Geneva put forward by the World Medical Association (WMA, 1948) is one example that reflects these aspects.

Before getting into a discussion of professional ethics, it is perhaps useful to clarify the confusion commonly seen among laypersons as well as some professionals about professional ethics and personal ethics, which sometimes appear to be mixed under the 'ethics' umbrella. Social work professor Allen Barsky (2010) contends that

> Professional ethics are rules that guide social workers or other professionals in the choices that they make in their professional capacities. Personal ethics are rules that guide people in their private lives, in their roles as parents, family members, friends, neighbours, citizens and so forth. (p. 5)

As briefly covered in the Introduction, using the example of a medical doctor who refused to assist in an abortion because of his personal beliefs, the distinction between professional ethics and personal morals may get blurry. Personal morals are concerned with right and proper conduct, which are strongly influenced by one's cultural or religious backgrounds (Corey, Corey & Callahan, 2003). Each person has his own personal ethical framework in which he himself decides what values he will live by, the type of person he is, the type of person he will become and the outcomes he wishes to achieve. Black (2003) concurs with this idea and adds that 'in making professional ethical decisions, the person is required to decide and perform actions on behalf of the organisation for which they work' (as cited in MacVean & Neyroud, 2012, p. 11).

The essence of professional ethics is the principle of service to others, which is not the case in personal ethics. Wueste (1994) posits that

> …on the basis of their expertise and the importance of the work that requires it, professionals claim to be and have been recognised as being governed (in their professional conduct) by role-specific norms rather than the norms that govern human conduct in general. (p. 11)

Personal ethics and professional ethics may, however, intersect in many areas of everyday activities, both professional and personal. According to Dyer (1988), most professions involve a relationship with a person who needs a professional service, and he goes on to say that 'it is the ethics of that personal relationship of service as much as the knowledge of the practitioner that defines a profession and distinguishes a profession from a trade' (as cited in Wueste, 1994, p. 2). Houser et al. (2006) believe that 'a difference between these two concepts concerns to some degree the objective versus subjective interpretation of right behaviour' (p. 1). The conflict between professional ethics and private morals appears to be one of the main sources of ethical dilemmas and will often be included in codes of ethics as an area that needs to be balanced by the professionals. Professional codes help define a profession and, having a code of ethics, therefore, is an integral part of any business that calls itself a profession (Houser et al., 2006), and yet professional codes of ethics do not necessarily consider private morals. Kaufman (1957) points out the altruistic nature of professional canons of ethics and the fact that they are not designed for a bad person who wants to know how much he or she can ignore rules and laws without getting into trouble but are drawn up for good persons or ethical persons, as buoys to assist them in charting their professional conduct. Kaufmann also cautions against overzealous adherence, trying to avoid even the slightest suggestion of ethical impropriety, as 'it may hinder the attainment of other important social interests' (p. 657).

Shortcomings of Codes of Ethics

Some authors argue that professional codes of ethics have limitations because they do not cover many issues encountered in professional practice and 'may increase conceptual confusion' (Keith-Spiegel & Koocher, 1985). Hughes (2013) has this criticism of some elaborately worded codes of ethics: 'the production and enforcement of professional standards can serve a variety of purposes, many of them related to the interests of the profession and its members rather than those of its clients or the public' (p. 12). It goes to show that on the one end of the spectrum lies the inherent deficiency of dot-point or rule-bound types of codes where their application may cause problems for their practitioners; whereas a more elaborate one, on the other end, runs the risk of focusing too much on the professions themselves and their own interests rather than the people they serve. Similarly, Neukrug et al. (1996) point out one major shortcoming of codes of ethics, highlighting that ethical decisions based solely on professional codes would be limited, as the codes could not possibly be able to account for all ethical dilemmas.

Houser et al. (2006), in a similar vein, observe that codes of ethics primarily examine the issues only from the professional's perspective without giving much consideration to the views of clients, and there may be conflicts among different professional codes. Laster and Taylor (1994), commenting specifically on the interpreting profession, argue that

> …an ideal interpreter is neutral, well-dressed, punctual and, most importantly, follows the codes of ethics to the letter. Yet, in many ways, the 'ideals' represented in the codes of ethics are not readily attainable. Nor is the fictional interpreter presented in the Codes a necessarily desirable 'ideal'. (p. 205)

They also argue there are a number of shortcomings in codes of ethics and they elaborate in detail:

- The codes confuse business rules, such as those governing the operation of an interpreting and/or translation agency and ethical principles on the other hand, which require contextual knowledge before they can be applied.

Professional Ethics

- The codes fail to acknowledge that ethical principles cannot be static; they must be flexible enough to accommodate changing social and legal values.
- The codes lack annotation or explanation. This suggests to neophyte interpreters that all they need to do is choose a rule, memorise it and apply it…. Answers to ethical 'dilemmas' are seldom straightforward, and ethical choices cannot be reduced to unthinking applications or 'rules'.
- There is no unified code of ethics… to be effective, a code needs authority, machinery for enforcement and professional support in the form of authoritative advice to members on ethical problems in practice. Most importantly, ethical norms need to be more than declarative; to be effective they need to be internalised by members through education and peer supervision.
- The codes are not effectively incorporated into professional education.
- There is dissatisfaction with the existing codes of ethics.
- The codes are frequently presented as sets of rules, which deny the need to debate and question ethical principles.
- The codes take no account of the demands made of interpreters to assume multiple roles.
- The codes are silent about the importance of variables such as gender and ethnicity.
- The codes fail to acknowledge the need for interpreters to make informed judgements about a situation, to act 'ethically'. (Laster & Taylor, 1994, pp. 205–206)

Preston (2014), paying attention to the same issue, lists the following as the major concerns about the misuse of codes:

- Sometimes codes are adopted for the wrong reasons. The code is seen as a status symbol, a public relations exercise designed to protect the profession or organisation and its monopoly of a certain practice or commerce.
- A serious case of misplaced expectations for codes emerges when it is assumed that they should, and can, cover every contingency of misconduct, or that once declared they become immutable, almost holy writ.
- More fundamentally, it is sometimes asserted that codes have severe limitations as instruments of ethics, and that in their regulatory capacity, they undermine the possibility of a mature, open-ended, autonomous and reflective ethical response, diminishing personal responsibility. (p. 215)

These shortcomings discussed by various scholars highlight two major areas of concern with codes of ethics or professional standards – a lack of emphasis on the interests of the clients or the society and a lack of provision of an overarching principle to guide ethical decision making and the exercise of *discretion*. McConkey (1985, as cited in Morrissey & Redd, 2006) also highlights the absence of overarching frameworks to guide ethical decision making by professionals positing that 'at the moment, the assumptions underlying many codes of professional conduct seem to be a mixture of moral relativism masking a legal formalism together with some utilitarian consequentialism and some assumptions of natural law' (p. 1).

Fullinwider (1996) proposes that these shortcomings can be addressed by bringing the people and society to the forefront of a code of ethics and reflecting this clearly right at the outset. He advocates that the primary role of a code of ethics should be to promote professionals' *moral self-understanding*, claiming that

> Regardless of how it is designed or presented, a code of professional ethics needs to serve to support moral understanding by connecting a profession to a moral purpose, thereby helping professionals to see their practices as 'performance for public good'. (p. 73)

Fullinwider (1996) further proposes that a code should state the service ideal of the profession, and the specific rules of conduct in accordance with that ideal. Through the code, both the professional and the users/beneficiaries of the professional service alike can identify the performance for public good that makes the profession more than a skilled job that is done for financial reward. He suggests that a professional code should start with a preamble describing the profession's moral purpose and role within society at large, by clearly stating the needs of the persons directly served by the profession. The following Code of Ethics of the Law Institute of Victoria has these desirable features such as proposed by Fullinwider, starting with a statement of the direct need served by the legal profession.

> As a member of the Law Institute of Victoria (LIV), I/we acknowledge the role of our profession in serving our community in the administration of justice. We recognise that the law should protect the rights and freedoms of members of society.
>
> We understand that we are responsible to our community to observe high standards of conduct and behaviour when we perform our duties to the courts, our clients and our fellow practitioners. (Law Institute of Victoria, n.d.)

Similarly, the Police Code of Ethics in the state of Victoria, in Australia, opens with a preamble that first states the role played by the police within the broader society and the direct need served by the police:

> The Victoria Police mission is to provide a safe, secure and orderly society by serving the community and the law. Our members have a duty to preserve the peace, protect life and property, prevent offences, detect and apprehend offenders and help those in need of assistance. (Victoria Police, n.d.)

With regard to policing as a profession, Neyroud (2003) proposes the following seven principles as a foundation to 'do the right things for the right reasons and thus police in an ethical manner' (p. 584).

- Respect for personal autonomy – derived from the ethics of duty, respecting individuals' rights, treating the public and colleagues with dignity and respect, not using either as a means to an end
- Beneficence and nonmaleficence – police officers helping people without harming others
- Justice – respect for human rights and for morally respectable laws
- Responsibility – requiring officers to justify their actions
- Care – emphasising the interdependence of police, individuals and the community
- Honesty – a key virtue central to the legitimacy and authority of policing
- Stewardship – emphasising trusteeship over the powerless and over police powers (p. 584)

Given professional ethics specifically deals with, or should deal with, how professionals, often in their fiduciary role, should use the specialist skills and the knowledge they have for the benefit of people they serve, it may be helpful to begin by finding out a profession's core value and purpose through 'philosophical inquiry into the ethics of a particular occupation or profession ... to uncover the major purposes or ends that do, and should, govern the behavior of people in that occupation' (Miller et al., 2006, p. 10). For example, the Declaration of Hawaii urges psychiatrists to serve the best interests of patients and apply professional skills and knowledge only for legitimate diagnostic and therapeutic purposes and preserve patients' confidences (Bloch & Pargiter, 1996, p. 183). Dr. Harold Shipman, aka Dr. Death, in the United Kingdom was responsible for the deaths of an estimated 250 patients. He was charged and convicted. He was using his medical skills and knowledge to harm trusting patients, usually lonely pensioners. He abused the trust of vulnerable people who relied on him. He could have helped them, using his medical skills and knowledge, but he chose to harm them. It is these professional skills and knowledge that the society expects will be performed to the highest standards and will be regulated either by law or self-regulated by professionals themselves, or a mixture of both.

Codes of Conduct

As we pointed out earlier, we have chosen to separate the discussion of professional ethics (ethics that relate to the provision of the core professional service) from a discussion of codes of conduct (conduct issues that are relevant to almost all professions). Keith-Spiegel and Koocher (1985, as cited in Parsons 2001) assert that

> …the primary reasons for ethical codes are to protect the public from unethical or incompetent professionals and to protect the profession from unethical practices by any of its members…They are simply guidelines that require selection and application to individual situations using the helpers [sic] best personal and professional judgment. (p. 41)

Codes of conduct, however, are designed to cover the practical issues that are relevant to a profession under the guidance of codes of ethics, and, at times, can become prescriptive as well as descriptive.

In the healthcare setting, for example, what is covered can range from maintaining health records securely and hygiene matters in the workplace to energy saving initiatives and proper use of facilities. In policing, complying with legislative requirements or strict adherence to procedures and processes may be accorded more emphasis. Snyder (1994, p. 16), in describing how to be a professional translator, makes the following suggestions on one's conduct to improve one's professionalism.

1. Know yourself.
2. Know what you are doing.
3. Be honest.
4. Be accurate.
5. Be neat.
6. Use a separate phone line for business if you work at home.
7. Dress like a professional.
8. Be friendly.
9. But don't get too personal.
10. Honour commitments.
11. The customer is always right.
12. Be patient.

13. Be humble.
14. Be tolerant of differences.
15. Be sympathetic.

They are all good suggestions, but with the exception of a few such as accuracy or knowing yourself (meaning the limits of your skills and competence) that are relevant for interpreters and translators directly, most are common sense, good practices that society expects from anyone who claims to be providing a professional service or an occupational service. As much as these are good practices, the fact that they are included in the codes of conduct also indicates that there must have been issues in the past that prompted organisations or associations to include them in the codes. For example, as a user of interpreters and translators, Metropolitan Police Standing Orders for Working With Interpreters (2007) stipulate conduct standards for freelance interpreters booked from external agencies such as

> 4.1 (8) Interpreters will notify officers their expected time of arrival when asked to attend at a police station. If unavoidable delay is experienced, the officer should be alerted and reasons given.
> 4.1 (13) Interpreters will not publicise their services within Metropolitan Police premises, including the distribution of personal business cards or publicly available material. (pp. 10–11)

Common Areas of Concern

Some concepts appear in the codes of most professions and are worth examining in detail here. Laster and Taylor (1994) list competence, impartiality, conflict of interest and confidentiality as areas most professional codes deal with. With respect to interpreters and translators, Hale (2007) identifies, in order of frequency, confidentiality, accuracy and impartiality/conflict interest as the most common areas in industry-specific codes around the world (Ozolins, 2015, p. 320). We shall, for the rest of the chapter, discuss these key aspects of most codes of ethics in three broad groups: impartiality, conflict of interest and privacy and confidentiality.

Impartiality

In professions where one professional deals with one client, the professional acts in the best interests of that client to maintain the fiduciary relationship, which is defined as a relationship in which one person trusts (or at least is entitled to trust) another to exercise judgment on his behalf (Miller et al., 2006, p. 212). For example, a lawyer is ethically and legally required to be partial to his or her client and defend the rights of this client. This is why a lawyer cannot represent, say, both a woman and a man who are going through a divorce. He or she would need to represent only one of the parties, as it would be almost impossible to be impartial.

Being impartial, according to the *American Heritage Dictionary*, is being 'not partial or biased; unprejudiced' and is synonymous with being 'fair'. It is linked to objectivity in decision making, which the same dictionary defines as 'uninfluenced by emotions or personal prejudices', which is again, is synonymous with being 'fair'. While impartiality focuses on being fair by not taking sides, objectivity relates to not allowing emotions and feelings to influence professional decisions. In professional ethics 'fairness' is owed to the clients who benefit from the professional service.

Being impartial appears to have slightly different interpretations in different settings. In the filed of police psychology, Heilbrun (2001) defines it as 'the evaluator's freedom from significant interference from factors that can result in bias' (pp. 36–37). As opposed to focusing on the agency of the professional in question, Fisher (2009) highlights the extent of impartiality in terms of who is covered in a psychologist's assessment: 'psychologists have an ethical obligation toward every party in a case, no matter how many and how named' (p. 1). In legal settings such as courts, Hendley (1996) offers his view about judges: 'in finding facts and applying general principles of law or community standards, the impartial judges are not predisposed in favor of either disputing party (including governmental parties) on political or personal grounds' (p. 115).

In other professions such as arbitration or mediation, often at least two opposing parties are involved and each has very different interests and objectives; but they are both assisted by the same professional – a mediator or arbitrator. This is a similar setting to interpreting where there are two separate parties involved. Impartiality in these professional settings where there are two clients or parties who need the services of the professional refers to 'lack of bias in favour or against one of the parties' (Mosk & Ginsburg, 2012, p. 381). For example, in international arbitration settings, involving international judges and lawyers, Megret (2014) believes that 'essential to the idea of impartiality is the ability of individuals to hoist themselves above their national identity to reach a sort of noumenon of internationalism' (p. 108).

Critics, however, claim that maintaining true impartiality is an illusion, because being biased is a part of human sympathy and therefore humans will always be inclined to pick one side (Barry, 1989). For example, with respect to judges, Hendley (1996) argues that 'impartiality can rarely be achieved completely. No decision maker can ever be completely impartial. Judges have values. They have ambitions. They may have some lingering dependence on, and loyalty to, those to whom they owe their job' (p. 115). It is therefore critical that professionals be aware of such tendency and exercise caution when impartiality is rightly expected by the service users.

Conflict of Interest

Another factor that may lead to bias is conflict of interest. According to Davids (2008), 'a conflict of interest arises whenever the private interests of someone in a position of public authority do not coincide with their official duties such that private interests may impinge on the performance of the official duty' (p. 1).

Conflict of interest is said to occur in two forms: perceived (due to a connection or interest that may be interpreted by others as a conflict of interest) or actual (where there is a direct link between the parties involved or the subject on hand and the professional involved). The way a perceived or actual conflict of interest is dealt with seems to be a more important issue than whether there is in fact a conflict of interest. Preston (2014) asserts that 'the fundamental and essential course of action is the ethical management of conflicts of interest' (p. 157). This tells a professional that others who are involved should know about the potential conflict of interest and those people, not the professional, should make the decision about the course of action that needs to be taken.

Privacy and Confidentiality

As we discussed earlier, people seeking professional help often disclose information that is not available to others, and this makes them vulnerable. Maintaining privacy and confidentiality, is therefore, a critical aspect of professional practice. Warren and Brandeis (1890) refer to privacy as the 'right to be let alone' (p. 195). Parker (1975) suggests that 'privacy is control over when and by whom the various parts of us can be sensed by others. By "sensed" is meant simply seen, heard, touched, smelled or tasted' (as cited in Sharma, 1994, p. 211).

However, in contemporary public life, privacy and confidentiality statements or guidelines commonly refer to the treatment of information about individuals or the business in question. Privacy generally refers to information that can identify a person including name, date of birth, address, photo or any other features of a person such as physical appearance. Confidentiality, on the other hand, has a broader meaning, in that it refers to a commitment undertaken by a professional not to disclose any information, including identifying information, discussed in his or her dealings with his or her client to anyone (Parsons, 2001). Although it is common courtesy not to share information disclosed to you because the client trusts you and expects that you respect his or her privacy and confidentiality, nevertheless 'common courtesy' is not enough. It is worth pointing out that different cultures may have different views and practices in relation to confidentiality, so the norms related here are mainly from the Western tradition. The rights to privacy and confidentiality are frequently explicitly included in codes of ethics of private and public organisations and agencies. In some highly sensitive settings, such as health and legal, they are legislated rights and are enforced by law. In addition, breaches of confidentiality betray the fiduciary nature of the relationship between the professional and the client. Because clients trust the professional, the expectation is that their privacy and confidentiality will be respected.

In professional life, however, these two rights carry more weight than in private life. This is because highly sensitive personal information or details are or have to be disclosed or revealed, in the course of professional services, and the treatment of this information confidentiality becomes not just a courtesy, but an obligation. Alexandra and Miller (2009, p. 149) propose that respect for confidentiality must be based on two objectives: preventing harm and building trust between a professional and his or her client. For example, violations of confidentiality, even in highly sensitive professional settings such as counselling, are among the common complaints against counsellors made to state licensing boards (Neukrug et al., 2001).

How are these two concepts applied in settings where interpreters and translators are involved to provide services within a police activity such as an interview or telephone intercepts? As discussed earlier, interpreters and translators, as professionals facilitating communication, have a separate role from the police officers who are tasked to enforce the law. Interpreters and translators in this setting occupy a role similar to that of a pathologist, an IT technician or a medical doctor who is providing his or her services within a police activity. In the course of providing their services, these professionals will inevitably gain access to personal details and information about the individuals involved in the police activity at hand as well as that of other individuals or matters. Although privacy and confidentiality afforded to individuals and organisations are part of the code of ethics of certified interpreters and translators, they are also enforced by law, as the breaches may lead to serious consequences beyond the immediate individuals involved. For example, breaches may lead to identification of police operations, victims or witnesses. A piece of information may not sound sensitive in many everyday settings but because it involves a police matter it may be significant. Benn (1988) holds that the disclosure of some general information may have more impact than usual if it involves a high-profile person because of his or her public role, in which case it would have to be treated as private.

In some settings, however, information that is exchanged between a professional and a client is more strictly protected. A good example is professional privilege, which protects information discussed between a professional and a client. Parsons (2001) explains that 'while confidential material covers most of what transpires between the client and the practitioner, privilege belongs only to certain defined "protected relationships" such as a physician and patients; lawyer and client...' (p. 120). This also has implications for interpreters and translators who are employed in these settings.

Summary

Society expects all professions to adhere to a code of ethics. Most professions have a code of ethics and/or code of conduct to set good practice standards for their members.

It is common to see some confusion about professional ethics and personal ethics. The essence of professional ethics is the principle of service to others and the high standards in delivering this service – an area that is not the concern of personal ethics. Professional ethics are often enforced by the relevant professional association or even by law, whereas personal ethics are individual choices and it is up to the individual whether to comply or otherwise.

Codes of ethics are a major step in professionalisation and demonstrate to the members of the profession the expected standards they should practice. However, critics have identified some shortcomings, pointing to the fact that codes of ethics are often rule based and rigid, and they are designed to serve the interests of the members of the profession, rather than sufficiently considering the needs of the clients. Fullinwider (1996) asserts that a code of ethics must first promote the moral self-understanding of the public good a profession serves. This can subsequently act as an overarching principle in making ethical decisions in many dilemmas that cannot possibly be encapsulated in every detail in the codes of ethics. This overarching *moral force* behind a profession can also promote voluntary compliance with codes of ethics.

Many professions have a separate code of conduct, which is designed to guide everyday behaviour and conduct, not necessarily directly linked to the core professional activity. The most common areas of concern for all professions are invariably impartiality, conflict of interest and privacy and confidentiality during the delivery of professional service.

Professional Ethics for Police Interpreters and Translators

5

The test of professional or public ethics is not that of satisfying one's personal conscience, but of acting in ways that are consistent with the duties entrusted to one in a public or professional role.

John Uhr
Cited in Preston, 2014, p. 158

Introduction

Increasingly more and more police activities involve the engagement of interpreters and translators to overcome language barriers that emerge during what are normally routine activities. The most common activities are police interviews with suspects, taking statements from witnesses or victims and translating evidence such as telephone intercepts or transcripts. Section 9.5.2 of the Adequacy of Interpretation in the Victorian Criminal Proceedings Manual by the Judicial College of Victoria, Australia, where judges and magistrates are trained, states that

> A high standard of interpretation is also required when the accused is being questioned by police. Errors in interpretation of questions or answers may make the record of interview unreliable by materially affecting the:
> - degree to which the accused can be said to have answered the questions asked;
> - meaning of any admissions made during the interview;
> - impression given to the jury of how the accused responded to police questioning, with consequential affects on the accused's perceived credibility and responsiveness (*NT v. R* [2012] VSCA 213). (Judicial College of Victoria, n.d.b)

Laster and Taylor (1994) assert that, in police activities where there are language barriers, interpreters and translators make policing more efficient and may prevent important evidence being excluded because it is considered unreliable. This is especially important during police cautions in Australia and the United Kingdom, or the Miranda Warning in the United States, when a suspect is told his or her rights, especially the right to a lawyer and the right to silence. Although, ideally, interpreters and translators will work in these settings as neutral facilitators of communication, involvement of interpreters and translators will inevitably change the dynamics. It will never be the same as two people communicating directly in the same language, as physically there is someone else in the setting. The involvement of a third person will inevitably give rise to issues that would not be a part of a direct communication. Some of the issues arising from these dynamics will also inevitably involve ethical issues that must be dealt with by professional interpreters and translators because of the unique position they hold in the setting. This chapter discusses professional ethics and code of conduct issues for interpreters and translators in police activities and uses case studies to illustrate the points of contention. The authors also try to offer guidance that may be of assistance to professional translators and interpreters and to police officers who have to work through them.

We need to emphasise at this point that our discussion relates only to professional interpreters and translators, rather than others such as bilingual staff members or uncredentialed persons who are called on to assist with communication in a police activity, as is evidenced in literature that reports all kinds of doubtful behaviour due to a lack of understanding of the profession. Ozolins (2015) emphasises the implications of this distinction for ethics by stating

> …the 'professional' proviso is crucial, because if interpreting is not carried out by a professional, then the responsibility resides only in the participant who hired or invited the particular person to interpret, for that person may not see themselves as professional, nor having any particular ethical responsibility. (p. 319)

The work provided by interpreters and translators in various settings is subject to guidelines emanating from these relevant professions and is governed by their relevant interpreting and translating organisations' own codes of ethics. Some of the more well-known and generally accepted codes are summarised in the text that follows. The full and current versions of these codes and guidelines are publicly available on these organisations' respective websites.

The Australian Institute of Translators and Interpreters' (AUSIT) Code of Ethics includes the following standards for its members:

- Maintain professional detachment, impartiality, objectivity and confidentiality
- Strive for excellence through continuous regular professional development
- Decline work beyond their competence

- Promote working conditions, relationships and an understanding of roles that facilitate collaboration and quality service delivery
- Adhere to dispute resolution procedures (Australian Institute of Translators and Interpreters, 2012)

The European Association for Legal Interpreters and Translators (EULITA) covers ethical issues for its members under the following headings:

Professional Competence
Accuracy
Obstacles to Performance Quality
Impartiality
Confidentiality
Protocol and Demeanour
Solidarity and Fair Conduct
(European Legal Interpreters and Translators Association, 2013)

The UK Chartered Institute of Linguists (CIOL) does not have a code of ethics; instead it has a general set of principles of professional conduct covering the following aspects:

1. Professional judgement
2. Linguistic competence
3. Subject competence
4. Professional competence
5. Continuing professional development
6. Responsibilities to clients/employers
7. Responsibilities to fellow language professionals and to the Chartered Institute of Linguists
8. Responsibilities to other agencies, public bodies and society (CIOL, 2015)

Institutional users of interpreting and translating services also developed guidelines to express what they expect from the interpreters and translators. For example, the Metropolitan Police brief for interpreters includes the following summary points:

- Competence – working in languages they are competent in
- Accuracy – without any addition, omission or colouring
- Impartiality
- Dignity and respect
- Confidentiality
- Conflict of interest

- Not accepting gifts or favours
- Not delegating their tasks
- Not promoting their services for further work
- Professionalism and integrity (Metropolitan Police, 2007)

Another good example reflecting the expectations of institutional users of interpreting and translating services is the benchcard prepared for the New York State Unified Court System titled *Working with Interpreters in the Courtroom*. It states that a judge can observe the following conduct to determine if the interpreter is delivering an effective service, revealing a number of pointers that service users may turn to for indications of the quality of interpreting they receive.

- Are there significant differences in the length of interpretation as compared to the original testimony?
- Does the individual needing the interpreter appear to be asking questions of the interpreter?
- Is the interpreter leading the witness, or trying to influence answers through body language or facial expressions?
- Is the interpreter acting in a professional manner?
- Is the interpretation being done in the first person? For example, while verbally translating what is being said in court, the interpreter will relay the words as if he or she is the person speaking. If the interpreter has a question, does he or she address the Court in the third person (e.g. 'Your honour, the interpreter could not hear the last question…') to keep a clear record? (The New York State Unified Court System, n.d.)

Codes for the interpreting and translating profession developed by different associations or organisations share many common features. Some of the features relate to the core activities of interpreting and translating such as accuracy, while others are more concerned with conduct issues such as punctuality and not personally promoting their own services. Ozolins (2015, p. 320) reports on two meta-analyses of interpreters' and translators' codes by Schweda-Nicholson (1994) and Hale (2007), and observes that most codes appeared to be deontological (duty-based) in nature. Schweda-Nicholson (1994) looks at nine, mostly North American, codes, whereas Hale (2007) analysed seventeen codes around the world. Confidentiality, accuracy and impartiality/conflict of interest are the top three areas most codes cover, followed by accountability/responsibility for own performance, role definition, professional solidarity and working conditions (Ozolins, 2015, p. 320).

The Value of the Primary or Preexisting Relationship

Professions serve different needs in society and each profession generally has its own code of ethics. Various codes for different professions may have overlaps as well as differences, causing certain ethical issues to arise when two or more professions come into contact. Although many professionals from time to time work *with* other professionals in the course of their duties, such as police officers having to work with paramedics, doctors, lawyers and social workers, it is inherent in the work of interpreters and translators that it always takes place *within* other professional activities. This makes issues around violation of or crossing professional role boundaries a more likely and immediate ethical concern in comparison to some other settings in which other professionals work. As a result the *Standard Operating Procedures* of the Metropolitan Police (2007) for working with interpreters highlights their expectation of the interpreter's role boundary in Section 4.5, 'Role of Interpreter': 'The interpreter should not take control of any situation in which they have been asked to interpret' (p. 9). This importantly demonstrates the clear demarcation of roles this police force wishes to draw in situations when they need to engage interpreters and translators. It is, therefore, warranted that we begin the rest of this chapter by examining interpreters' and translators' role boundaries before moving on to other areas of ethical issues. Some of the issues we discuss in the text that follows can very well be categorised under multiple headings; this is because that they can be viewed and analysed from different perspectives and each is equally valid.

The sort of professional activities we are referring to as constituting primary relationship are, for example, the likes of interviews between a parent and a teacher, consultations between a medical practitioner and a patient, counselling sessions between a psychologist and a patient, legal consultations between a lawyer and a client, meetings or negotiations between two trade delegations, speeches delivered by a presenter to an audience and so forth. In these encounters the two parties normally carry out their business directly, either in a one-to-one setting, or sometimes more than one individual may be involved in each side. For example, a person who feels unwell makes an appointment with a medical professional. At the appointment, the health professional will typically ask a series of questions designed to get some details such as the medical history of the person, most recent events or activities and the nature and intensity of the symptoms. The health professional may then explain what the problem is and prescribe medication or may ask for further tests to help with the diagnosis. This is the professional–client relationship between a health professional and a person who needs help for a health problem. Similarly, an encounter between a lawyer and a client may start with the client contacting the lawyer to make an appointment about seeking advice regarding a divorce matter, or a dispute with a landlord or business partner or a criminal matter. The lawyer would then obtain information about the matter that is the issue and would provide advice and information as appropriate. Some of the information the lawyer needs to have access to before providing appropriate legal advice may be in another language. For example, in a dispute over an inheritance, some documents may relate to properties in another country and would need to be translated. These transactions or activities would normally take place in a one-to-one relationship in a language that both the professional and their client are fluent in. Roy (2000) also highlights that these settings are not casual social interactions: 'speakers interact to accomplish a purpose (or purposes). They bring with them different expectations about the way they want to accomplish their goals through talk' (p. 5).

This desire to achieve their purpose (or purposes) in the interaction through talk dictates the language used by the speakers. Each party is responsible for what he says and what he does not say, how he says it, and so forth. This constitutes the *primary* (Michultka, 2009, p. 160) or *preexisting* (Gentile, Ozolins & Vasilakakos, 1996) relationship between the two parties in which interpreters or translators work in. When the speakers do not share a common language, but still need to carry out the business they have with each other, they will require language assistance. In many formal settings, this assistance will be provided by an interpreter or translator. An interpreter needs to be involved to interpret for both parties. This constitutes another professional–client relationship embedded within the original primary relationship described earlier.

Tasked with providing an essential service within a primary relationship, a professional interpreter should only be a means for communication between two parties who do not have a common language, similar to a conduit for communication. This is not in the sense that he or she should be 'a machine', 'a device', 'a pipe' or 'invisible', but in the sense that the main business that is part of the primary relationship still remains to be taken care of between the parties. Niska (1990) contends that 'the principle of information transfer is… to conceal, to add or to change nothing' (as cited in Schweda-Nicholson, 1994, p. 82) and that this defines the conduit role of the interpreter. Schweda-Nicholson (1994, p. 82) quotes Dan Barnes, a retired chief of language services at the US Department of State, who described the role of interpreters as a 'pane of glass', through which light passes without alteration or distortion. She says this analogy represents a role that allows for the communication of ideas without modification, adjustment or misrepresentation.

More specifically in the legal domain, in particular in courtroom settings, the much misconstrued instructions from judges and lawyers for interpreters only to translate (interlingually what is said) but not to interpret (i.e. infer, extrapolate or hypothesise what is meant by the speaker) reinforces their need for language service providers to work within their primary relationship with their clients/interviewees, and leave them to complete their business or transaction without undue interference from the interpreter (orally) or translator (in written format) other than the linguistic transfer between two languages. The interpreter is not and cannot be a part of the primary relationship at any stage apart from being a communicative link for both parties. For example, if the business is between a doctor, who is providing medical advice, and a patient, who is receiving medical help, this remains the same. An interpreter does not become a party by either providing medical advice or receiving medical help. An interpreter or translator cannot justify changing the primary relationship by overstepping his or her role boundaries as a language service provider. In the next section, we expand on this notion about the role of interpreters and translators working within a primary relationship.

Primary or Preexisting Relationship between Police and Suspects/Witnesses

Similar to the primary relationships in many professional fields described earlier, there are many occasions when police officers need to speak to people in the community to obtain information that cannot be obtained from other sources. These include talking to victims or witnesses of crimes, offenders or persons of interest in an investigation, or at information sessions for community members (Mulayim et al., 2015).

The notion of 'polis' in ancient Greece and Rome referred to the governance of the city-state for the common good and was embedded in ideals of citizenship and public service (Barrie, 2010). In *Lectures in Jurisprudence*, Adam Smith (1763) referred to police 'as the second general division of jurisprudence…which properly signified the policy of civil government, but now means the regulation of inferior parts of government such as cleanliness, security and cheapness or plenty' (as cited in Cannan, 1896, p. 422). In modern civic societies, a core function of the police is to effectively maintain social order. This is achieved by civic obedience in both personal encounters with police, as well as in people's everyday compliance with the law (Murphy & Cherney, 2012).

A survey conducted by police researchers McGurk, Carr and McGurk (1993) found that the interviewing of witnesses and suspects is in the top four of the most frequently conducted tasks in day-to-day policing; furthermore, from the point of view of police officers, their three most important investigative duties are taking statements, interviewing witnesses and interviewing suspects. The centrality of conducting interviews is confirmed by a more recent study by O'Neill and Milne (2014) of sixty-four police officers in England and Wales, where 54.6% of the respondents ranked interviewing suspects as the most frequent crime investigator activity, followed by other activities such as case file preparation, attending scenes, attending court and interviewing witnesses. According to Yeschke (2003), in the United States, real and documentary evidence of crimes makes up about 20% of all evidence presented in courts of law, whereas testimonial evidence (from interviews) accounts for the remaining 80%. As forensic linguist Dr. Kate Haworth (2006) puts it, '…the police interview is not only a means of evidence gathering, but also becomes a piece of evidence in itself submitted to the court at trial' (p. 741).

For suspects, police interviews are the most significant stage in their journey in the criminal justice system. This is when they need to explain their version of events, thereby setting the course for their defence. Often the success of the defence will depend on what they said or did not say in the police interview. Laster and Taylor (1994) observe that most criminal proceedings are decided based on the confession of the suspects in the police interview, which seems to agree with Gudjonsson's (2003) findings that decisions on 60% of criminal proceedings over more than twenty-five years in England were based on confessions from suspects in custodial interview. Obviously, securing confessions in the criminal justice system brings advantages such as increasing the likelihood of defendants being convicted and sparing victims and witnesses from giving evidence in court (Kebbell, Hurren & Robert, 2005), consequently saving court time; reducing the burden on victims and witnesses; and, if an early guilty plea is entered, mitigating the sentence. From this point of view, carefully administering suspect interviews with an aim to secure confessions is undoubtedly an institutionally and societally desirable outcome. However, ethical interviewing has to be at the forefront of interviewing practice to avoid false confessions that facilitate nothing but miscarriages of justice.

When short of confessions, resorting to questioning/interviewing victims and witnesses of crime becomes central to criminal justice. Their police statements often become one of the most credible types of evidence later in the court proceedings, as they are often taken soon after an incident while relevant information is still fresh in their minds. Owing to lengthy criminal justice processes, a case may not come before a court for months or sometime years. This makes the initial statements or complaints given to the police highly critical. All the details of an incident as expressed by a witness or victim need to be captured in the statement accurately.

When Language Assistance Is Needed
The Standard Operating Procedures for Metropolitan Police (2007) describe the role expected of an interpreter to be '…to facilitate communication between two parties who do not share a common language…They will interpret to each party everything which is said in the other language' (p. 9). The

two parties in this setting, namely a police officer and a suspect or witness/victim, already have a preexisting or primary professional relationship. The police officer needs to investigate a criminal activity and it involves talking to a witness/victim or interviewing a suspect. They are, however, unable to undertake that professional activity because of a language barrier and they have to include someone else in this setting to assist them. This then means the primary relationship or preexisting relationship has changed by default. It is not one person talking to another person directly. They are undertaking their transactions or business via another means. The question now is not if an interpreter or translator should intervene or not in this primary relationship, as he or she is already physically present in the event. Where an interpreting service is called for, the situation may be open to intervention, justified or unjustified, by the interpreter (Mulayim et al., 2015). The question is how much further he or she can intervene and whether he or she can justify any intervention or not. Can we justify the level of intervention in an interpreted event as Roy (2000) defends: 'Because the two primary speakers in interpreted events do not know the other's language, the interpreter is the only participant who can logically maintain, adjust and if necessary, repair differences in structure and use' (p. 6). In forensic contexts such as a police interview, cross-examination in court or a psychiatrist consultation, interpreters may find it difficult to justify when engaging in 'repairing differences in structure and use' when admissibility of evidence is called into question. The significance of preserving speech features including mistakes and errors is concurred by Laster and Taylor (1994): 'If an interpreter corrects linguistic mistakes made by a witness in a court or tribunal, even if these are obvious and unintended, or lengthens or embellishes their statements, this interferes with the judicial officers' ability to assess the credibility of the witness' (p. 212). In suggesting interpreters take on a role beyond a communication link, Roy (2000) is of the view that 'the interpreter is an active, third participant who can influence both the direction and outcome of the event, and that event itself is intercultural and interpersonal rather than simply mechanical and technical' (p. 6). One has to ask, in a police interview or a forensic assessment, for example, are the other parties in the communication aware that the 'direction' or the 'outcome' has been influenced by the interpreter? On being questioned, an interpreter may have to assess carefully whether this influence can be justified.

Pellegrino (1991) asserts that 'No professional can function properly without discretionary latitude. The more discretionary latitude we permit our professionals, the more vulnerable we become' (p. 74). This points to a need for interpreters and translators to exercise their professional latitude carefully because they are often the only persons in the communicative event who know what is said in both languages and may need to justify the level of discretion used in making professional decisions. Preston (2014) concludes that posing meta-ethical questions such as 'what reasons can we give for ethical attitudes and behaviours?' will guide us to the core concern of ethics – the justification for our decisions and actions. Rachels (1991) states that

> …a moral judgment … must be supported by good reasons. If someone tells you that a certain action would be wrong, for example, you may ask why it would be wrong, and if there is no satisfactory answer, you may reject that advice as unfounded. In this way, moral judgments require backing by reasons, and in the absence of such reasons, they are merely arbitrary. (p. 438)

The relationship between an interpreter/translator and the clients, in which the interpreter/translator undertakes the provision of language services so that the parties can communicate, is fiduciary in nature. This is in the sense that the clients have placed utmost trust and confidence in the language assistance they receive from the interpreter or translator in order for them to undertake their business in primary relationship. This relationship between interpreters and translators and their clients therefore calls for following duties to be fulfilled.

- Meeting their communication needs
- Maintaining confidentiality
- Maintaining impartiality

These duties shape the *conduit* role, interestingly favoured and even demanded by people who rely on translating and interpreting services in legal settings, including police settings, but much despised by some academics in translating and interpreting studies (Ozolins, 2015, p. 328).

The expectations of the role of an interpreter by police officers in investigative interviewing are well reflected by Shepherd (2007): 'The interpreter must know from the very first meeting that you [the police officer] wish to take active control of the interview even though you do not speak the individual's [the interviewee's] language' (p. 173). Shepherd also offers the outline of a briefing that a police officer should administer with the interpreter before an interview by instructing the interpreter to:

- Use the direct approach to interpreting [i.e. use first person]
- Work with you [i.e. the police officer] to keep the pace of the exchange down
- Not speak on the suspect's behalf
- Not engage in side conversations with the suspect
- Not talk at the same time as you [i.e. the police officer] or the suspect
- Stop you [i.e. the police officer] or the suspect when necessary [in order to interpret]

- Check if he or she is in any doubt as to what is being said by you [i.e. the police officer] or the suspect – and let you know about this doubt
- Not compress or alter whatever is said by you [i.e. the police officer] or the suspect (Shepherd, 2007, p. 172)

It is absolutely essential for an interpreter or translator to acknowledge and respect this primary relationship, with all its dynamics and features. The involvement of an interpreter or translator in this relationship is required *solely* for maintaining this relationship, using the skills and knowledge of an interpreter or translator to overcome language barriers. The only thing that has changed is the way the two parties communicate, that is, they are communicating indirectly via the interpreter, rather than directly. This means that an interpreter must only do what the two parties entrusted them to do – to help them communicate. The parties will be making decisions or taking actions on the assumption that whatever the interpreter says, or the translator writes, is actually the words of the other party. This is the trust placed on the interpreter/translator within a preexisting or primary relationship. This trust would then lead to the expectation that an interpreter or translator should not engage in any activity that would undermine this trust. This is the reason why interpreters and translators must do their very best in the oral or written form of communication they deal with to be *accurate*, which is always hailed by interpreting and translating academics and taken for granted by lay people or users of interpreting and translating services but rarely is it remarked on *why* accuracy is paramount.

A respondent in a survey of a group of translators and interpreters working for the International Criminal Tribunal for the former Yugoslavia said, when asked about the most challenging duty in the experience,

> …dealing with the (possibly) deliberate ambiguity in some source documents so that the translation also retained ambiguity without introducing possible interpretations apparently absent in the original (a tricky area at the best of times, let alone in a forensic context). (Elias-Bursać, 2015, p. 41)

In the same survey, a respondent interpreter answers that the most challenging aspect for him or her was that 'I had to change my interpretation style (after fifteen years of freelance work on the Paris private market), because everything said in the courtroom must be interpreted for the record' (Elias-Bursać, 2015, p. 41). Considering these requirements, debates about whether the interpreter/translator should be faithful to the speaker/author/source text or listener/reader/target text, as are commonly seen in translation and interpreting studies, are out of place in this context. The debates are from the perspective of the interpreter or translators. The fidelity of interpreters or translators must first be to the *trust* placed in them by the people who rely on their service. In this sense, the service-oriented role of interpreters or translators should be understood as a *'commitment'* (Beauchamp & Childress, 2009, p. 7) or *'pledge'* (Koehn, 1994, p. 56) to serve a need, rather than a description of what they do. *Service-oriented interpreting* or *translating* places the commitment and pledge to serve the communication needs of the parties in a primary relationship and the trust these parties has in them.

As we discussed earlier, the act of interpreting and translating can never be reduced to a technical or mechanical task, as it involves interaction between human beings who are undertaking an activity, such as a police interview, with each party having different aims, objectives, perspectives and intentions, not to mention different backgrounds and personalities. The communicative intent of a person who places a particular emphasis on a word in an utterance through intonation and stress, makes a sarcastic statement, is flippant or deliberately produces incoherent statements cannot be conveyed effectively by mechanical or technical means. This is when interpreters and translators exercise their autonomy the same way as other professionals in deciding the latitude they apply in their rendition guided by, most importantly, the communication taking place in the primary relationship and the trust that has been bestowed on them by the participants in that primary relationship. As aptly expressed by Gentile et al. (1996), 'the most effective interpreter, the one who is most "in control", is the one whose presence effects the least amount of disruption or change to the normal behaviour (linguistic and otherwise) of the other parties' (p. 53).

As a result, to *respect* the preexisting or primary relationship between his or her clients (e.g. a police officer and a suspect) means an interpreter/translator will convey oral utterances or written texts expressed in one language as accurately as possible into another and will not engage in any activity that may violate the boundaries of the primary relationship. Gentile et al. (1996) assert that

> ...the fundamental skill is the ability to maintain a clear focus on the interpreter's role as an abstract construct, while evaluating each situation and issue and making decisions which are consonant with that role but also take into account and cater for the singularity of each situation. (p. 38)

Parsons (2001) further holds that '...all boundary crossings (i.e. departure from commonly accepted professional rules and practices) can become problematic and need to be avoided' (p. 137).

In practice, however, certain decisions or actions of an interpreter or translator, knowingly or inadvertently, may intervene in the primary relationship whether it is fiduciary in nature or not. Unless these can be justified, a key aspect of ethical decision making, they could be regarded as breaches of the role entrusted to an interpreter or a translator.

To Intervene or Not to Intervene

> Like other professionals, interpreters constantly exercise discretion in their choice and performance of role. Recognising that there may be legitimate reasons for departing from a conduit role, and understanding the ethical and legal consequences of the choice will help interpreters to resolve some of their existing role conflicts.
>
> **Laster & Taylor, 1994, p. 225**

The verb *Intervene* comes from the Latin words *inter* + *venīre*, meaning to come between. The act of *unjustified intervention*, in our discussion of ethics for interpreters and translators who act as a communication link between two parties, refers more to the sense of taking 'a decisive or intrusive role ... in order to modify or determine events or their outcome' (*Collins English Dictionary*) but also includes aspects of the legal meaning of this word in the sense that 'to *interpose* and *become a party to* an action between others, especially in order to protect one's interests' (*Collins English Dictionary*).

First, the sheer physical presence of an interpreter or translator in a police activity or interview already creates a certain level of intervention (compared with a monolingual setting in which the police officer and the suspect/witness or other persons speak the same language). Second, the core task of interpreting and translating involves a series of choices made by an interpreter and translator, as 'the concepts and ideas expressed by each speaker have been "processed through [the] mind via perception, classification, recollection and utterance"' (Byrne & Heydon, 1991, p. 776). The question then is not so much about how an interpreter or translator can be made invisible but how their visibility remains within the confines of the role they are required for. An interpreter's or translator's practices or decisions can be assessed only by whether his or her intervention is 'justified' or 'unjustified' when viewed from the standpoint of his or her professional role in the police activity such as an interview – in other words, serving the direct need of both parties to communicate with each other. This role and the tasks needed to fulfil this role can be the only justifications for intervention by an interpreter or translator. Any decision or action that cannot be justified in such a way would potentially lead to mixing or violation of professional role boundaries (Parsons, 2001).

An interpreter or translator must not intervene in the primary relationship between a police officer and a victim/witness/suspect, without justification.

Case Study

Lee (2016) documents a South Korean murder case in which a Russian single mother was accused and later convicted of murdering her four-year-old child with her Korean ex-husband. The extracts below show the interview conducted the day after the incident between the interviewing police officer (Pol 1) and Alisa, the woman's thirteen-year-old daughter from her previous marriage in Russia. A Russian-Korean interpreter (Int) was engaged to facilitate the communication.

576 Pol 1: [Tell her to] tell us in details [sic] what she knows.
577 Int: Please give us details about yesterday's accident.
578 Alisa: Well, I went to school yesterday. Mum was at home with the little one. Mum must have taken her to kindergarten and gone to work. In the evening, I picked up the little one, went home and we stayed around/hung out. I fed her and [we] watched TV, and went to bed.
579 Int: Did you sleep, right?
580 Alisa: Yes, the little one and I went to bed... [omitted]
581 Int: Last night, right? Do you mean... [omitted]
582

. *[exchanges between Int and Alisa omitted]*
.
588
589 Int: In the evening, right? Alright. Thank you. Yesterday, she spoke at length, she says the child went to the kindergarten yesterday too. The child, to the kindergarten. She also went to school and came home. She went to the kindergarten herself to take her younger sister home. Alisa says ... [omitted]

After the interviewing officer posed the question in turn 577 enquiring what happened yesterday, it took an extraordinary twelve turns between the interpreter and Alisa before the interpreter finally rendered Alisa's account into Korean in turn 589. In the omitted turns, the interpreter was constantly checking with Alisa his understanding and asking additional questions, so that he put forward a chronological account in summary format in turn 589 for the interviewing police officer. From an ethics point of view, the exchange between the interpreter and Alisa should have taken place between the police officer and Alisa, if the former chooses to do so. Taking over the interviewing officer's role in this way is unjustifiable. This is what should have happened: simply interpret whatever Alisa says in the previous turn and leave the interviewing officer to ask whatever question he or she sees fit. In addition, rendering a summary of twelve turns of lengthy exchanges from turns 577 to 588 in turn 589 by the interpreter violates the accuracy principle of ethics, with much nuanced detail Alisa provided lost in translation. The trust that Alisa and the interviewing officer bestowed on the interpreter is completely breached – Alisa's story was not conveyed faithfully, and the police interviewer did not get to hear the utterances straight from Alisa, so that he could then determine the direction that he wanted to pursue with the inquiries.

The following excerpt shows that, after a lengthy exchange between Alisa and the interpreter without involving the police interviewer in which Alisa said that she thought her mother went downstairs with a torch and that was when her mother found her younger sister lying on the ground, the interpreter rendered a summary account that contained factual inaccuracies in turn 807.

807 Int: ... at first, <u>her mother looked through the window, she could see with some light the child fallen there</u>, so Natasha called an ambulance and what not...the three of them found the baby later. (N.B. Natasha is a friend of the mother.)
808 Pol 1: Then, [she] did not go down as soon as she saw her. (N.B. [The mother] did not go down as soon as the mother saw her child from the apartment window.)
809 Int: She's not saying exactly, exactly when. But she says her mother saw first. It's her mother that saw first. (N.B. Alisa is not saying exactly, exactly when...)
810 Pol 1: That's right. Then Natasha and herself did not seem [sic] themselves at the time, right? But after hearing from her. (N.B. Then Natasha and Alisa did not see themselves at that time.)
811 Int: Yes, yes.
812 Pol 1: Normally you'd go straight downstairs, right?
813 Int: Right, calling...

Contrary to the norm to interpret in first person, the use of reported speech by this interpreter creates confusion about who is who. Notes are inserted by the authors in the above excerpt for the purpose of clarity. From turn 808 to turn 813, by the interpreter again deprived Alisa of her right to answer the questions posed the police interviewer by engaging with the police interviewer on her behalf. This case reported by Lee (2016) is riddled with a litany of breaches of the interpreter's codes and is a textbook case of how interpreting should not be done. One may rightly question whether the interpreted evidence had affected the outcome of the case. The accused was convicted and sentenced to fifteen years' imprisonment (Lee, 2016). During the court trial, when

Alisa spoke through a different interpreter, she denied aspects of her statement made with the police discussed above. But when the interpreting issues were raised in the appeal in the Supreme Court, the court ruled that Alisa's statement during the police interview was more credible and accurate because she was interviewed shortly after the incident and she had no reason to speak against the interest of her mother (Lee, 2016). The appeal was not successful.

The authors must point out that although on the one hand this case study shows the significant implications of interpreters' understanding of their role and conduct, it should equally be emphasised that the police interviewer bears the responsibility for maintaining the integrity of his or her primary relationship with his or her interviewee by guarding against unjustified encroachment by interpreters whose business in the encounter is solely to facilitate their communication with their interviewee and nothing more.

Other Areas of Concern in Police Settings

It is impossible to come up with a comprehensive list of all the issues that can arise in police activities in which an interpreter is engaged. This is essentially due to the fact that interpreting and translating involve human interaction between parties in an essentially forced encounter between a police officer, who needs to investigate a crime or offence, and a suspect or witness/victim in that crime or offence. This setting can have a whole range of dynamics depending on the cooperative attitudes of the interviewee, and their intellectual, psychological and verbal competence to deal with the interview, which would be different from other settings such as interpreting or translating in a conference, a business setting, a medical appointment or parent–teacher interview.

There are, however, some areas in which interventions by interpreters or translators appear more often and where justification needs to be monitored closely by parties to the primary relationship as well as by interpreters and translators themselves. We group and discuss them in the rest of the chapter under four headings, which are identified as key areas of ethical concerns for all professions: competence, impartiality, conflict of interest and confidentiality (Laster & Taylor, 1994).

Competence

When interpreters and translators work in legal contexts, including police, the level of competence they are expected to possess is well defined by Laster and Taylor (1994). They contend that the benchmark should be set at putting the person(s) receiving the service 'on the same linguistic footing' (p. 209) as a native speaker of the other language the person does not speak. They do not say 'to be on the same legal knowledge or cultural knowledge footing'. It is because even native speakers of English may have varying degrees of legal knowledge and information and not all are on an equal footing with everyone else in society. Native speakers of English may also struggle to understand what is going on in a formal process in a criminal justice setting or what options they have in a criminal matter. However, help and assistance can be sought by native speakers of English from other players in the setting, such as lawyers, court staff, social workers and so on, for them to function effectively in the situation. This opportunity needs to be offered, linguistically, to a non- or limited English speaker, as opposed to the popular misconception by the general public and sometimes even professionals who allocate all those roles to the interpreter. This then sets the benchmark, the authors believe, for the level of competence expected of interpreters and translators. They need to be competent enough to comprehend and convey the verbal or written messages and the nonverbal features of a communication so the parties involved are, as much as possible, on the same linguistic footing. Parsons (2001) explains that competence does not mean being perfect, saying 'To suggest one is competent implies that the individual is capable of performing a minimum quality of service that is within the limits of his or her training, experience and practice, as defined in professional standards or regulatory statutes' (p. 156). This precisely conforms to the authors' position explained earlier.

Me Interpreter!

A CHINESE CASE

A Chinese defendant stepped forward at the City Court this morning, when called to answer a charge of hawking without a licence.

After the case had commenced it was intimated that the defendant was quietly sitting down in court with his coat off. The judge asked the Chinaman who had stepped forward and had occupied the place given to defendants, what he had to do with the case? 'Me Interpreter', answered the Chinaman. Subsequently The Judge then asked, 'You want an Interpreter yourself?' The alleged Interpreter said 'No; (pointing to defendant) tell me come up'.

The Daily News
Australia, 1911

As we discussed in the Chapter 2, a claim to the title of 'profession' refers to serving a need of society directly with *specialised skills and knowledge* and *autonomous decision making*. Consequently a professional refers to someone who is competent in undertaking that profession as expected by the members of society. The core competence of the interpreting and translating profession is the 'exact transfer of the original spoken (or written) message into the other language' (Laster & Taylor, 1994, p. 211) so as to place the person receiving the language service 'on the same linguistic footing as an English-speaking person within the system' (p. 209). This is borne out in the following protest by an accused person who was being tried at the International Criminal Court and assisted by a simultaneous interpreter:

> *The Accused*: [Interpretation] Mr. Antoneti, at the beginning of the Status Conference, you, yourself, said that the reliability of simultaneous interpretation was 80 per cent. I need 100 per cent reliable translation, if we're talking about transcripts that are being admitted, transcripts from other cases (...). Because I have the simultaneous interpretation on paper and it's only 80 per cent reliable, well what does that ... where does that leave me? (Elias-Bursać, 2015, p. 90)

This is a legitimate question by a defendant in a high-stakes hearing. He is facing being locked away for years at the conclusion of this trial. It is only fair that he expects 100% accuracy.

Much attention usually, legitimately, focuses on the bilingual linguistic ability of the interpreter when it comes to competence, scrutinising his or her transferring ability in finding an acceptable equivalent word or expression in the target language with maximum accuracy. However, a number of other actions that may be taken by an interpreter or translator could seriously undermine the trust clients have and expect in the competence of an interpreter or translator. Such actions may be unethical or unacceptable, or even illegal in some circumstances, unless they can be justified. These actions are grouped under the current heading of competence, and deserve further discussion to raise awareness both for interpreters/translators and other parties in an interpreted activity, for example, a police interview.

Filtering, Omitting or Summarising Content
One issue, more than any other factor, that often undermines the competence of and trust in an interpreter or translator and is difficult to justify is when filtering, omitting or summarising of content happens: hence all the 'lost in translation' stories in which the length of a client's speech appears to be much longer or shorter than the interpreter's speech. This does not immediately mean there is filtering or summarising or addition, as this may be a natural result of conveying meaning between two different languages and cultures and can be justified in some situations (Mulayim et al., 2015).

From an Australian newspaper *Barrier Miner* (Broken Hill, NSW: 1988–1954) dated 21 June 1892:

Alleged Embezzlement

A Chinese interpreter Wanted.

At the Police Court this morning, before Mr. C.L.C. Badham, P.M., after a few inebriates had been appropriately dealt with, a Chinaman, who on his arrest by Constable Mackie had given the name of Ham Sung, was charged with being identical with one Ham Goon Tin, accused of embezzling a sum of money from AhLouy at Menindie recently. The prisoner stated that he knew no English, an assertion which was scarcely borne out by the constable's evidence; an interpreter being called for, another Mongolian lounged nonchalantly into court, and, with hand in pocket, assured the magistrate that he knew English 'a lill bit', and kissed the book. He would doubtless have sworn just as cheerfully over the blowing out of a match or the decapitation of a rooster. When the magistrate read the charge, which was of considerable length, the interpreter, addressing the accused, muttered something like 'Ho ki li', and in response to the natural query of the bench, smilingly gave his assurance that in about three syllables he had compressed the meaning of several sentences. The bench, however, was dubious, and remanded the prisoner for the presence of a more verbose interpreter.

Alleged Embezzlement
Barrier Miner, Australia, 1892

From an ethics point of view, what we are concerned with is when this filtering, omission or summarising occurs because an interpreter believes the content is not relevant, too complicated or not important for the other party to know. The reason for this may also include the interpreter or translator making a judgement as to whether the content is culturally or morally relevant or offensive or not. These decisions should be a matter for the parties in the original primary relationship. Their trust in the interpreter or translator is to meet their communication needs, not to think or judge on their behalf. The New York State United Court System has the following points in the Code of Ethics for its court interpreters to address precisely such issues, although they categorise these points under the heading of accuracy:

- Provide the most accurate interpretation of a word despite a possible vulgar meaning. Colloquial, slang, obscene or crude language, as well as sophisticated and erudite language, shall be conveyed in accordance with the usage of the speaker. An interpreter is not to tone down, improve or edit any words or statements.
- Not simplify or explain statements for a Limited English Proficiency (LEP) or deaf or hard of hearing impaired person even when the

interpreter believes that the LEP speaking or deaf or hard of hearing person is unable to understand the speaker's language level. If necessary, the LEP or deaf or hard of hearing person may request an explanation or simplification. (UCS, 2008, pp. 7–8)

Case Study

The following transcripts are from an interview between Australian journalist George Negus and the then Libyan leader Colonel Muammar Al-Gaddafi in 2010, broadcast on *Dateline*, a current affairs program on SBS TV in Australia.

Colonel Muammar Al-Gaddafi [Translation]: The authority is with the people, in the end. Authority lies with the Libyan people who rule and so all other options are out.
George Negus: How do you find out what the people want?
Colonel Muammar Al-Gaddafi [Translation]: The people say now they are exercising authority. Other options might be proposed but they are alternatives to the people's authority. The people are free.
George Negus: So it wouldn't really upset you if they said 'We don't like the Gaddafi system'?
Colonel Muammar Al-Gaddafi [Translation]: For forty years I have not been the ruler, the authority has been with the people. They take nothing from me or add anything to me.
George Negus: Interestingly enough, I'm exactly the same age as you, and in 1969, when you had your bloodless coup, I started in journalism. It is a strange coincidence. I also had a Volkswagen car like your Beetle. But, we say in the West that people should have certain things on their tombstone – certain words on their tombstone. What do you think people will want to see on Muammar Gaddafi's tombstone? Gaddafi an angel or Gaddafi a villain?
Interpreter [Translation]: **Sir, what do you want to be written about you?**
Colonel Muammar Al-Gaddafi [to the Interpreter]: **No, I heard a different question.**
Interpreter [To Al-Gaddafi]: **No, I mean, sir …. How do I say it, I mean, in hundreds of years, what do you want written about you?**
Colonel Muammar Al-Gaddafi [to the Interpreter]: **He used other words.**
Interpreter: **Sir, I don't want to say them.**

(Boldface added, SBS, 2010)

In this interview, the interpreter, who believes the journalist's question involving the word 'villain' may offend the ruler, distorts and omits content based on his judgement about what is offensive and not, interprets as *'Sir, what do you want written about you?'* However, Gaddafi spoke some English and understands parts of the questions and is aware that some distortion and filtering has occurred and brings this to the attention of the interpreter. What is significant here is that even as a dictator or an authoritarian ruler at the time, Gaddafi was assuming that whatever the interpreter said was actually what the journalist had said. He was not expecting that his interpreter, probably on his payroll at the time, should be softening or culturally mediating content. A negotiation with the interpreter then ensues, first by him protesting *'No, I heard a different question'* and then *'He used other word'* and the interpreter avoiding interpretation of what had been said exactly. Instead he tries to *justify* his distortion and omission with the excuse *'I did not want to say it'*. It was not because there was a linguistic gap or a culture-specific term that he could not manage. It was simply because he did not want to interpret because he 'thought' it would be offensive. The direct need, however, that Gaddafi, was *expecting*, and *trusting*, his interpreter to serve, even in his position of power at the time as an authoritarian ruler, was to assist him with communication with the journalist. With the benefit of some English skills Gaddafi questions the interpreting when he realises there was some distortion. This then raises a serious concern, one that is probably felt in many interpreted interviews, 'What if he had no English at all, not a word of English?', as many suspects and witnesses in police settings do not. Then Gaddafi and journalist George Negus would be having two separate conversations, as they would be asking and answering different questions. This is where the vulnerability lies, for both parties, not just the person who cannot speak the language of the interviewing person. Some commentators who are in favour of assigning interpreters and translators a range of other roles such as a 'mediator' or an 'advocate' ignore this fundamental expectation. The authors argue that it neglects the trust the parties in the primary relationship place on interpreters and translators, the context in which they undertake to assist communication for the activity or business those parties are having to take its course. The role boundaries for interpreters and translators, therefore, should not violate the preexisting relationship they operate in.

Schweda-Nicholson (1994, p. 88) relates to Schuker's comments about a lengthy court trial where the most common error was the omission of parts of long statements or sentences, using one such statement that included a long list ('boots, oilskins, shovels, rakes, plastic bags') as an example. Schuker (as cited in Schweda-Nicholson, 1994, p. 88) explains it is imperative in a legal setting to capture and convey every single item in the list whereas in other settings such as conference interpreting one may do with a general description 'cleanup equipment' or 'boots, shovels, etc'.

In a police activity, such as an interview with a suspect, taking a statement from a witness or telephone intercepts, all content, no matter how irrelevant, trivial or offensive they may sound to an interpreter or translator, needs to be conveyed as closely as possible using the linguistic and paralinguistic means available to an interpreter. This applies to the utterances made by both the questioning and the answering sides. The questions and statements by the police officer also need to be conveyed to the suspect or witness without filtering, omission or summarising. If one party uses offensive language, makes racial comments or jokes against the other, the other party should not be denied knowledge of this. In a normal, monolingual interview, the parties would hear everything that is said to them and would have the opportunity to respond or ignore. This should not change due to the presence of an interpreter or translator in the middle. This is how the authors insist the conduit role should be understood, one that accentuates the interpreter's and translator's duty to meet their clients' communication needs.

Case Study

Q. What time did you wake up?
A. Ahh about seven, eight o'clock.
Q. What did you do then?
A. We had breakfast like we used to do and **then**, ohh have, had a shower together. Had breakfast, then I said to Petra, well I'll see you on Monday. She usually goes home on the Sunday a lot, **likes to go home to her parents on the Sunday and just, 'cos she doesn't get to see her parents very much.**
Q. And what'd you do?

(A transcript of the police interview with Martin Bryant, n.d.)

The above interview is from Australia's worst mass shooting event in 1996 where nineteen-year-old Martin Bryant shot dead thirty-five people and injured a further twenty-three. Imagine how the section in bold in a different case may be critical for an alibi. If it was an interview where the suspect spoke a different language and an interpreter was used, leaving out or summarising the bold segments because the interpreter decided that it was not significant would not be justified.

Case Study

A victim of a road rage incident is reporting the incident to the police:

Police Officer: So, the other car cut in front of you and the guy came out and then, what happened?

Witness: [in LOTE] Uhm, he had something in his hand, the thing that you use to change wheels, he threw it at my car.)
Interpreter: He had a wheel brace in his hand and he threw it at my car.

This summary of what the witness said would not be acceptable, as it does not reflect what the witness actually says, even though the witness may in fact be referring to a wheel brace (or lug wrench). What the interpreter did was to express his or her opinion and this cannot be justified in a police interview. The interpreter should have interpreted all that was said, and if there was any ambiguity it would be within the police officer's role, not the interpreter's, to clarify what is meant by the witness.

Interpreter Giving Instructions or Prodding Speakers

One of the commonly observed ethical concerns, even with some experienced interpreters, relates to mixing or violating professional role boundaries during police interviews. It can be an intentional act to support one of the parties or simply the result of not having proper training to know that this is beyond their role in that police interview.

Case Study

Police Officer: Do you remember closing the door before going to bed?
Interpreter: [in LOTE] Do you remember closing the door before going to bed?
Suspect: [in LOTE] How can I remember? It has been 4 months?
Interpreter: [in LOTE] You need to answer, yes or no.
Suspect: [in LOTE] No.
Interpreter: No.

In a police interview setting as above, it is not within the interpreter's role to prod the interviewee to answer in a certain way, or redirect the course of the interview to get it 'back on the right track' for the interviewing officer, or instruct the interviewee that they have not answered the questions correctly (Mulayim et al., 2015). In police interviews, it is the interviewing officer who is in charge of the interview and responsible for what is said and how it is said. If the police officer thinks the suspect or witness's answer is not relevant, it is up to the officer to ask the suspect/witness to answer the question, and tell the suspect/witness not to answer a question with another question. Interpreters must be acutely aware that clarifying instructions or suggesting examples of proper ways of responding is not within their role; rather, this is entirely the prerogative of the professionals in the primary relationship. This was an unjustified intervention by the interpreter and therefore is not acceptable as professional interpreting practice (Mulayim et al., 2015).

Case Study

Police Officer: Did you produce a gun at the kebab van when the owner refused to serve you?
Interpreter: [in LOTE] Did you produce a gun at the kebab van when the owner refused to serve you?
Suspect: [in LOTE] I don't have a gun.
Interpreter: I don't have gun.
Police Officer: I did not ask if you owned a gun. Did you produce a gun at the kebab van?
Interpreter: [in LOTE] I did not ask if you owned a gun. Did you produce a gun at the kebab van?
Suspect: [in LOTE] I said, I didn't own a gun, didn't I?
Interpreter: [in LOTE] You already said that. He is asking if you took it out. You must answer the question.

Giving instructions or prodding the speaker to answer a question in a certain way, as seen in the preceding example or judging whether an answer is repetition or not, is not within the role of an interpreter and cannot be justified. It would undermine the competence expected by the users of the interpreting service. That a suspect provides the same answer repeatedly may have some significance as far as the police officer is concerned. For example, it may imply that the answers have been rehearsed. Similarly, a suspect may be deliberately not answering a question.

Giving Advice, Opinion or Information

The involvement of an interpreter in a primary relationship between a police officer and a suspect or witness is needed because they do not have a common language and need a way to communicate. This should remain the sole purpose for the presence of an interpreter. However, because of the unusual position the interpreter occupies, in a metaphorical sense, between the two parties, and a whole range of interpersonal communication dynamics, interpreters may be asked to do something or asked for advice or information by either party, or interpreters themselves may feel compelled to take some action or volunteer advice or information. Laster and Taylor (1994) quote a lawyer saying:

> Strictly speaking, they should be professionals, the interpreters. It is a profession. It would be difficult for them because a person who has been picked up and charged is obviously extremely stressed out... It would be very hard for the person in that situation not to ask someone else who does speak that language and does understand, to do things with them. It's just natural, and I guess it would be a matter for the individual interpreter. There are facilities, though. It just depends on what context... If they were interpreting in a conference in the Remand Centre there are social workers, and Salvation Army people and

welfare workers within the Remand Centre; it would be fairly simple just to leave a message. But then again, it depends on how they have been called to the Remand Centre – they may have been called by lawyers acting for someone within the Remand Centre to come and interpret. (p. 221)

Generally speaking, giving advice or information is not within the role boundary of an interpreter or translator, unless it is advice or information directly related to the core reason for their presence – facilitating communication and that advice or information is needed either to improve communication or resolve a breakdown in communication between the parties involved. Advice or information that has nothing to do with meeting communication needs by conveying meaning from one language to another cannot be justified, if questioned or scrutinised. The Standard Operating Procedures for working with interpreters and translators for the Metropolitan Police (2007, p. 10) explain that extra information on linguistic or cultural issues can be justified 'where it impacts upon comprehension of the message'.

British forensic psychologist Eric Shepherd (2007) has the following to say about interpreters from the point of view of investigative interviewers as service users of interpreters. He holds that interpreters should not act as 'intermediaries', which is another independent profession by its own right normally possessing speech or language therapist qualifications and working with vulnerable suspects and witnesses in English and Welsh courts by ensuring communication is as complete, coherent and accurate as possible (Intermediary Programs in England and Wales, n.d.; Ministry of Justice, 2012).

> An interpreter performs the task of communicating verbally, giving as accurate as possible a rendering of what you or the interviewee are saying to each other... An interpreter is responsible for providing an accurate transfer of meaning from one language to another.
>
> He or she is allowed to intervene to ask for clarification, accommodation of the interpreting process, and to alert you and the interviewee – and any other third party present – to possible misunderstanding and missed cultural inferences.
>
> He or she must not act as an intermediary, i.e. must not explain the question to the interviewee nor explain the interviewee's responses. Intermediaries who fulfil this role with witnesses come from a range of professional backgrounds, including speech and language therapy, psychology, education and social work. When the interviewee is a suspect, the intermediary occupies the role of an appropriate adult under para 1.7 of Code C to the Police and Criminal Evidence Act 1984. (p. 171)

Shepherd (2007) cautions against confusing the roles of interpreter and intermediary by pointing out that 'It is certainly the case that many interpreters on their own initiative take on the role of intermediary, and in doing so may make the task of managing the interview much more difficult' (p. 172). In England and Wales, there is a registration system for intermediaries, who belong to a separate profession usually possessing qualifications in speech pathology or language therapy responsible for facilitating communication between a defendant, witness or other party and the legal system to ensure the communication is as complete, coherent and accurate as possible (Communication Matters in the Courts, n.d.; Intermediary Programs in England and Wales, n.d.).

The difficulties Shepherd describes explain service users' preference of receiving such communication service under a conduit model in order for every professional in the setting to play his or her role appropriately according to his or her expertise. An understanding and appreciation by interpreters and translators, as part of their competence, of such an expectation or even demand, for strictly defined role boundaries is critical when working in police settings as well as other criminal justice settings including courts.

Case Study

Judge Orie: …When you spoke to those who interviewed you and when you described your relationship with Mr. Nikic, do you remember what you used what your family relationship, or your relationship, with Mr. Nikic was? Do you remember the word you used in your own language? Could you just give that word, if you remember?

Witness: [interpretation] They asked me, Who is he to you? I said, Relative, friend; 'relative' meaning distant relative. We have a relationship of mutual respect from way back, but I don't understand why my counsel is grilling me on this point and splitting hairs.

Judge Orie: Could I ask the interpreters, perhaps. The word witness used, is that a word which would make it possible to understand it as a wider relationship rather than a close relationship, such as a cousin? I'm not listening to the English channel, so if perhaps the English interpreter could…

Interpreter: 'Relative' is a very general word and that's the word that the witness used, 'rodzak', meaning literally relative. He doesn't specify any kind of relationship close or distant.

Judge Orie: Yes. Would it be… and I am asking you more or less now as experts, would it be imaginable that if someone uses this word that in a… well, let's say, a quick translation, it could be interpreted as 'cousin'? Is that something you could imagine?

> *Interpreter:* Your Honour, with all due respect, we should not be answering questions of this kind. There are all sorts of interpretations throughout the former Yugoslavia. Maybe somewhere.
>
> *Judge Orie:* Yes, I fully respect that you consider yourself not to be in a position to answer this question. Perhaps I should not have asked it. (Elias-Bursać, 2015, p. 86)

The example above shows the interpreter resisting, and rightly turning down, a judgement call imposed on him/her because such intervention, although invited, if complied with, may be unjustifiable and simply be personal conjecture.

On the contrary, when an interpreter or translator volunteers advice, opinion or information beyond his or her role, it may be viewed as a sign of incompetence and not welcomed by the service users. Section 4.1 of the Standard Operating Procedures for working with interpreters and translators for the Metropolitan Police (2007) (2) reads 'Interpreters will interpret and translate accurately and faithfully between their listed languages to the best of their ability, without any addition, omission, advice or personal opinion tainting the message' (p. 10). Similarly, Gibbons (2007) found in a study of NSW police officers that they were reluctant to call an interpreter for a number of reasons. Among other things such as budgetary considerations, concerns that the interpreter would serve as an advocate for the suspect is relevant for the present discussion, and it is unfortunately a real concern for the service users. Interpreters should not be or appear to be an advocate for a suspect or witness. Advocacy is another domain covered in the setting by other professionals such as their lawyers, legal guardians and social workers, who have qualifications or professional credentials or membership in a profession.

Case Study

> *Police:* Now, did you have any lawful reason for physically assaulting your daughter?
>
> *Interpreter:* [in LOTE] Did you have any lawful reason for physically assaulting your daughter?
>
> *Suspect:* [in LOTE] She needs to obey her parents. In my culture, girls stay home with the parents until they get married.
>
> *Interpreter:* He says she needs to obey parents. In my culture, girls stay home until they marry. I think that is right. In some traditional families, people still expect their daughters to live with the parents until they get married. Of course it would not justify hitting but you should see why he did it.

The example above relates to a suspect who is being interviewed for allegedly hitting his daughter for disobeying his instructions. The intervention by the interpreter, that is, providing his or her personal views on cultural practices, is beyond the transfer of messages originating from the speakers in the primary relationship, and therefore totally unjustified. A big question mark should immediately be attached to the interpreter's competency.

Case Study

Just before a police interview starts in the interview room:

Suspect: [in LOTE] Mr Interpreter, you would have done these police interviews many times. Shall I answer the questions or shall I make a 'no comment' interview?

There are a couple of issues at play here. If the interpreter answers this question, he or she may be undermining their impartiality, which will be discussed in detail under the next section heading. From the point of view of the current discussion, offering advice or information to the suspect, be it an example such as the above or a question about whether the suspect should contact a lawyer or a support person or other matters such as whether the suspect will get a copy of his or her statement or interview record at the end of the interview, will have consequences in that it may influence the decisions or actions of one of the parties. Therefore, the source of that advice – the interpreter – will be held accountable, if not liable. This is so, even if all parties in the communication agree for the interpreter or translator to provide that advice or information. Matters such as these are within the police officer's role to attend to, rather than for the interpreter to overstep the role entrusted to him or her and provide advice to the person being questioned.

One thing that may not be recognised sufficiently in the interpreting and translating profession is that in many Western countries, providing professional advice is strictly regulated and unless a person is qualified to provide advice and his or her professional role allows him or her to do so, giving advice and information should be avoided, as it may be illegal or have legal implications. For example, giving legal advice is highly regulated in many countries, as it means the legal advice is based on a person's specific circumstances and may lead him or her to take a certain course of action in a legal matter, which may in turn affect his or her rights and obligations. As this task falls under the professional practice of lawyers or attorneys, people who are not qualified should avoid such activities.

Having an understanding and appreciation of this notion is paramount for interpreters and translators, because they have direct contact with the people they are serving and it is inevitable that they will be asked for advice by either party, who may not be clear about the role boundaries of an interpreter or translator. First, such requests should be conveyed to the other party so they are aware of the request for advice or information. In fact, as both parties rely on the interpreter for communication, interpreters must avoid having conversations with one of the parties without telling the other party what the conversation is about. This will prevent a perception that the interpreter serves one party more than the other. Subsequently the interpreter can decide whether the advice or information is needed for the facilitation of communication, and if it is related to their role in that setting. For example, answering a police officer's question about whether particular legal terminology or a certain legal process would pose difficulties in interpreting or translating into another language of an area that has a totally different legal system would be justified, as it relates to the role of the interpreter or translator in facilitating the communication.

Inaccuracies and Distortions

> If you assume reality reflects an independent world like a mirror, then meaning is what mirrors that reality, and distortion is what deviates from it. If I am standing in front of a cow, and I call it a horse…the chances are that someone will tell me I am distorting reality.
>
> **Degramont, 1990, p. 1**

Distortion occurs when accuracy is compromised. Therefore when discussing accuracy in interpreting and translating, the most scrutinised aspect is the act of distortion

Accuracy is defined in the *Oxford English Dictionary* as

- The quality of being correct or precise, as in 'we have confidence in the accuracy of the statistics'.
- (*technical*) The degree to which the result of a measurement, calculation or specification conforms to the correct value or a standard.

Distortions in interpreting and translating refer to changing the meaning of utterances or texts during the transfer process. Distortions may be related to linguistic competence either in comprehension of an utterance or in expressing the same into the other language. Laster and Taylor (1994) acknowledge the challenges of maintaining accuracy:

> Interpreters are required to make instantaneous and irrevocable decisions about how to interpret from the source language. Inevitably, the interpreter will sometimes choose an inappropriate equivalent term, or there will be ambiguities in the source language which allow more than one valid interpretation. (p. 183)

Interpreters and translators have a duty to be accurate (Laster & Taylor, 1994). The authors argue that the notion of accuracy in translating and interpreting should be understood in the technical definition quoted earlier: 'the degree to which something conforms to the correct value or a standard'. In interpreting and translating, *the 'correct value or a standard' is what was said or written by the parties and how it was said or written.*

Case Study

A: Did you and C travel back to your house together?
B: My car wasn't working.
Interpreter: My car wasn't working, so I couldn't give him a ride. (Jacobsen, 2002, p. 138)
A: How do you get on at work?
B: They are giving me a raise next month.
Interpreter: I'm getting on very well. (Jacobsen, 2002, p. 140)

In the examples above, the correct value or standard is not adhered to by the interpreter. In the first example, the interpreter adds 'so I couldn't give him a ride', which is not uttered by B, although it may well be what B means. Similarly, in the second example, the rendition provided by the interpreter 'I'm getting on very well' negates B's utterance completely, although it may be what B means pragmatically. The authors argue that these changes do not conform to the correct value and standard of their original utterances, and there is no justification for the change for linguistic or transfer reasons. Such an attempt on the part of the interpreter to make clearer or explicit the speaker's meaning is beyond the role of an interpreter and is a decision that should be left with the primary speakers in the communicative event to work out, just as in mono-lingual communication where no interpreters are involved.

Accuracy in interpreting and translating should not simply be understood as 'the quality of being accurate' as in the first definition listed earlier. The quality of being accurate is for the speakers or authors who have produced the original utterance or text to decide and justify. For example, if a suspect says 'I remember I left my house at 2pm', whereas in his earlier answer, he said 11am, he/she is responsible for the accuracy of this. Any correction of this by the interpreter would not be justified.

The level of accuracy in a police interview covers all that is said by the parties, including all the 'imperfections', 'syntactic mess' and 'corruptive details' (Drew, 1990, p. 40). These make up the 'correct value or a standard' to test the accuracy of an interpreter or translator. In practice, these can also include false starts, repetitions, level of formality and self-corrections by a suspect or witness, which may be of significance to a police officer but appear trivial or irrelevant to a layperson. This is by no means an easy task to achieve.

> Evidence given through an interpreter loses much of its impact, and this is so in spite of the expert interpretation now readily available. The jury do not really hear the witness nor are they fully able to appreciate, for instance, the degree of conviction or uncertainty with which this evidence is given; they cannot wholly follow the nuances, inflictions, quickness or hesitancy of the witness; all they have is the dispassionate and unexpressive tone of the interpreter... These matters may operate unfairly either to the advantage or to the disadvantage of the witness involved. (*Filios v. Morland* (1963) 63 SR (NSW) 331 at 332-3 per Brereton J) (Laster & Taylor, 1994, p. 114)

Whether this expectation can be fully met or not is a discussion to be had. But what is clear is that, in a range of settings, accuracy is a manifestation of a number of negotiated factors for the purpose at hand. Parsons (2001) rejects the idea that competence for professionals is synonymous to being perfect; rather, it means that the professional is 'capable of performing a minimum quality of service that is within the limits of his or her training, experience and practice' (p. 156). By the same token, interpreters (and translators) cannot be perfect; but they can try to the best of their abilities. The accuracy issues, therefore, that we focus on in this book are the ones that result from deliberate interventions by an interpreter or translator.

Chinese Interpreter Fined for Incorrect Translations

> Evidence of an understanding between Chinese in Sydney, where by countrymen who get into trouble are found bail, was given at the Central Police Court Sydney, when Charles Tein, a Chinese, was charged with having given an incorrect translation of answers while acting as interpreter. Tein admitted that he was a member of the 'Go You Clan', and that he always attended the court to act as bondsman for members of the Clan who got into trouble. He was fined £10.
>
> **Chinese Interpreter**
> *The Maitland Daily Mercury Australia, 1928*

Inaccuracies and distortions on the interpreter's or the translator's part may also be intentional. The service users expect and *trust* that the interpreting is accurate or a piece of translation is accurate. Distortions for the purpose of this discussion under professional ethics, however, are those resulting from an interpreter or translator making a linguistic choice, such as choosing one expression over another, based on his or her personal interests, political or religious beliefs and views or cultural assumptions. In addition, Laster and Taylor (1994) also list gender issues and ethnic background as commonly encountered factors in deliberate distortions. In other words, distortion is when interpreters and translators deviate from how interpreting or translating should be done if one were to base decisions solely on the linguistic and contextual features of the utterances devoid of other considerations infused by the interpreter or translator. This is when interpreters and translators should firmly uphold their objectivity, which is defined by Gaukroger (2012) as being free of influence from prejudice or biases and is viewed as one of the most distinguishing human traits. There is not much primary research that investigates factors leading to deliberate distortions by interpreters and translators. Elias-Bursać (2015) gives an example in which a defendant assisted by a simultaneous interpreter at a trial discovered that the interpreter was adding the words 'your Honours' to his evidence to make it more respectful according to the conventions of the Court. The defendant, however, protested that he deliberately did not want to address the bench with words of respect, as it was not part of his culture to do so. He pointed out that the interpreter inserted the words 'your Honours' without his knowledge or consent.

Impartiality

> The need for impartiality and the appearance of neutrality is arguably the greatest in formal proceedings.
>
> **Laster & Taylor, 1994, p. 217**

Maintaining impartiality in professions in which at least two different parties need the services of the same professional means an undertaking to be unbiased and a commitment to serve all parties equally. Interpreters and translators have an unusual position compared with most other professional–client relationships in that the other two parties who have a primary or preexisting relationship both rely on the services of the interpreter or translator to undertake the business they have at hand. Such business or matter can be a consultation, medical assessment or a police interview with a victim of crime. It means interpreters and translators, a common communicative link between a police officer and a suspect or witness, have their own relationship with both parties and 'the obligation to remain impartial is owed to all the parties present in the legal setting' (Laster & Taylor, 1994, p. 217). Interpreters and translators' ethical obligation to serve equally all parties in a communicative event 'no matter how many and how named' (Fisher, 2009, p. 1) is similar to Fischer's assertion with respect to that of psychologists'. This is a critical ethical standard for interpreters and translators. Biased or partial interpreting or translation cannot possibly be credible, as it would be affecting the professional decisions and would be disadvantaging one of the parties. One of the things that would be compromised by biased interpreting or translating is accuracy, which is 'the ultimate objective if interpreting' (Laster & Taylor, 1994, p. 115).

A biased or partial interpreting or translation cannot possibly be credible.

Impartiality in an interpreted communication can manifest and be categorised into three aspects: attitudinal, linguistic and interactional.

1. *Attitudinal*

    Interpreters and translators are rightly autonomous persons with their own values and worldviews. It is commonplace that the subject of the communication for which they are providing their service is something about which they have different personal views or judgement – and that is quite acceptable. For example, an interpreter relates that 'I felt physically sick when I interpreted for an incest case in a police interview' (Lai, Heydon & Mulayim, 2015, p. 10).

Case Study

An interpreter in a police interview of a suspect for allegedly sexually abusing his daughter thinks the man is not credible and believes what he did was horrible. Throughout the interview he thinks this man should be jailed forever and not see his children ever again.

Situations like this may influence the transfer decisions made by the interpreter or translator from one language into another, and lead to distortions as discussed in the previous section. Interpreters and translators are entrusted with accuracy and should not let their personal views, beliefs or opinions interfere with their performance. If this is in doubt, it may be best for the interpreter to bring it to the attention of the police officer and offer to withdraw from the assignment.

While one always has the recourse to withdraw from an interpreting or translating assignment, in the following section we focus on cases when one decides to persist. It then becomes important that one remains attitudinally neutral to respect the primary relationship the interviewing officer has with the interviewee.

British forensic psychologist Professor Ray Bull (2013, 2014) reports that, according to two highly experienced US interviewers – O'Connor and Carson – the respect shown by interviewers to child molesters appears to be the primary reason that they confess. These two professional interviewers recommend that interviewers need to demonstrate an understanding of the interviewee's view of the world, develop rapport, communicate in a nonthreatening and nonjudgemental way and show empathy and respect for the interviewee as a human being. Bull (2013,

2014) also draws attention to a 2006 Australian study on male prisoners convicted of sex or violence crimes (some had confessed, and some had pleaded not guilty but had subsequently been found guilty). It is reported that the interviews of those who confessed had been more ethical, humane and less domineering than those of the deniers. This is an important reminder to interpreters and translators working in this kind of context to re-create such interviewing approaches faithfully in their rendering for the interviewee. Noteworthy in this 2006 Australian study is that only half of these convicted offenders said that they attended the police interview having already decided whether to deny or confess – 20% had decided to deny and 30% to confess – whereas the remaining half actually did not decide one way or another. The study also noted that some guilty suspects who (prior to and/or at the beginning of the interview) may be considering whether to confess could subsequently decide not to simply because of the way they are being interviewed (Bull, 2014, vi). Extending this research outcome to an interpreted police interview, one would be extremely concerned that such negative interactional dynamics, instead of coming from the police officer, could come through from the interpreter because of a biased preconception formed during the interview.

A review of a relatively significant amount of literature from around the world in Bull's 2013 paper and a subsequent 2014 book unequivocally concludes that a more humanitarian interviewing style is more likely to elicit truthful and comprehensive information from the interviewee. Interpreters and translators working in police interviewing contexts should be made aware of this consensus and understand its significant implications for interviewing outcomes. While the police interviewer tries hard to embody humanity and empathy in his or her interview with the interviewee, the interpreter must be mindful of maintaining his or her attitudinal neutrality and convey truthfully such humanity and empathy the interviewer trusts would be conveyed in his or her interpretation to the interviewee. Failing to do so, as the literature suggests, might have implications for the police in terms of their task to elicit voluntary confession, which, in turn, hinders the goal of achieving desirable justice outcomes.

2. *Linguistic*

As explained before, interpreters and translators wield considerable power in an interpreted communication, because participants must trust what the interpreter says is exactly what the other party says. Such power can be used by a 'biased interpreter' (Schweda-Nicholson, 1994, p. 86) to
1. Omit certain things altogether
2. Invent material that was never spoken
3. Alter what is said so as to help or harm one side or the other

4. Emphasise matters that were not accentuated in the original version or, conversely, downplay a point which was clearly stressed

When an interpreter or translator is unable to stay impartial in the communication he or she is facilitating, this can manifest in his or her demeanour as is analysed in the previous section on attitude as well as in the linguistic performance as discussed under 'Inaccuracies and Distortions'. Schweda-Nicholson (1994) concurs by giving the example of interpreters 'eliminating profanity, making ungrammatical items into grammatical ones and otherwise altering material, all with the stated goal of making a witness or patient "look better" (more intelligent, worldly, educated or refined than he or she is)' (p. 87).

3. *Interactional*

Interpreters and translators are often positioned physically in between the parties they are assisting, in addition to their notional third-party position in the originally bilateral communication. In this sense, dispute mediation as a profession can be said to have similar dynamics. Gibson (1999) regards neutrality in dispute mediation to be multifaceted, therefore leading to difficulty as to how the mediator should act, in that in the classic sense the mediator is supposed to refrain from intervening in the substance of the dispute and should not attempt to alter the power imbalances (Benjamin, 2001). Such an ideological position is close to what the authors believe.

Elias-Bursać (2015) refers to the following exchange from a defendant in a trial at the International Criminal Court, where Vojislav Šešelj snapped at an interpreter for laughing at what he was saying.

The Accused: [Interpretation] Please, I don't think the interpreters should be laughing while interpreting into the Serbian language for me. Let them assume a normal tone of voice and not giggle. I don't think it's a good idea for interpreter to be laughing along as they are interpreting.

Judge Antonetti: [Interpretation] Let me remind the interpreters because it's not the first time we have a problem of the kind. The interpreter at all times must be extremely neutral and because of this must express nothing through his voice, neither laughter or anything. (p. 56)

This is a good example of the expectations that involved parties have of interpreters to not only be impartial but also appear to be so. The parties who rely on the interpreters can infer ideas from the actions and words of interpreters, even if they may be quite innocent actions or utterances.

Laster and Taylor (1994) state, in a police interview setting,

> For the Non English Speaking Background [NESB] suspect, the interpreter is the only non-police person present and, not surprisingly, they regard the interpreter as a quasi-advocate, affording them some 'protection'. In some communities, there is even an explicit expectation that the interpreter should protect the client and 'fix' the legal problem. (p. 124)

Although the rhetoric of impartiality often finds its way into regulations and statements or guidelines for engaging interpreters, and parties may well believe in this, some practices may in fact create a perception that this is not so. In police settings, how the interpreters are physically seated and positioned in an interview room, or how one party appears to be having a conversation in one language, without letting the other party know what the conversation is about, may also contribute to the perception of bias in the interpreter or translator. This needs to be handled with care, especially in highly sensitive matters and also where mental health issues may exist with a suspect or witness.

The non-English-speaking suspect or witness's misconception of the interpreter's role is further reinforced by the interviewing officer's expressions such as 'this is your interpreter' or 'Ms. X is going to interpret for you today', which portrays the interpreter as partial to one party. Furthermore, some innocent actions by the police officer and interpreter may be interpreted very differently. Imagine a situation in which the police officer walks into an interview room with an interpreter, appearing to be having a conversation and laughing. The suspect to be interviewed may observe this and conclude that the interpreter is working for the police and may trick him or her into admitting things or revealing information that he or she may otherwise be unwilling to reveal, whereas the interpreter and the police officer may simply be exchanging a few lines about how parking is problematic in the city center or that the weather has been too hot or cold recently.

It is not uncommon for clients of interpreters to ask them for assistance beyond communication because of things such as being of the same religious or ethnic background or the interpreter having been paid for by one party. If an interpreter or translator feels his or her professional decisions or actions are being influenced by any of these factors, his or her impartiality would be compromised and to continue would be unethical. Both parties who are served by an interpreter and translator (in this case, members of the police force and suspects and witnesses) need to be provided with language services equally so they can undertake their primary relationship, for example, police interview, witness statement or complaint about a process. If one of these parties is served less than the other, claims of bias will inevitably emerge and it may have implications for the admissibility of a police interview or witness statement as evidence in a future court case. Parsons (2001) comments on the professionals working in the human services context, stating that 'if a helper's objectivity becomes compromised, the professional nature of the relationship may be threatened' (p. 139). He lists a number of ways a professional's objectivity may be compromised to different degrees, including

1. *Simple identification*, which occurs when a helper identifies himself/herself with the client because something about the client's experience or story causes the helper to relate to the client's story or experience and even see himself/herself in the client's shoes
2. *Transference*, in which the helper uses the context of the helping relationship and presence of the client to express his own feelings, beliefs or desires, often subconsciously
3. *Dual relationships*, in which the helper has two or more roles with the client, including personal friendships and family relationships. In these kinds of multiple relationships, there is the increased likelihood of a loss of professional objectivity and boundary violations (Parsons, 2001)

Although the aforementioned situations relate to counsellors and the relationship with their clients, they are equally relevant for the work of interpreters. It is not uncommon for interpreters to interpret for a client who has a similar experience or story of, say, migration, as the interpreter (simple identification), or to add the interpreter's own feelings of settlement hardship or cultural/religious beliefs in the fiduciary relationship with their client (transference), or to act both as an interpreter and an advocate/cultural mediator at the same time (dual relationship).

Conflict of Interest

It is not uncommon for an interpreter who interpreted in a police interview to find out they are interpreting at the hearing of the same case, as it sometimes takes months, if not years in some cases, before a matter is heard in court. The interpreter may simply be unaware of the matter. This information may also not be immediately available to the other parties involved (e.g. defence team, prosecutor, the court). The best practice would be for the interpreter to advise the prosecutor that he or she was the interpreter in the police interview as well. The reason is that once an interpreter interprets in a police interview, they then actually become a witness and may be called in to give evidence. Furthermore, the defence team may also raise concerns about the quality of interpreting at the police interview and this can leave the interpreter in an awkward position.

Preston (2014) writes that a conflict of interest is not unethical as long as it is managed appropriately, explaining that 'the fundamental and essential course of action in the ethical management of conflicts is the *recognition* and *disclosure* of the conflict' (p. 150, emphasis in original).

Case Study

An interpreter, X, is booked for an assignment that involves a recorded interview of a suspect who allegedly defrauded members of a seniors' club in a scam. Interpreter X finds out the identity of the suspect just before the interview starts and recognises that it is an association the interpreter's father attends as well.

In interpreting and translating, the key to handling any concerns about conflict of interest is to advise the other parties of the existence of a real or perceived conflict of interest, as Interpreter X in the preceding example should do. Once the other parties involved are informed, a number of actions can be considered to make all parties feel comfortable about the process. These may include

- Withdrawing from the assignment so another professional can help the client
- Allowing the professional to continue to provide services, once the consent of all interested parties is obtained

Interpreters and translators should always remember that having a conflict of interest is not a problem in itself; what matters is how it is handled by the interpreter and the translator. The Metropolitan Police (2007) Standard Operating Procedures for interpreters and translators states in 4.1 (9) that 'Interpreters will disclose any conflict of interest, whether personal or financial, which arises from an assignment and will withdraw from the assignment or continue only with the informed consent of all parties' (p. 10).

So far we have approached impartiality and conflict of interest issues from an interpreter's perspective, in the sense that a publicly funded interpreting service is expected to serve equally the party providing government service as well as the party receiving the service. However, in the United States, for example, Berk-Seligson (2009) observes that the overlooking of possible bias when police officers or associates of police officers act as interpreters in their questioning of suspects is not uncommon. She reports that 'defense attorneys of persons convicted of various sorts of crimes are increasingly becoming aware of the inherent conflict of interest present in situations where law enforcement officers unexpectedly play the role of interpreter' (Berk-Seligson, 2009, p. 21). Evidence obtained in this way by police may not be admissible in some jurisdictions, as it would be considered against the principle of natural justice.

Privacy and Confidentiality

> Breaching a client's confidentiality can have devastating consequences.
>
> **Laster & Taylor, 1994, p. 223**

Privacy and confidentiality are very important aspects of the practice in the interpreting and translating profession, as in many other professions. Interpreters and translators especially occupy an unusual position, as they acquire highly confidential information about their clients during the course of their assignments that is often not available even to the closest relatives or friends of suspects or witnesses. In other words, the private or confidential information is not shared with them directly. It is shared between, say, a police officer and a witness, in the course of reporting a crime or investigating an alleged offence. Regardless of how they acquire the information during the course of their professional service as interpreters or translators, they are ethically and legally bound to respect privacy and keep information confidential.

As we discussed earlier, professionals have special skills and knowledge and serve a need of the people, and in this capacity, 'treating communications as confidential is critical to establishing a trust relationship with clients' (Laster & Taylor, 1994, p. 222). To access the services of an interpreter or translator, people will have to disclose highly personal details about themselves or their families or other people or organisations they are associated with. This is identified as one of the aspects that make people vulnerable in a relationship between a professional and those who need to access the professional's services because this information is not available to others in the society. This also applies to interpreters and translators who are trusted with highly sensitive details during police activities from interviews to telephone intercepts and translation of evidence. The confidential information may relate to the future direction of a police investigation, for example, to the identities of some well-known community members or business or sports personalities being revealed in an investigation about fraud or sexual abuse. Disclosing confidential information, including assignment details, even if it is broadly or vaguely worded may lead to the identification of people or organisations in a case and may have serious consequences legally and socially. Laster and Taylor (1994) assert that 'The concern for breaches of confidentiality was the reason for some victims of domestic violence not preferring to seek the assistance of an interpreter' (p. 223).

A breach of confidentiality by an interpreter or translator is a breach of trust, and is therefore unethical.

The seriousness of respecting privacy and confidentiality in some professional areas such as legal and health services is also reflected in a range of legislation that regulates and provides for penalties for breaches. Miller, Blackler and Alexandra (2006) explain that professional confidentiality should be maintained, as it is

1. The subject of a promise on the part of the professional to the client not to disclose the sort of information in question to others
2. Enshrined in the law so that the professional has a legal duty not to disclose this information to others (p. 210)

Professional translators and interpreters are advised to undertake a privacy/confidentiality training course to learn about relevant legislation and guidelines in their states or countries and how these may have implications for their work.

On the flip side of the coin, professionals are also expected to hold in trust the best interests of society. For example, if a lawyer becomes aware that a client is likely to kill someone, he or she is released from solicitor–client privilege in the interest of protecting society; and dentists are expected to release our records if it helps to identify our bodies (Beaton, 2010, p. 5).

In many jurisdictions in the West, a suspect has the right to speak to a lawyer for legal advice. In interpreted interviews, it is not uncommon to engage an interpreter for both the interview and the legal advice session (in the absence of police officers), and the information an interpreter becomes privy to during a suspect's conversation with his or her lawyer or attorney is covered by the 'Legal Professional Privilege'. This term refers to protection of documents, conversations or correspondence from disclosure if these relate to providing legal advice or are part of a legal proceeding (Victorian Government Solicitor's Office, 2007).

This also extends to an interpreter who is present in that session. If the contents are freely disclosed by an interpreter or if an interpreter is forced to disclose the information (without explicit permission of the lawyer and the suspect), such disclosure would constitute a breach of 'Legal Professional Privilege' (Laster & Taylor, 1994).

Such reasoning can be traced back to a much earlier case of *Du Barré v. Livette* (1791), in which case Chief Justice Lord Kenyon was asked to compel the interpreter to disclose the conversations between the defence counsel and his client Livette – one of the accused in a jewellery theft case. Counsel for Du Barré argued that in another case the year before, Justice Buller decided that a Catholic prisoner's confession to a Protestant clergyman was compellable. However, Lord Kenyon held that the interpreter in this case should be protected by legal professional privilege just as Livette's lawyer himself, because the lawyer could not fulfil his proper function without the involvement of the interpreter (Thompson, 2011). In other words, because the relationship

Professional Ethics for Police Interpreters and Translators 105

between the defendant and his lawyer was privileged and because it was necessary to have an interpreter for the purpose of their communication, everything said before that interpreter was equally in confidence as if said to the lawyer when no interpreter was present (Roberts-Smith, 2009, p. 14).

In other sensitive settings, there are similar regulations to protect the confidentiality of information. For example, in Australia, the Administrative Appeals Tribunal (AAT) has a specific legislation about an 'entrusted person' and how their right to confidentiality is protected. This is a tribunal that handles merits reviews of administrative decisions made by Australian government ministries, departments and agencies under Australia's Commonwealth laws (AAT, n.d.). The Administrative Appeals Tribunal Act 1975, Section 66, defines an 'entrusted person' to be any of the following:

a. a person who is or has been a member of the Tribunal;
b. a person who is or has been an officer of the Tribunal;
c. a person who is or has been a member of the staff of the Tribunal;
d. a person who is or has been engaged by the Tribunal to provide services to the Tribunal during a proceeding before the Tribunal. (AAT, 1975)

Interpreters and translators providing service to the AAT fall in category (d) above; they are, therefore, afforded the same protection when it comes to the confidential information they become aware of in the course of their work. Section 66 of the Act stipulates that such confidential information is not to be disclosed:
Protected documents and information

1. An entrusted person must not be required to produce a protected document, or disclose protected information, to a court except so far as necessary for the purposes of carrying into effect the provisions of this Act or another enactment conferring powers on the Tribunal.
2. An entrusted person must not be required to produce a protected document, or disclose protected information, to a parliament if:
    a. the document or information relates to a Part 7-reviewable decision within the meaning of the Migration Act 1958; and
    b. the production or disclosure is not necessary for the purposes of carrying into effect the provisions of this Act or another enactment conferring powers on the Tribunal. (AAT, 1975)

Summary

This chapter examined key ethical issues for police interpreters and translators, which we approach from the point of view of the professional role they play. The chapter first discussed the value of understanding the primary or preexisting relationship between a police officer and a suspect, victim or witness. The role of an interpreter or translator in this relationship is to respect this primary relationship and provide a competent and impartial communication link to both parties. This role defines the boundaries within which an interpreter or translator can move. The first consideration in any ethical decision making for interpreters or translators should be to consider if the action they intend to take would be within their role boundaries or not. Any departure from this role would be a violation of their role boundaries, unless it can be justified.

This chapter also examined ethical issues in common areas of competence, impartiality, confidentiality and conflict of interest through case studies involving police interviews.

Compliance with Codes of Ethics
A Wicked Problem

6

Professional ethics, as many professionals themselves insist, is too important to all of us to be left only to professionals. The pressing challenge for the future is to forge, in principle and in practice, a union of the traditional idea of the autonomous profession (preserving its ethics of service) and the modern demand for accountability (acknowledging an ethics of responsibility).

Dennis F. Thompson
Director Emeritus, Edmond J. Safra Center for Ethics
Harvard University

Introduction

Codes of ethics adopted by professional associations and organisations are generally recommendations for good practice and maintaining the status of the profession. Whether one complies or not is a voluntary decision. Some aspects in the codes such as being polite to clients are merely advisory and there are no prescribed remedies for violations or even procedures for determining whether a violation has occurred or not. However, a person who breaches these codes may not be regarded as professional by members of society and may not receive work from users of his or her services.

In some well-developed and highly organised professions such as medicine or law, however, there is a registration authority that can enforce codes for their profession, through a range of processes including suspension or cancellation of a licence or membership or other administrative penalties. Some codes of ethics involve basic human rights (e.g. privacy and confidentiality) and fall under some act or regulation and can be enforced by law.

One undisputed fact about codes of ethics is that, despite well stated, all-encompassing codes covering the highest standards of practice, ethical breaches of some sort occur all the time in any profession, and they occupy considerable time and effort to remedy. Being ethical goes beyond simply knowing. It requires practising. Sternberg (2015) highlights the gap between knowing the rules and practising by saying

> In ethical reasoning as in creativity, there may be a large gap between thought and action. Both often involve defying the crowd, and hence even people who believe a certain course of action to be correct may not follow through on it. (p. 225)

Laster and Taylor (1994) highlight the damage noncompliance can inflict not only on the individual practitioner but also on the profession he or she represents: 'All too frequently, professionals consciously and unconsciously disregard ethical principles. If this behaviour goes unchecked, it will eventually reflect on all members of the occupational group and severely erode their claims to professional status' (pp. 203–204).

Many police forces have established some sort of ethical standards units or sections to monitor, investigate and resolve ethical breaches by members of the police forces. This is hardly any different for interpreters and translators. Whether they are staff interpreters or translators or work as freelancers or subcontractors, the ethical breaches have implications for the police agencies that engage the interpreters and translators within their activities. Schweda-Nicholson (1994) reports of a study by the New Jersey Supreme Court Task Force on Interpreter and Translation Services that included a survey of New Jersey judges about their perceptions of ethics among interpreters. They found only 25% of the judges were completely satisfied with the interpreters' ethical knowledge and compliance.

Case Study

When I go to the heart doctor, my interpreter likes to talk to the doctor in English. He tells everyone that he went to medical school back in his country. The doctor hardly pays any attention to me, and the interpreter tells me not to ask so many questions, just to do what the doctor instructs me to do. (Golley, 2008, p. 4)

One senior manager from a major language services agency in Australia reports that the overwhelming majority of complaints raised about interpreters relate to ethics and conduct issues, as opposed to common assumptions about linguistic insufficiency:

> As most professionals don't speak the NES client's language they are generally not in a position to comment on the interpreter's linguistic skills and interpreting abilities...
> Common concerns raised by clients are:
>
> - Interpreters failing to attend assignments
> - Interpreters running late

Compliance with Codes of Ethics

- Interpreters having side conversations with the NES client without interpreting this to the professional
- Interpreters overstepping their boundaries and providing advice and advocacy to NES clients (Personal communication, July 15, 2015)

Similar issues are also reflected by other agencies. A social worker/counsellor from inner city Melbourne, who has more than twenty-five years of experience and has worked with interpreters in numerous counselling sessions owing to the highly multiethnic makeup of the suburbs she works in, says:

I am full of praise of the professionalism of many interpreters who worked with and helped me to communicate with my clients who are often emotionally distressed and are vulnerable. However, you also get bad apples. Some of the interpreters find counselling sessions too slow and too long and you can tell from their actions and looks that they'd rather be somewhere else. I often brief the interpreters before the session begins to inform them of what to expect from the therapeutic process, which is much slower than with case work because of the processing of internal states and emotions etc. Still some interpreters become irritated and restless during the session.

Some of the memorable experiences I had with interpreters over the years would be:

- Chewing on gum during the session
- Loud sighing during the session
- Stating impatiently, 'This is very repetitive'
- Knitting during a session
- Interacting with the client as though they are family
- Conducting a separate conversation with the client, disregarding the counsellor
- Giving the counsellor advice about what she should say and do for the client.

Personal communication, September 25, 2015

What this feedback from the industry and stories we discussed in previous chapters tell us is that noncompliance continues to be a persistently difficult issue to resolve in the profession, and this is true also of many other professions. According to the 2013–2014 Annual Review of Public Service Interpreting by the National Register of Public Service Interpreters in the United Kingdom, police, being the major users of the registered interpreters, recorded the highest number of complaints to the National Register (see Figure 6.1); and where there was a finding against a registered interpreter, categories that received the highest percentages of breaches are (see Figure 6.2) the interpreters' 'integrity' (13%), their act to bring the profession into 'disrepute' (10%) and their inability to 'uphold [the] profession' (7%).

110 Ethics for Police Translators and Interpreters

Analysis of complaints
3.2 Complaints by complainant type 2012–2014

Police are the major users of registrants and therefore are the major source of complaints. NRPSI will sponsor some complaints itself; for example, breaches of the code that come to light as part of the registration process.

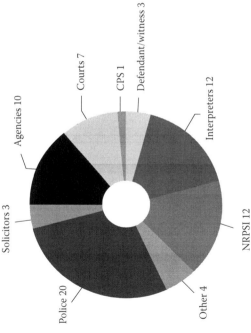

Figure 6.1 Distribution of complainants. (From NRPSI (2014). *NRPSI Annual Review of Public Service Interpreting in the UK 2013*, p. 17. Retrieved 2 December, 2015, from http://www.nrpsi.org.uk/downloads/NRPSI_Annual_Review_of_Public_Service_Interpreting_in_the_UK_2013.pdf.)

Compliance with Codes of Ethics

3.5 Sections of NRPSI Code of Conduct breached 2012–2014

Where there was a finding against a Registrant, this shows which sections of the NRPSI Code of Conduct were breached. More than one section might be breached in a particular complaint.

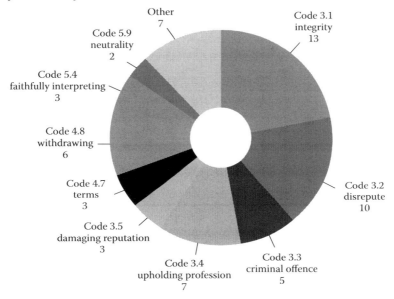

Figure 6.2 Distribution of code of conduct breaches. (From NRPSI (2014). *NRPSI Annual Review of Public Service Interpreting in the UK 2013*, p. 19. Retrieved 2 December, 2015, from http://www.nrpsi.org.uk/downloads/NRPSI_Annual_Review_of_Public_Service_Interpreting_in_the_UK_2013.pdf.)

The difficulty in ensuring all members of a profession abide by their ethics makes it a wicked problem. Rittel and Webber (1973), who came up with the concept of the 'wickedness' of problems, albeit in the area of urban planning, explain that the meaning of 'wickedness' in the sense they use is similar to 'malignant' (in contrast to 'benign') or 'vicious' (like a circle) or 'tricky' (like a leprechaun) or 'aggressive' (like a lion, in contrast to the docility of a lamb) (p. 160). Here we use the term 'wicked' in the sense of 'difficult to resolve'. Compliance with codes of ethics relies largely on the use of discretion. The use of discretion, in turn, relies on the following subjective factors:

1. *First, understanding and identifying an ethical dilemma is subjective.* Gardner (2014) highlights subjectivity in understanding, and points out that 'some people will experience a particular issue as an ethical dilemma that others see as straightforward' (p. 127).
2. *Making a judgment about what action to take relies on professionals' personal interests, special value sets and ideological predilections that differ widely.* This impacts on the solution. Rittel and Webber (1973)

state, that unlike, for example, a chess problem or a maths equation, in which 'the problem-solver knows when he has done his job and there are criteria that tell when the or a solution has been found. Wicked problems don't have a set criteria.... There is no immediate and no ultimate test of a solution to a wicked problem' (p. 163).
3. *There are no set rules that can apply to all situations.* 'Wicked problems do not have an enumerable (or an exhaustively describable) set of potential solutions, nor is there a well-described set of permissible operations' (Rittel and Webber, 1973, p. 164). This idea reflects the similar limitations codes of ethics try to address.
4. *Every wicked problem is essentially unique.* '[B]y "essentially unique" we mean that, despite long lists of similarities between a current problem and a previous one, there might always might be an additional distinguishing property that is of overriding importance' (Rittel and Webber, 1973, p. 164). This is similarly true for noncompliance with codes of ethics. Each ethical dilemma has some distinguishing feature(s) as well as common ones. In each situation, justification for the action taken is unique in a way as well, as Ritell and Webber (1973) propose: 'People choose those explanations which are most plausible to them' (p. 166).

It is obvious that there is no easy answer or solution for noncompliance and almost everyone will have a differing opinion on ways of remedying the wicked problem of noncompliance. What is obvious is that as much as persisting with promotion of the current codes, there is a need to seek new approaches to influence cognitive rationalisation and reasoning in a range of ethical dilemmas a professional may come across in everyday practice.

The Value of Moral Self-Understanding in Compliance

> The role of a code in stimulating moral self-understanding is important. It not only supplies a vocabulary but also helps *create* the community of users. (Fullinwider, 1996, p. 83; emphasis in original)

We have so far discussed some of the traditional and recognised approaches to ethics in general, mainly normative ethics and then offered various definitions of what a profession is and used a schema proposed by Fullinwider (1996) as a tool to look at two professions that are the focus of this book: policing and interpreting and translating. We then discussed professional ethics, that is, ethics issues that relate to the use of professional skills and knowledge, codes of conduct and general considerations expected of almost any profession that provides a service to the community.

In this section, we discuss a different approach to dealing with issues concerning noncompliance with regard to professional ethics. This is because there are some issues and perceived shortcomings of the bullet-point codes of ethics commonly adopted by associations and organisations. Preston (2014, p. 220) notes that a number of concerns exist:

- When codes of ethics are being used more for public relations or a gate keeping exercise in some professions
- When codes are assumed to cover almost all contingencies in professional practice and, once adopted, become almost holy writ and resist change
- Most significantly, when codes may actually defeat the purpose and undermine the exercise of open-minded, autonomous and reflective ethical decision making, thus diminishing personal responsibility

Referring to a list of ethical rules in bullet points may not be much help in guiding a professional decision, because they may be too general or simply not exhaustive of all possible scenarios. Laster and Taylor (1994) argue that 'as experienced interpreters well know, the variety of ethical problems that arise in practice is infinite, and no amount of re-reading the (many) codes of ethics brings one any closer to resolving them' (p. 206). Beauchamp and Childress (2001) also maintain that

> Unfortunately, some professional codes oversimplify moral requirements, make them indefensibly rigid, or claim more completeness and authority than they are entitled to claim. As a consequence, professionals may mistakenly suppose that they satisfy all relevant moral requirements if they obediently follow the rules of the code, just as many people believe that they discharge their moral obligations when they meet all relevant legal requirements. (p. 7)

These perceived shortcomings and similar concerns in the face of infinite combinations of situations that may arise, especially for interpreters and translators who always work within another professional–client relationship, point to a need for different approaches in situations in which a professional ethical issue needs to be assessed and an action decided on. Laster and Taylor (1994) conclude that 'ethical principles, such as confidentiality, impartiality, accuracy and competence, can be stated relatively easily, but each depends upon the exercise of informed discretion by individual interpreters, and the development and enforcement of overarching norms by the profession as a whole' (p. 224). Inghilleri (2012) also agrees that it is necessary to evaluate further and reconsider the current codes of ethics that guide interpreter training and practice. She suggests that 'an important step in undertaking this exercise must be to extend understandings of what actually might constitute ethical behaviour in interpreted communicative contexts beyond those currently in place; that is, beyond questions of duty and impartiality' (p. 34). To improve compliance with ethics in policing, on the other hand, Elliot and Pollock (2014) propose a comprehensive approach to professional ethical decision making: 'Supervisors should routinely discuss ethics – including ethical models, cognitive rationalisations, and the results of unethical conduct on officers, agencies and communities – while paying special attention to the reasoning processes and values underlying an officer's decision' (p. 250). Fullinwider (1996) and Preston (2014) argue that enforcement is not necessary to stimulate moral self-understanding. Senior members of a profession can achieve it by consistently practising it and 'their conduct, in turn, exerts a pull on less established members to obey as well. The profession operates by a strong sense of personal honour and emulation which is sufficient to check wrongdoing' (p. 87). Preston (2014) makes a similar point, highlighting the place of moral autonomy in ethical decision making and compliance: 'Doing something just because you are commanded to do it, or just because others are doing it, or because you will be punished if you do not do it, are immature reasons for ethical action…' (p. 209). He goes on to suggest that, for a professional, 'the essence of moral autonomy…requires owning and acting on a value system that is internalised rather than merely adopted because it is prescribed by an external authority' (Preston, 2014, p. 209).

These observations lead us to consider new approaches to the way professional interpreters and translators justify ethical decisions, with a focus on the perspective of people who benefit from the services of interpreting and translating. We propose that the *moral force* behind the interpreting and translating profession must be spelt out clearly in the codes of ethics. This can be best done by promoting *moral self-understanding* of the following two key factors in the relationship an interpreter or translator has, in the context of this book, with a police officer and a victim, witness or suspect. We contend that these factors can act as an overarching principle for cognitive rationalisation and help promote voluntary compliance in a range of situations a professional may come across in their practice. These two factors are

1. Commitment to the defining interest of the profession of interpreting and translating, which connects the profession to a moral purpose
2. Fidelity to the trust placed on them by the parties who are assisted to maintain professional trust and regard

For interpreters and translators as professionals who provide a service required by two other parties to communicate, the defining interest must relate not only to the interpreters and translators' understanding of how an ethical dilemma should be resolved/handled, but also to the recognition that the primary relationship between their two (or more) service users must remain at the forefront of any decision that must not be tampered with, distorted or altered. The discussions about the role of translators and interpreters emanating from the translating and interpreting field has traditionally revolved around the handling of the complexity of two languages at once. In doing this, in the case of interpreting, the interpreter becomes an interlingual oral text producer between the primary speakers so every other turn is done by the interpreter, and this makes the interpreter a communication coordinator. All these roles are justified apart from the fact that the emphasis of the overarching primary relationship under which these activities take place is not sufficiently recognised. Those people who require the services of a professional interpreter or translator seek such services because they need a communication link to express their wishes, thoughts, views, doubts, feelings, anger, emotions or positions on an issue to the other party or organisation (e.g. housing office, disability services, government or private agency, police interview, court hearing and so on) and are unable to do so because the medium of communication – a common language – is missing. This need for communication is, and should be, the main consideration in any decision a professional interpreter or translator makes. Any decision or action that does not respect the preexisting or primary relationship between the parties would lead to a mixing or violation of role boundaries. Parsons (2001) is adamant about maintaining professional boundaries and holds that '…all boundary crossings (i.e. departure from commonly accepted professional roles and practices) can become problematic and need to be avoided' (p. 137).

An analogy of where a profession's fidelity should be directed can be found in the legal field. The general public in the adversarial systems by and large agree that the role of lawyers is first, to respect the law and its procedures and second, to represent their clients 'zealously' within the bounds of the law. They work under the principles of partisanship, neutrality and non-accountability, allowing them to pursue the lawful objectives of their clients zealously, regardless of their own personal views about the moral merits of a case or their client's character. They are *not* held accountable for the moral worth of their client's actions or objectives; otherwise they may compromise their position in making full legal representation of their client. Such a conception is 'grounded in their fidelity to the law and its institutions' (Inghilleri, 2012, p. 58), as they must be 'committed to the principle of universal access to justice, regardless of their own personal views of the actions of a particular individual' (Freeman, 1966, 1922; Yellen, 1998/99, as cited in Inghilleri, 2012, p. 58).

Debates about negotiating the interpreter's identity always come to the fore when discussing their roles. Going by Rudvin's (2003, p. 180) definition of identity, it can be categorised into personal (or private) identity and public identity. Personal identity operates both at the collective cultural level and at the individual level, with the latter being conditioned by the interpreter's life experiences, whereas the former may be less idiosyncratic and more group-based on national or ethnic inclinations. And Rudvin talks about the hybridity of these two aspects contributing to the personal identity assumed by the interpreter. On the other hand, the interpreter's public identity, according to Rudvin, is related to the professional identity, which is often dictated by rigid professional codes of ethics. For example, Rudvin contends that in a medical interpreting setting, the hospital's institutional identity, the patient's understanding and expectations of the institution and the patient's own view of health and illness all have impacts on the interpreter's own professional code of ethics. She further states that

> ...it is precisely at this interface between different professional-institutional identities that the parameters of the interpreter's role can become very confusing indeed.... The problems that tend to crop up when discussing the interpreter's role – impartiality-neutrality bonding – are precisely those that are affected by the balancing or negotiating of professional identities. (p. 182)

The authors agree that the interpreter's personal identity and public identity are always interacting and competing with each other. It may be helpful to remind interpreters that the struggle in this tug of war of identities may be a result of viewing the interaction from the 'me' perspective – how we project ourselves in this triadic interaction. If we remind ourselves about the overarching primary relationship and come in and change focus to what the doctor and patient, or the police officer and interviewee, want to achieve, it may remove much of the confusion we create for ourselves. It must also be pointed out that when discussing interpreters' role boundaries, identity confusions and ethical behaviours, much of what the translating and interpreting literature relates to are ad hoc and untrained persons who happen to speak the two languages. Although these untrained persons provide rich sources for academic analysis of their ethical dilemmas, both on linguistic and nonlinguistic fronts, they should not be regarded as professionals, and thus the issues they encounter should not be regarded as the norm for professional interpreters.

The first and foremost principle in ethical decision making for an interpreter or translator should be an understanding of the defining interest of – the moral force behind – his or her profession.

With a sound understanding of the defining interest of their profession, interpreters and translators could be more consistent in their ethical decisions and the quality of their moral engagement, as they will have greater consensus and reflect more closely the values that define the purpose of their involvement in a dialogue between a police officer and a suspect or witness. This is also why professional codes need to highlight to practitioners what they should do and why, and in doing so describe the *defining interest* of the interpreting and translating profession and its implications for their ethical and conduct decisions. The code should not only supply rules to cover areas of concern, or distrust, which are by all means useful for professional interpreters and translators, but must also actively stimulate moral self-understanding to help *create* a community of professionals united in a *common moral purpose* that is not subject to individual interpretation.

This also has implications for building professional trust and professional regard, which is the second factor, we argue, that can help achieve higher self-compliance in a wide range of professional settings. Pellegrino (1991) argues that the importance of trust in professional relationships had been neglected and, as a result, an ethics of distrust emerged, with stringent rules and contracts to regulate professional activity to control professional decisions and conduct and eliminate the need for trust entirely. He states that 'the ethics of distrust is perilous, self-defeating and ultimately impossible to practice. It is sounder to acknowledge the ineradicability of trust and to restructure the ethics of our professions even more solidly on this foundation' (Pellegrino, 1991, p. 70). He also stresses the need to define the moral purpose of a profession, highlighting 'such an ethic of trust must be based in the "internal morality" of each profession – those ethical obligations that arise in the nature of each profession, the kind of human activity each profession encompasses' (p. 76).

Barber (1983) identifies three key expectations of people who seek help from a professional who possess specialised skills and knowledge – in our case, interpreting and translating skills to facilitate communication:

1. They will act within a persistent moral order.
2. They will perform their technical roles competently.
3. Roles that require a special concern for others, such as the fiduciary role, will be faithfully fulfilled.

These are also what is expected of an interpreter and translator with the assumption that any discretionary latitude needed to undertake the core professional role will be exercised 'with circumspection – neither intruding nor presuming too much nor undertaking too little' (Barber, 1983, p. 73), which reflects Pellegrino's definition of the professional relationship between a doctor and a patient. A professional interpreter and translator should be faithful to his or her role in meeting these expectations, rather than the narrow conception of being faithful to the spoken or written text he or she deals with – the authors would argue. Zaner (1991) asserts that 'professional trustworthiness may be more accurately characterised as the essential promise that trust is warranted and always an issue to be made good on in the course of the (professional) encounter' (p. 57). Interpreters' or translator's fidelity should be to the trust the parties have in them, that they will make good their promise to interpret and translate truthfully. This arises from the rule of *credat emptor* that encompasses the trust or credence the 'buyer' (or beneficiaries) of professional services gives to those professional services (Hughes, in Wueste, 1994).

It is always claimed that interpreters should be faithful in their interpretation, taking into account the pragmatics of the communicative situation, as well as factors such as whether there is a linguistic equivalent in the two languages, whether the discourse conventions allow the target language to be framed in a similar way, or whether the target culture provides a similar social framework to situate the idea, and so forth (Janzen & Korpiniski, 2005, p. 181). American Sign Language scholars Janzen and Korpiniski contend that 'since language use and language choices are always subjective in nature, an excellent interpretation has less to do with ethics than with expertise' (p. 181). On the contrary, the authors, as have argued so far, are of the view that the interpreter's self-moral-understanding of the their role in the primary relationship as well as their sense of fidelity to the trust bestowed upon them by the service users as their only means of communication will guide them to behave appropriately. There is no doubt that linguistic errors can be made by the most ethical of interpreters, as is pointed out by Janzen and Korpiniski (p. 181). This should be addressed in the training and credentialing of interpreters and translators to ensure minimum acceptable competency. The more important thing is to instil a sense of self moral-understanding so unethical behaviour, such as deliberately changing the message from what is intended or not caring whether the message remained intact as pointed out by Janzen and Korpiniski (p. 181), can be eliminated. As discussed earlier, achieving and maintaining professional trust and gaining respectful regard, where users/beneficiaries of this esoteric service give credence or trust, that is, *credat emptor* (Hughes in Wueste, 1994), to the professional's services, contributes to the professionalisation of interpreting and translating more than anything else.

The fidelity of an interpreter or translator should, first and foremost, be to the trust the other parties have in him or her.

The emphasis, in this fiduciary relationship, first and foremost is on the expectation of the parties who need the special skills and knowledge possessed by an interpreter/translator, not what an interpreter/translator thinks that role should be. This is because the primary relationship is between these two parties, not with the interpreter/translator. It would be very difficult to justify an action, say softening the offensive language of one of the parties

Compliance with Codes of Ethics 119

to maintain peace in the room, if the other party expects, and trusts, that everything that is said, regardless of whether or not it is rude or not, is being interpreted. The example given in Chapter 5 about Gaddafi's precise need for an unfiltered version of rendition illustrates this point. Possibly the best way for an interpreter or translator to develop a sound awareness of this is to reflect on the question 'what would I expect if I were in their shoes?'

This professional role boundary of an interpreter or translator working within a police activity has implications for the way interpreters and translators are engaged by the police forces. Some of the current practices may need to be reviewed to incorporate changes in processes through which the role of interpreters and translators can be clarified for both the police officers and the members of the public, be they suspects or witnesses or others.

The Need for an Oath/Affirmation for Police Interpreters and Translators

As outlined earlier, most professions develop their own codes of ethics for their members and also provide guidance for those who are not members of that association but practise the profession. Again, as we noted, codes of ethics include, generally, not only statements that define the core activity of that profession, but also, sometimes, other aspects of conduct guidelines, from being punctual, dress codes, to fees and charges. The practical aspects included in the code of conduct can change depending on where the profession is practised. For example, a doctor working in a company or a lawyer in the legal team of a university would be subject to more rules and expectations than a fellow professional who works from their own practice. Because of this diversity of practice it would be a challenge to come up with an all-inclusive set of rules that can apply in all settings everywhere. However, with a code of ethics that is based on the professional role, a reasonable attempt can be made. Similar to the all-encompassing 'Heal and Do No Harm' for medical doctors, or 'Decide without Fear, Favour or Affection' for judges, the essence of the professional role can be captured in a preamble or oath to precede specific codes of ethics and codes developed by individual associations or agencies and used to promote the moral self-understanding of an interpreter or translator in any setting and remind members of the role boundaries they have to keep to to guide their decisions. In fact, in the legal system there are practices that are good examples of this. Laster and Taylor (1994) remind us that 'since the early days of law, the oath has been a way of impressing witnesses with the solemnity and significance of their actions' (p. 169). For this purpose, in Australian courts, if an interpreter is required, he or she is sworn in before a witness is sworn in and gives evidence. Although it may be variations among jurisdictions in terms of such oath and affirmation according to the Evidence Act 1995 (NSW) (AUSTLII, n.d.), Oaths Act 1867 (QLD) (Queensland, 2012, pp. 15–18), and Evidence Act 2008 (VIC) (Judicial College of Victoria, 2012), they all read something like 'I swear by Almighty God/do solemnly and sincerely declare and affirm that I will well and truly interpret the evidence that will be given and do all other matters and things that may be required of me to the best of my skill and ability'.

The New York State Unified Court System developed a Benchcard for Judges titled *Working with Interpreters in the Courtroom*. It recommends that interpreters should be sworn in essentially for two purposes: formalising the interpreter's presence will highlight 'the importance of adhering to the principles of good court interpreting' and 'when the interpreter states his or her name, it is a good opportunity to inquire whether any party knows the interpreter' to identify any potential conflicts. The Benchcard, therefore, proposes the following sample interpreter oath:

> Do you solemnly swear or affirm that you will interpret accurately, completely and impartially, follow all official guidelines established by this court for legal interpreting or translating, and discharge all of the duties and obligations of legal interpretation and translation? (The New York State Unified Court System, n.d.)

Although these oaths/affirmations are largely based on the technical perspective of interpreters and translators in criminal justice settings as a conduit, they are not totally devoid of the social aspect of 'meeting a need of the society', which Fullinwider proposes as essential for moral self-understanding of the professional role. This is implied in the expression 'and all other matters and things', or 'discharge all of the duties and obligations', which affords some flexibility to accommodate instances in which an interpreter or translator may be asked when working in other court procedures. Laster and Taylor (1994) draw attention to the expected role of an interpreter described in the oath/affirmation: 'Interpreters are not required to swear or affirm that they interpret "flawlessly"....Interpreters have a duty to be accurate...The standard is that of a competent professional who owes an ethical duty to the court' (p. 167).

As well as committing an interpreter to the legally binding task he or she is required to do, an oath or affirmation also serves a purpose in identifying the role of the interpreter and translator in a setting that is shared with other professionals, including judges, barristers and other court staff all operating in the same case, which includes people who have language barriers. There does not appear to be a similarly concise preamble in highly sensitive forensic settings such as counselling sessions or mental health assessments. Interestingly, this practice also appears to be missing in police procedures. The common practice in Australia in police

Compliance with Codes of Ethics 121

interviews or other police activities, such as phone intercepts, is for an interpreter to be asked to sign an affidavit at the end of the activity, if the matter is going to court, as the interpreter becomes potentially a witness and can be called to a witness examination in a future contested hearing. This affidavit will state that the interpreter interpreted everything correctly to the best of his or her skills and ability. There does not appear to be a practice at the start of the police activity, regardless of whether the matter will go to court or not, whereby interpreters or translators undertake an oath or affirmation as a preamble for highlighting the professional role they have in that setting – meeting the communication needs of the police officer and the victim/witness/suspect in a process of criminal justice – and reminding them and others in the room of the solemnity and significance of their actions.

The Standard Operating Procedures for working with interpreters and translators for the Metropolitan Police (2007) includes a recommended framework to serve as an introduction along the lines of

- (Interpreter's name) is an interpreter. He/she is not a police officer. The interpreter is independent. He/she is a professionally qualified interpreter.
- Interpreters have strict rules about how they work. The interpreter will interpret everything we say. He/she will not add, leave-out or change the meaning of our words. The interpreter will not help you. The interpreter will not give his/her ideas. You must not talk privately to the interpreter. I will decide what the interpreter does. If we know the interpreter has broken any of these rules, we will take action to make sure it does not happen again. (p. 20)

The introduction is definitely a useful one and would help to clarify the roles in the interview. It, however, appears to place the onus to manage at least some of the dynamics of the event on the suspect. What may also work as well, similar to the court or tribunal processes, is an oath or affirmation, along the lines of

> I swear by Almighty God/do solemnly and sincerely declare and affirm that I will well and truly interpret the contents of this interview and do all other matters and things that may be required of me to the best of my skill and ability.

This can be put on record at the start of a police interview in a police preamble where a suspect is reminded of his or her rights. This may serve to remind the interpreters and translators of the legally binding role they play in that setting. Understanding of the formal role can then guide him or her in making ethical decisions on a whole range of dilemmas that may arise during a police activity, the listing of which would be a futile attempt. The other parties in the setting, police officers and victims/witnesses/suspects, would also be clear about the service to be provided by the interpreter in that setting. This is likely to increase compliance with ethical codes by minimising unjustified intervention by interpreters and translators and lessen undue demands and requests from other parties involved. Such a practice would also further strengthen the evidence obtained by the police in critical police procedures in an increasingly diverse policing environment in an ever globalised world with extraordinary security issues.

Use of Personality Measures in Screening for Suitability

Our discussions about ethics and professions in general and in particular about the interpreting and translating profession point to a need for a high degree of agency from the professionals in making ethical decisions. Whether it is rule-based or role-based professional ethics, making a decision requires considering alternatives and using discretion. As the almost daily occurrences of ethical breaches demonstrate, people can make completely different decisions on the same ethical dilemma. This is because, often, ethical decision making is not a linear, step-by-step, formulaic process. Factors such as personality, feelings, emotions, assumptions, cultural upbringing and state of mental well-being influence how people judge a dilemma or behave in a particular way. These are part of human life and the society we live in, and it is difficult to control these factors.

In professional ethics, however, we are dealing with a confined group of people (e.g. doctors and patients) in a well-defined section of society (e.g. people who need medical care). Also, professional ethics is concerned not with broad issues of personal morality but with how ethical decision making can best be influenced during the practice of a profession. In our case, professional ethics is concerned with how interpreters and translators conduct themselves while providing a competent and impartial communication link within another professional activity, which involves a primary, and often, fiduciary relationship.

Interpreters and translators are frequently engaged in policing activities where there is a language barrier between a police officer and a suspect or victim/witness. A significant number of these settings also include highly sensitive investigations and/or highly traumatic events. These police activities can potentially cause anxiety and stress to the vast majority of ordinary members of society as well as the police officers themselves. The American Institute of Stress ranked policing in the top ten high-stress jobs in the United

States (Dempsey & Forst, 2015). They quote criminologist Michael Pittaro, who summarises the gravity of stress in policing aptly:

> The research strongly suggests and most people would agree that a certain amount of stress is evident in most, if not all, professions; however, law enforcement has the dubious honour of being recognised as one of the most stressful professions in the world. The harmful effects and debilitating impact of stress, can lead to a multitude of physical, emotional, psychological and behavioural problems that not only affect the individual officer, but the officer's family, partner, fellow officers and of particular interest, the community with which the officer has sworn to serve and to protect are also at risk. (p. 169)

Interpreters and translators work with police officers closely in many highly stressful tasks. It is inevitable that they would be exposed to stress factors, albeit not always as long term or as ongoing as for police officers. A study by Lai, Heydon and Mulayim (2015) of 271 public service interpreters, largely based in Victoria, Australia, found there is a real concern that they may acquire vicarious trauma both personally and professionally. The study reveals that about four in five interpreters surveyed report experiencing distress after being exposed to assignments involving 'traumatic client material' (p. 4). Although the majority of affected interpreters and translators report feeling disturbed only for a short period, such disturbance may impact on their performance during the affected period. Two other major European studies (Baistow, 1999; Loutan, Farinelli & Pampallona, 1999) also point to similar outcomes, although the percentage of the interpreters and translators surveyed who reported experiencing distress as a result of their professional engagement is lower – about two thirds. Lai et al. (2015) therefore call for better awareness, self-care strategies and briefing/debriefing processes to be afforded by training and service users. This is because by leaving the issue unaddressed, interpreters' perceived cognitive processes, and therefore their perceived performance, as well as their emotional well-being during and after their assignments, are likely to be significantly impacted, which may even become a reason for interpreters and translators to leave the profession, as some respondents in the study expressed.

Furthermore, interpreters are often subjected to demands by police officers and suspects or witnesses to achieve their respective agendas in such assignments. In addition, both police and suspects/witnesses justifiably raise concerns associated with interpreter competence, impartiality, possible conflict of interest and confidentiality.

Some interpreters' and translators' behaviour and conduct that are of concern to the people in the primary relationship may result from the interpreter or translator's personality traits. This then raises the question of how interpreters and translators are selected to work in these environments. At present, the selection of interpreters and translators for training or employment appears to rely largely on assessment of language skills only. Certain security agencies may employ specific selection tools, including psychometric testing for their employees, but such procedures may not necessarily take into account interpreting and translating staff. If the selection of interpreters and translators is solely based on linguistic criteria, it is neglecting the candidates' ethical reasoning ability, critical personality traits and ability to handle stress, all of which may have impacts to the professional context which their service is sought for in the first place.

The authors, as a result, have identified the need for a specific aptitude test for the purpose of making a more comprehensive evaluation of prospective interpreters and translators working with the police. Aptitude tests are typically used in the selection phase to measure applicants' suitability for their future career (Cook, 2009). Gamez and Collins (2014) note psychological testing in screening applicants for police training commenced as early as 1950. These tests continue to be used to select individuals who will have successful employment and 'who will not engage in problematic behaviour' (p. 39). Some of the most common generic screening tests (Gamez & Collins, 2014, pp. 37–38) include

- Minnesota Multiphanic Personality Inventory-Revised (MMPI-2), a self-reporting test designed to assess personality and psychopathology characteristics
- NEO Personality Inventory-Revised (NEO-PI-R), a self-reporting test designed more for organisational settings measuring five traits of conscientiousness and emotional stability
- Personality Assessment Inventory (PAI), preemployment screening of law enforcement personnel for psychopathology

A scientifically developed and empirically trialled aptitude test or instrument can provide objective, reliable and valid information that will assist in predicting career success and satisfaction. In view of this, the authors, in collaboration with two psychologists, have developed a specific personality test for interpreters and translators, named Translator Interpreter Personality Screening (TIPS) Test. The test can both assist in identifying specific areas of concern that needs to be targeted in interpreter training and also can be used as a screening tool in addition to linguistic assessment by police agencies. The test includes interpreting/translating specific issues as well as sections to identify psychographic profiles. The psychographic profile includes measures of the candidate's social desirability (deception measure), normal personality (Big Five Traits), psychopathology (at risk) and personality disorders (depression, anxiety, stress). A prototype TIPS Test was designed in 2015, and the pilot study was presented at an international police symposium. The finalised tool will be useful for selecting trainees for interpreting and translating in general and, in particular, in police settings, and will also provide material useful in police training.

Summary

Most professions have codes of ethics and conduct and some forms of enforcement. However, noncompliance remains an issue that is difficult to resolve in many professions including interpreting and translating. It appears that the causes of noncompliance and solutions often involve multiple factors and conditions, and the most realistic objective is to minimise noncompliance, rather than trying to eradicate it.

Current status quo calls for new perspectives and approaches. For translating and interpreting, one of the shortcomings in the codes appears to be a lack of emphasis on the direct need served by the profession and the trust of the people who benefit from this service. An overarching principle for cognitive rationalisation can help promote voluntary compliance in a range of situations a professional may come across in their practice. These two factors are

1. Commitment to the defining interest of the profession of interpreting and translating, which connects the profession to a moral purpose
2. Fidelity to the trust placed upon them by the parties who are assisted, to maintain professional trust and regard

One other step to improve compliance can be screening professionals for certain undesirable attitudes. This can be done by way of a personality inventory specific to interpreting and translating professionals in police settings.

Police interviews are one of the most common police activities interpreters are engaged for. These interviews often make up the key evidence in prosecutions. It may be a good idea, to improve the quality of interpreting, to include a formal oath or preamble at the outset of the interview to formalise the interpreter's presence and remind the interpreter as well as others of the role of the interpreter in that setting. This is an established practice in court and tribunal hearings.

Epilogue 7

Translating and interpreting are professions, not merely occupations.

Ethics and ethical conduct have always occupied a significant part of public debates as well as philosophical inquiry. Going by the news stories in the media almost every second day involving some ethical breaches by politicians, public servants or professionals, a growing interest in ethics is not surprising.

The main questions of 'How should one behave in an ethical dilemma?'; 'How can one justify their ethical decision?' and 'How can people's ethical decisions be influenced?' have led to many theories and approaches, be it in the classic writings of Greek philosophers such as Plato and Aristotle, in the holy books of the major religions, or the moral traditions of Eastern religions and philosophy. Secular thinkers such as Immanuel Kant (1724–1804), Jeremy Bentham (1748–1832) and John Stuart Mill (1806–1873) contributed immensely to the philosophical debates in normative ethics, underpinning the later development by more contemporary thinking in postmodern terms offered by sociologists such as Zygmunt Bauman. Further development has occurred in the more recent branching into applied ethics in various human activities in areas such as business, politics and medicine and on into the current development in striking a balance between Ethics of Justice vs. Ethics of Care, the former being autonomy- and objectivity-oriented and the latter focusing more on the building of harmonious relations.

While meta-ethics deals with the broader philosophical debate about the need for ethics at all, normative ethics attempts to provide frameworks that can be used as a tool to guide our decisions (Kuusela, 2011). In other words, with normative ethics, the focus is on 'theories which aim to guide our conduct, to help us decide what we ought to do and how we ought to live' (Preston, 2014, p. 17). Although developed centuries ago, three major normative ethics theories continue to inform ethical debates to this date: virtue theory (focusing on the agent, i.e. the person, who performs an act), deontology (the act itself) and consequentialism (the consequences of the act, represented by utilitarianism). Utilitarian theory detailed in the works of classical Utilitarians, Jeremy Bentham and John Stuart Mill, focuses on the consequences of an action that will bring about the greatest good for the greatest number of people (*Stanford Encyclopedia of Philosophy*, 2014). Deontology, in contrast, advocated by Kant uses the categorical imperative that one should only do what is one's duty, as long as it can be universalised, ignoring the consequences of that action. It is therefore considered a nonconsequentialist approach. Virtue theory, lastly, was originally proposed by Plato and established more particularly by Aristotle (*Stanford Encyclopedia of Philosophy*, 2012). The Virtue Ethics approach does not consider duty or consequences of an action, but focuses on virtues of the agent, that is, the person. It uses the maxim that one should try to be a good person, and a good person will do the right thing (Banks, 2014; Ryan, 2001). For example, integrity, which is commonly included in codes of ethics, is a virtue.

This book focuses on professional ethics (rather than personal ethics), which is an essential part of professionalisation and is frequently demanded by society. Professional ethics can be defined as 'the ethics of role' (Preston, 2014), and it is essential to nut out what is understood by the term 'profession' together with its role boundaries to enable discussions of ethics for any particular profession. The essence of professional ethics should, importantly, be recognised as the service for the public good. Ethicist Robert Fullinwider (1996) proposes the following maxim to identify the direct need a profession serves in society:

The Profession of … serves … needs of persons.

The defining interest of a profession, Fullinwider argues, can connect a profession to a moral purpose. He further proposes two more characteristics for an activity to be considered a profession:

1. Having specialised skills and knowledge that cannot be automated, as autonomous decision making and discretion are needed in making professional decisions.
2. People may be vulnerable while accessing the services of the professional.

Many professions, including the traditional professions of medicine and law, fit this definition. Medical doctors meet health needs of individuals by using their specialised skills and knowledge to diagnose a health problem and then deciding on the most appropriate treatment or procedure for that problem. Patients often follow the instructions and recommendations of the doctor without questioning because they trust the doctor more as a representative of a profession than as a person. This reliance on the professional skills and knowledge of the doctor makes them vulnerable.

Epilogue

If we run the translating and interpreting activity through Fullinwider's schema, the defining interest of the profession of translating and interpreting can be formulated as

> The profession of translating and interpreting serves a need for competent and impartial communication when there is a language barrier need between at least two persons who do not share a common language.

This critical role in communication constitutes the public good directly served by the interpreting and translating profession. Although interpreters and translators can be found to work in a wide range of contexts in which people communicate to conduct their business, this book specifically focuses on the police setting. In modern civic societies, a core function of the police is to effectively maintain social order. This is achieved by civic obedience in both personal encounters with police, as well as in people's everyday compliance with the law (Murphy & Cherney, 2012). The focus for this book is intended to acknowledge the importance of the role police play in modern societies, and more specifically, the centrality of interviewing civilians in the course of their work, much of which these days needs to be conducted through the services of interpreters (sign language or spoken language) and translators when a common language is lacking. McGurk, Carr and McGurk (1993) confirmed that the interviewing of witnesses and suspects is in the top four of the most frequently conducted tasks in day-to-day policing, and from the point of view of police officers, their three most important investigative duties are taking statements, interviewing witnesses and interviewing suspects. A more recent survey by O'Neill and Milne in 2014 also confirms police officers' self-reported activity of highest frequency in handling volume crime to be interviewing suspects.

When servicing their clients' communication needs, interpreters and translators make autonomous decisions, using their specialised skills and knowledge, to convey what is said or written in one language into another. Borrowing from the model proposed by Claude Shannon (1948; see Figure 3.1), credited as the father of modern communication theory, a message created from the information source normally wades through a noise source to reach the receiver end. In this monolingual communication setting, this noise source can be an impediment to successful communication ranging from the physical environment in which the communication takes place, the receiver's physiological impairment, cultural stance or psychological state, to semantic or syntactical infelicities in the original message in the first place. Similarly, in conversation analysis according to Professor Paul Drew (1990), the original message frequently contains syntactic mess, false starts, unfinished clauses or sentences, hesitancies, repetition of words and so on. This makes it an unenviable job for interpreters and translators who have to deal firstly with such noise issues intralingually as the receiver of the message, and subsequently interlingually as the transmitter of the recreated message in another language to the actual receiver. This essentially creates a 'nested loop – a loop within a loop' (refer Figure 3.2), with 'noise' issues in each loop.

It is unlikely that, at least with current technology, a routine or automated way of undertaking this interlingual communication act could operate reliably enough in many formal, high-stakes settings such as police interviews or cross-examinations in courts where it is not just what people say, but also how they say it, that is equally significant. People hardly use language in strict adherence to rules of grammar or syntax, either deliberately or because of literacy, physiological or medical issues. Regardless of the reasons for this, apart from transferring the meaning, things such as the intention, for example, sarcasm, scepticism, approval and disapproval, need to be expressed as much as is practicably possible.

Serving people's needs immediately raises the issue of vulnerability and trust. As soon as a professional who has specialised skills and knowledge in a particular field comes into contact with someone who needs those specialised skills and knowledge, a relationship of trust commences. People who are in need *trust* that specialised skills and knowledge will be used by the professional to the highest standards to meet their needs. This reliance on the professional makes clients vulnerable, as they hand over control over aspects of their lives to the professional. A professional, in his or her unique position, can help them or harm them.

When professionals offer their services to people who are in need of the services, they make a commitment or pledge that they have the specialised skills and knowledge to meet the client's needs. In turn, the client has the expectation that he or she will necessarily be protected by the professional's code of ethics from harm. Like many other professions, various interpreter and translator organisations and professional associations around the world have developed their guidelines and codes, covering common areas of competence, impartiality and confidentiality in predominantly bullet-point, rule-based form.

For any practitioner in any profession, knowing the codes of ethics and conduct does not necessarily mean practising them. Laster and Taylor (1994) identified the need for an overarching tool in guiding professional discretion in ethical decision making by interpreters and translators; and they concurred that a professional interpreter (or translator) may be able to recite all the codes in a Code of Ethics, but it does not mean that the code would offer sufficient guidance for practitioners in exercising discretion in the many choices they need to make in their practice. As it would be impossible to include all the potential ethical and conduct issues that may arise in interpreting and translating, there is a need for expounding an overarching principle or common approach for cognitive rationalisation to guide ethical decision making and promote voluntary compliance. In this light, professional organisations for translators and interpreters can play a critical role in guiding and monitoring their members' ethical conduct. They also can be a major force in fostering understanding and good practice standards with other professions they work with.

To design a universal tool for interpreters (for sign and spoken languages) and translators for this purpose, the dynamics of professional settings in which interpreters or translators provide a service must be well understood. When two parties need to communicate to undertake an activity, for example, a police interview or taking a statement from a witness, a relationship immediately commences between the police officer and the suspect or victim/witness. This can be called a primary or preexisting relationship, in the sense that it was formed before the involvement of an interpreter or translator. Where the parties in the primary or preexisting relationship do not share a common language to undertake the activity in question, they need, in many formal processes, the services of someone who is competent and impartial, to assist them with communication. The parties, therefore, *trust* that this service will be provided by an interpreter or a translator. This can be described as *service-oriented interpreting* and *translating*. The parties also trust that any discretionary latitude needed to undertake the core activities required to deliver service-oriented interpreting and translating will be exercised 'with circumspection – neither intruding nor presuming too much nor undertaking too little' (Pellegrino, 1991, p. 73), in the same way as one would see a professional relationship between a doctor and a patient. An interpreter's or translator's fidelity must first be to this trust. Just to remind ourselves, Zaner (1991) views professional trust as 'the essential promise that trust is warranted and always an issue to be made good on in the course of the (professional) encounter' (p. 57). And users/beneficiaries of this esoteric service must give credence or trust – *credat emptor* (Hughes in Wueste, 1994).

Informed by the appreciation of interpreters and translators' involvement in a preexisting relationship as discussed so far, guided by a sense of moral self-understanding, the authors propose the following overarching tool for the profession:

1. Commitment to the defining interest of the profession of interpreting and translating, connecting the profession to a moral purpose
2. Fidelity to the trust placed in interpreters and translators by the parties they serve

Ethical conduct relies on the use of discretion, which is subject to variables such as the agent's own personality, attitudes, cultural upbringing, emotions and mental state. This is especially challenging in interpreting and translating within police settings, which is arguably one of the most stress-filled professions in the world (Pittaro, as cited in Dempsey & Forst, 2014). Selection of interpreters and translators for training to date typically places emphasis on predominantly, if not solely, their bilingual proficiency; and when their service is called for by the police, there is normally no particular procedure to select those with more suitable aptitude to work in these highly stressful settings. A set of specifically designed personality screening inventories for those who will be engaged in police settings may therefore be a feasible solution for police interpreters and translators. A prototype aptitude test was designed by the authors in collaboration with two psychologists in 2015, and the pilot study was presented at an international police symposium. When this screening tool is finalised, in addition to more generic personality inventories, it can be used for the selection of candidates for interpreting and translating training or for employment; moreover, it will also be useful in helping to identify common areas of concern in noncompliance, thus informing what should be specifically addressed in training.

Translators and interpreters provide a critical service to society, and many of them do a great job, enabling members of the community to complete their business when they are faced with communication difficulties due to language barriers. However, as is evidenced by user feedback (see Chapter 6) on ethical behaviours by interpreters and translators, as in any other profession, there is room for improvement. The authors provided detailed analysis and examples of ethical issues categorised under competence, impartiality, conflict of interest and privacy and confidentiality, before proposing an overarching principle to guide ethical decision making. This book is ultimately intended to empower interpreters (for sign and spoken languages) and translators by connecting their profession to a moral purpose, which is key to voluntary compliance. It is hoped that the commitment to the moral purpose of the profession and fidelity to the trust bestowed by the people they serve will guide interpreters and translators in their professional practice, enabling them to scaffold an ethical construct that will assist in justifying decisions that they will be making in a wide range of ethical dilemmas.

Attributes of a Professional Police Interpreter and a Translator

Finally, by way of summarising our discussion of ethics, professions and professional ethics and compliance issues, we would like to propose what we believe are the attributes of a successful interpreter and translator. The attributes proposed here are not assumed to be finite and they focus mainly on police interpreting and translation settings. They are based largely on the characteristics of a profession proposed by Robert Fullinwider (1996) as a broad framework.

Professional police interpreters or translators should have

1. *Sound understanding of their service to society.*
   Understand the moral purpose of the profession of translating and interpreting – directly meeting the need for competent and impartial communication by individuals who don't share a language. The moral self-understanding of this commitment underpins their professional practice and ethical decisions.
2. *Competence in specialised skills and knowledge.*
   Convey what is said or written in one language into another precisely, using their linguistic and extralinguistic knowledge and cognitive transfer skills to assist both parties to be 'on the same linguistic footing'.
3. *Fidelity to the trust of people who benefit from interpreting/translating.*
   a. Appreciate the vulnerability of either party who needs assistance arising from an inability to understand at least part of a dialogue at any given moment.
   b. Appreciate the vulnerability of both parties arising from reliance on what was interpreted/translated.
   c. Respect the primary or preexisting relationship between the parties and avoid any unjustified intervention or boundary violation.
   d. Be committed to the trust of both parties and do not allow bias or conflict of interest to influence professional and ethical decisions.
   e. Appreciate the vulnerability of parties arising from having to disclose their confidential details to receive professional service and undertake to maintain privacy and confidentiality of information gained during professional practice.
   f. Be committed to building professional trust and maintaining respectful regard for the profession of interpreting and translating.

References

AAT (Administrative Appeals Tribunal). (1975). Administrative Appeals Tribunal Act 1975—Sect. 66. Retrieved 10 September 2015 from: http://www.austlii.edu.au/au/legis/cth/consol_act/aata1975323/s66.html.

AAT (n.d.). Administrative Appeals Tribunal: What we do. Retrieved 10 September 2015 from: http://www.aat.gov.au/about-the-aat/what-we-do.

Abbott, A. (1988). *The System of Professions: An Essay on the Division of Expert Labour.* Chicago: University of Chicago Press.

ABC (2012). Paramedics blamed for declaring crash victim dead. Retrieved 20 May 2015 from: http://www.abc.net.au/news/2012-04-13/paramedics-blamed-for-declaring-crash-victim-dead/3948608.

ABC (2014). Tyler Cassidy shooting: Police officer involved in teenager's death break their silence. Retrieved 22 March 2015 from: http://www.abc.net.au/news/2014-06-07/tyler-cassidy-shooting-police-officers-involved-break-silence/5506708.

AIIC (International Association of Conference Interpreters). (2012). Code of Professional Ethics. Retrieved 20 September 2015 from: http://aiic.net/page/6724/code-of-professional-ethics/lang/1.

Alexandra, A., & Miller, S. (2009). *Ethics in Practice: Moral Theory and the Professions.* New South Wales: University of New South Wales Press.

Alexandra, A., & Miller, S. (2010). *Integrity Systems for Occupations.* Surrey and Burlington: Ashgate.

Alleged Embezzlement. (1892, June 21). Barrier Miner (Broken Hill, NSW: 1888–1954), p. 2. Retrieved 10 October 2015 from: http://nla.gov.au/nla.news-article44085219.

Anderson, R. B. W. (1976/2002). Perspectives on the role of interpreter. In F. Pöchhacker & M. Shlesinger (Eds.), *The Interpreting Studies Reader.* London: Routledge.

Angelelli, C. V. (2001). Deconstructing the Invisible Interpreter: A critical study of the interpersonal role of the interpreter in a cross-cultural/linguistic communicative event. Dissertation Abstracts International, *62*(09), 2953. (UMI No. AAT 3026766.)

Around the World Etiquette for Gift Giving. (n.d.) Retrieved 1 September 2015 from: https://travelopinions.wordpress.com/2011/04/28/etiquette-of-gift-giving-guide-for-around-the-world/)?

A transcript of the police interview with Martin Bryant. (n.d.) Retrieved 2 August 2015 from: http://members.iinet.net.au/~nedwood/transcript.html.

AUSTLII. (n.d.). Evidence Act 1995—Schedule 1, Sect. 21 (4) and 22 (2). Retrieved 10 September 2015 from: http://www5.austlii.edu.au/au/legis/nsw/consol_act/ea199580/sch1.html.

Australian Institute of Translators and Interpreters. (2012). AUSIT Code of Ethics and Code of Conduct. Retrieved 2 September 2015 from: http://ausit.org/ausit/documents/code_of_ethics_full.pdf.

Australian Law Dictionary, 1st ed. (2010). Oxford University Press. Retrieved 1 September 2015 from: http://www.oxfordreference.com.ezproxy.lib.rmit.edu.au/view/10.1093/acref/9780195557558.001.0001/acref-9780195557558-e-1384.

Baier, A. (1986). Trust and antitrust. *Ethics, 96*, 231–260.

Baistow, K. (1999). *The Emotional and Psychological Impact of Community Interpreting*. London: Babelea 2000.

Banks, C. (2009). *Criminal Justice Ethics: Theory and Practice*, 3rd ed. Thousand Oaks, CA: SAGE.

Banks, C. (2014). Implementing democratic policing reform: Challenges and constraints in three developing countries. In B. D. Fitch (Ed.), *Law Enforcement Ethics: Classic and Contemporary Issues* (pp. 347–384). Thousand Oaks, CA: SAGE.

Barber, B. (1963). Some problems in the Sociology of Professions. *Daedalus, 92*(4), 669–688.

Barber, B. (1983). *The Logic and Limits of Trust*. New Brunswick, NJ: Rutgers University Press.

Barrie, D. (2010). Police in civil society: Police, enlightenment and civic virtue in urban Scotland, c. 1780–1833. *Urban History, 37*(1), 45–65.

Barry, B. M. (1989). *Theories of Justice*. Berkeley and Los Angeles: University of California Press.

Barsky, A. E. (2010). *Ethics and Values*. Oxford: Oxford University Press.

Bartels, L. (2011). Police interviews with vulnerable adult suspects. Report No. 21. Canberra: Australian Institute of Criminology.

Beaton, G. (2010). Why professionalism is still relevant. Retrieved 11 July 2015 from: http://www.beatonglobal.com/pdfs/Why_Professionalism_is_Still_Relevant-George_Beaton.pdf.

Beauchamp, T. L., & Childress, J. (2009). *Principles of Biomedical Ethics*. New York: Oxford University Press.

Benjamin, R. (2001). The risk of neutrality: Reconsider the term and concept. Retrieved 5 September 2015 from: http://www.mediate.com/articles/benjamin.cfm.

Benn, P. (1998). *Ethics*. London: UCL Press.

Benn, S. (1988). *A Theory of Freedom*. Cambridge, UK: Cambridge University Press.

Bennett, C. (2010). *What Is this Thing Called Ethics?* New York: Routledge.

Bentham, J. (1776, 1988). *A Fragment on Government*. Cambridge, UK: Cambridge University Press.

Berk-Seligson, S. (2009). *Coerced Confessions: The Discourse of Bilingual Police Interrogations*. New York/Berlin: Mouton de Gruyter.

Birzer, M., & Tannehill, R. (2001). A more effective training approach for contemporary policing. *Police Quarterly, 4*(2), 233–252.

Bloch, S., & Pargiter, R. (1996). Developing codes of ethics for psychiatrists. In M. Coady & S. Bloch (Eds.), *Codes of Ethics and the Professions* (pp. 193–225). Melbourne: Melbourne University Press.

Bokor, G. (1994). Ethics for translators and translation business. In D. L. Hammon (Ed.), *Professional Issues for Translators and Interpreters* (pp. 99–106). Amsterdam and Philadelphia: John Benjamins.

Bot, H. (2005). *Dialogue Interpreting in Mental Health*. Amsterdam and New York: Rodopi.

References

Botes, A. (2000). A comparison between the ethics of justice and the ethics of care. *Journal of Advanced Nursing, 32*(5), 1071–1075.

Brabeck, M. (1993). Moral judgement: Theory and research on differences between male and female. In M. J. Larrabee (Ed.), *An Ethics of Care: Feminist and Interdisciplinary Perspectives*. London: Routledge.

Brook, R. (1987). Justice and the golden rule: A commentary on the 3 recent work of Lawrence Kohlberg. *Ethics, 97*, 263–273.

Brouwer, G. (2007). Past Patterns Future Directions – Victoria Police and the problem of corruption and serious misconduct. Retrieved 12 July 2015 from: http://www.ibac.vic.gov.au/docs/default-source/opi-parliamentary-reports/past-patterns-future-directions—feb-2007.pdf?sfvrsn=4.

Bull, R. (2010). Investigative interviewing of children and other vulnerable witnesses: Psychological research and working/professional practice. *National Criminal Justice Reference Service, 15*(1), 5–23.

Bull, R. (2013). What is 'believed' or actually 'known' about characteristics that may contribute to being a good/effective interview? *Investigative Interviewing: Research and Practice, 5*(2), 128–143.

Bull, R. (Ed.). (2014). *Investigative Interviewing*. London: Springer.

Byrne, D., & Heydon, J. D. (1991). *Cross on Evidence* (4th ed.). Sydney: Butterworths.

Canale, M. (2013). From communicative competence to communicative language pedagogy. In J. Richards & R. Schmidt (Eds.), *Language and Communication* (pp. 2–28). London: Taylor & Francis.

Cannan, E. (Ed.) (1896). Lectures on justice, police, revenue and arms, delivered in the university of Glasgow by Adam Smith, reported by a student in 1763 (Glasgow, first published in 1776). London: Claredon Press.

Carr-Saunders, A. M., & Wilson, P. A. (1993). *The Professions*. Oxford: The Clarendon Press.

Childress, J. (1986). Applied ethics. In J. Macquarrie & J. E. Childress (Eds.), *A New Dictionary of Christian Ethics*. London: The Westminster Press.

Chinese Interpreter. (1928, July 14). *The Maitland Daily Mercury* (NSW: 1894–1939), p. 2. Retrieved 13 September 2015 from: http://nla.gov.au/nla.news-article125251052.

Cheetham, G., & Chivers, G. (2005). *Professions, Competence and Informal Learning*. Northampton, MA: Edward Elgar Publishing, Inc.

Chomsky, N. (1998). Reflections on language. In A. Kasher (Ed.), *Pragmatics: Critical Concepts* (pp. 21–36). London: Routledge.

CIOL (Chartered Institute of Linguists). (2015). Code of professional conduct. Retrieved 10 September 2015 from: http://www.ciol.org.uk/images/Membership/CPC15.pdf.

Cleveland, G., & Saville, G. (2007). Police PBL: Blueprint for the 21st century. Retrieved 10 May 2015 from: http://www.pspbl.com/.

Coady, M., & Bloch, S. (Eds.). (1996). *Codes of Ethics and the Professions*. Melbourne: Melbourne University Press.

Code C Detention, Treatment and Questioning of Persons by Police Officers, Police and Criminal Evidence Act 1984 (1984).

Colby, A., Gibbs, J., Kohlberg, L., Speicher-Dubin, B. & Candee, D. (1979). *Standard Form Scoring Manual: Part three from A*. Cambridge, MA: Centre for the Moral Education, Harvard University.

Collste, G. (2012). Applied and professional ethics. *KEMANUSIAAN, 19*(1), 17–33.

Communication Matters in the Courts. (n.d.). Intermediaries. Retrieved 25 September 2015 from: http://www.communicourt.co.uk/recruitment/.

Cook, M. (2009). *Personnel Selection: Adding Value through People*, 5th ed. West Sussex, UK: Wiley-Blackwell.

Corey, G., Corey, M. & Callahan, P. (2003). *Issues and Ethics in the Helping Professions*. Pacific Grove, CA: Brooke/Cole.

Cruess, S. R., Johnston, S. & Cruess, R. L. (2004). Profession: A working definition for medical educators. *Teaching and Learning in Medicine*, Winter, *16*(1), 74–76.

Dael, R. van, & Metselaar, C. (2001). The computing profession in the era of virtual organising. In L. Bloch Ramussen, C. Beardon & S. Munari (Eds.), *Computers and Networks in the Age of Globalisation* (pp. 187–198). New York: Springer Science+Business Media.

Davids, C. (2008). *Conflict of Interest in Policing: Problems, Practices, and Principles*. Sydney: Institute of Criminology Press.

Degramont, P. (1990). *Language and the Distortion of Meaning*. New York: New York University Press.

Dempsey, J., & Forst, L. (2014). *An Introduction to Policing* (7th Ed.). Clifton Park, NY: Delmar Cengage Learning.

Doyle, A. (n.d.). *Top 10 reasons for getting fired*. Retrieved 3 September 2015 from: http://jobsearch.about.com/od/firedtermination/a/wrongful-termination-reasons.htm.

Drew, P. (1990). Strategies in the contest between lawyer and witness in cross-examination. In J. N. Nevi & A. Graffam Walker (Eds.), *Language in the Judicial Process* (pp. 39–64). New York: Springer Science+Business Media.

Dyer, A. R. (1988). *Ethics and Psychiatry: Toward Professional Definition*. Washington, DC: American Psychiatric Publishing.

Edwards, S. D. (1996). *Nursing Ethics: A Principle-Based Approach*. London: Macmillan.

Elias-Bursać, E. (2015). *Translating Evidence and Interpreting Testimony at a War Crimes Tribunal: Working in a Tug-of-War*. Hampshire and New York: Palgrave Macmillan.

Elliot, K. A., & Pollock, J. M. (2014). The ethics of force: Duty, principle, and morality. In B. D. Fitch (Ed.), *Law Enforcement Ethics: Classic and Contemporary Issues* (pp. 231–256). London, New Delhi and Singapore: SAGE.

European Legal Interpreters and Translators Association (2013). EULITA Code of Professional Ethics. Retrieved 2 September 2015 from: http://www.eulita.eu/sites/default/files/EULITA-code-London-e.pdf.

Fisher, M. A. (2009). Replacing "Who is the client?" with a different ethical question. *Professional Psychology Research and Practice*, *40*(1), 1–7.

Flanagan, O., & Jackson, K. (1987). Justice, care and gender: The 4 Kohlberg-Gilligan debate revisited. *Ethics*, *97*, 622–637.

Freckelton, I. (1996). Enforcement of ethics. In M. Coady & S. Bloch (Eds.), *Codes of Ethics and the Professions* (pp. 130–165). Melbourne: Melbourne University Press.

Freidson, E. (1986). *Professional Powers: A Study in the Institutionalization of Formal Knowledge*. Chicago: University of Chicago Press.

References

Freidson, E. (2001). *Professionalism, The Third Logic: On the Practice of Knowledge.* Chicago: University of Chicago Press.
Fullinwider, R. (1996). Professional codes and moral understanding. In M. Coady & S. Bloch (Eds.), *Codes of Ethics and the Professions* (pp. 72–88). Melbourne: Melbourne University Press.
Gaio v. The Queen. (1961). *Melbourne University Law Review, 3*(2), 237–240. Retrieved 5 March 2015 from: http://www.austlii.edu.au/au/journals/MelbULawRw/1961/26.html.
Gamez, A. M., & Collins, G. G. (2014). Psychological evaluations of law enforcement applicants: The search for ethical officers. In B. D. Fitch (Ed.), *Law Enforcement Ethics: Classic and Contemporary Issues* (pp. 29–47). Thousand Oaks, CA: SAGE.
Gardner, F. (2014). *Being Critically Reflective in Holistic Practice.* Basingstoke, UK: Palgrave Macmillan.
Gaukroger, S. (2012). *Objectivity: A Very Short Introduction.* Oxford and New York: Oxford University Press.
Gentile, A., Ozolins, U. & Vasilakakos, M. (1996). *Liaison Interpreting: A Handbook.* Melbourne: Melbourne University Press.
Gerver, D. (1971). *Aspects of Simultaneous Interpretation and Human Information Processing.* Oxford: Oxford University Press.
GFK Verein (2014). *Global Study on Trust in Professions.* Retrieved 20 July 2015 from: http://www.gfk.com/news-and-events/press-room/press-releases/pages/gfk-verein-global-study-on-trust-in-professions—.aspx.
Gibbons, J. (2007). *Forensic Linguistics: An Introduction to Language in the Justice System*, 2nd ed. Oxford: Blackwell.
Gibson, K. (1999). Mediator attitude towards outcomes: A philosophical view. *Mediation Quarterly, 17*(2), 197–211.
Gile, D. (2009). *Basic Concepts and Models for Interpreters and Translator Training* (revised edition). Amsterdam and Philadelphia: John Benjamins.
Gilligan, C., Ward, J. V., & Taylor, J. M. (1994). *Mapping the Moral Domain.* Cambridge: Harvard University Press.
Golley, L. (2008). Medical interpreter ethics. Retrieved 3 August 2015 from: http://www.uwmedicine.org/uw-medical-center/documents/Medical-Interpreter-Ethics.pdf.
González, R. D., Vásquez, V. F. & Mikkelson, H. (1991). *Fundamentals of Court Interpretation: Theory, Policy and Practice.* Durham, NC: Carolina Academic Press.
Grieve, J., Harfiled, C., & MacVean, A. (2007). *Policing.* London: SAGE.
Gudjonsson, G. H. (2003). *The Psychology of Interrogations, Confessions and Testimony.* Chichester: John Wiley & Sons.
Hale, S. (2004). *The Discourse of Court Interpreting: Discourse Practices of the Law, the Witness and the Interpreter.* Amsterdam and Philadelphia: John Benjamins.
Hale, S. (2007). *Community Interpreting.* Hampshire and New York: Palgrave Macmillan.
Hall, P. (2008). Police speak. In J. Gibbons & M. T. Turell (Eds.), *Dimensions of Forensic Linguistics* (pp. 67–94). Amsterdam and Philadelphia: John Benjamins.
Heilbrun, K. (2001). *Principles of Forensic Mental Health Assessment.* New York: Kluwer Academic/Plenum.
Hendley, K. (1996). *Trying to Make Law Matter: Legal Reform and Labor Law in the Soviet Union.* Ann Arbor: University of Michigan Press.

Heydon, G. (2005). *The Language of Police Interviewing: A Critical Analysis*. New York: Palgrave Macmillan.

Houser, R., Wilczenski, F. L. & Ham, M. (2006). *Culturally Relevant Ethical Decision-Making in Counseling*. Thousand Oaks, CA: SAGE.

Hughes, J. (2013). Theory of professional standards and ethical policing. In A. MacVean, P. Spindler & C. Solf (Eds.), *Handbook of Policing, Ethics, and Professional Standards* (pp. 7–16). New York: Routledge.

Inghilleri, M. (2012). *Interpreting Justice: Ethics, Politics and Language*. New York and London: Routledge.

Intermediary Programs in England and Wales. (n.d.). Retrieved 5 September 2015 from: http://www.vicbar.com.au/GetFile.ashx?file=CPDAdjournedFiles%2FDOJ+-+Intermediary+Programs+in+England+and+Wales.pdf.

Internet Encyclopaedia of Philosophy. (n.d.). Applied ethics. Retrieved 1 September 2015 from: http://www.iep.utm.edu/ap-ethic/.

Jacobsen, B. (2002). *Pragmatic Meaning in Court Interpreting. An empirical study of additions in consecutively interpreted question-answer dialogues*. (PhD), Aarhus University, Aarhus.

Jakobson, R. (1959). On linguistic aspects of translation. Retrieved 1 May 2015 from: http://www.stanford.edu/~eckert/PDF/jakobson.pdf.

Janzen, T., & Korpiniski, D. (2005). Ethics and professionalism in interpreting. In T. Janzen (Ed.), *Topics in Signed Language Interpreting* (pp. 165–199). Amsterdam & Philadelphia: John Benjamins.

Judicial College of Victoria (n.d.a). *Victorian Criminal Proceedings Manual*, Section 9.5.1: Use of an interpreter. Retrieved 10 September 2015 from: http://www.judicialcollege.vic.edu.au/eManuals/VCPM/index.htm#27584.htm.

Judicial College of Victoria (n.d.b). *Victorian Criminal Proceedings Manual*, Section 9.5.2: Adequacy of interpretation. Retrieved 12 September 2015 from: http://www.judicialcollege.vic.edu.au/eManuals/VCPM/index.htm#27585.htm.

Kahane, E. (2000). Thoughts on the quality of interpretation. Retrieved 1 May 2015 from: http://aiic.net/page/197/thoughts-on-the-quality-of-interpretation/lang/1.

Kant, Immanuel (1785, 1998). *Groundwork of the Metaphysics of Morals*. M. Gregor (ed. & translator). Cambridge, UK: Cambridge University Press.

Kaplan, L., & Owings, W. A. (2015). *Educational Foundations*, 2nd ed. Stamford, CT: Cengage Learning.

Katan, D. (1999). *Translating Cultures: An Introduction for Translators, Interpreters and Mediators*. Manchester: St. Jerome.

Kaufman, I. R. (1957). The former government attorney and the cannons of professional ethics. *Harvard Law Review, 70*(4), 657–669.

Kebbell, M. R., Hurren, E. J., & Robert, S. (2005). Mock-suspects' decision to confess: The accuracy of eyewitness evidence is critical. *Applied Cognitive Psychology, 19*, 1–10.

Keith-Spiegel, P., & Koocher, G. (1985). *Ethics in Psychology: Professional Standards and Cases*. New York: Random House.

Kitchener, K. S. (2000). *Foundations of Ethical Practice, Research and Teaching in Psychology*. Mahwah, NJ: Lawrence Erlbaum Associates.

Koehler, W. (2015). *Ethics and Values in Librarianship: A History*. Lanham, MD: Rowman and Littlefield.

References

Klingberg-Allvin, M., Tam, V. V., Nga, N. T., Ransjo-Arvidson, A.-B., & Johansson, A. (2007). Ethics of justice and ethics of care values and attitudes among midwifery students on adolescent sexuality and abortion in Vietnam and their implications for midwifery education: A survey by questionnaire and interview. *International Journal of Nursing Studies*, 44, 37–46.

Koehn, D. (1994). *The Ground of Professional Ethics*. London and New York: Routledge/Taylor & Francis.

Kohn, L. (2001). *Daoism and Chinese Culture*. Cambridge, MA: Three Pines Press.

Kolb, R. W. (Ed.). (2008). *Encyclopedia of Business and Ethics and Society*. Thousand Oaks, CA: SAGE.

Kuusela, O. (2011). *Key Terms in Ethics*. London and New York: Continuum.

Lai, M. (2016). *Police Cognitive Interviews Mediated by Interpreters – An Exercise in Diminishment?* PhD thesis. Translating and Interpreting. RMIT University, Melbourne.

Lai, M., Heydon, G. & Mulayim, S. (2015). Vicarious trauma among interpreters. *International Journal of Interpreter Education*, 7(1), 3–22.

Langford, G. (1978). *Teaching as a Profession*. Manchester: Manchester University Press.

Laster, K. (1990). Legal interpreters: Conduits to social justice? *Journal of Intercultural Studies*, 11, 16–32.

Laster, K., & Taylor, V. L. (1994). *Interpreters and the Legal System*. Sydney: The Federation Press.

Laster, K., & Taylor, V. (1995). The compromised "conduit": Conflicting perceptions of legal interpreters. *Multiculturalism and the Law*, 6(4). Retrieved 10 May 2015 from: http://www.aic.gov.au/media_library/conferences/multiculturalism/laster.pdf.

Latimer, P., & Maume, P. (2015). *Promoting Information in the Marketplace for Financial Services: Financial Market Regulation and International Standards*. London: Springer.

Lauder, S. (2009, 30 July). Council workers sacked over free sandwich. *ABC News*. Retrieved 4 March 2015 from: http://www.abc.net.au/news/2009-07-29/council-workers-sacked-over-free-sandwich/1371772.

Law Institute of Victoria (n.d.). Code of Ethics. Retrieved 1 September 2015 from: http://www.liv.asn.au/getattachment/For-Lawyers/Ethics/Code-of-Ethics/Code-of-Ethics—17-4-14.pdf.aspx.

Leanza, Y. (2007). Roles of community interpreters in pediatrics as seen by interpreters, physicians and researchers. In F. Pochhacker & M. Shlesinger (Eds.), *Healthcare Interpreting: Discourse and Interaction* (pp. 11–34). Amsterdam and Philadelphis: John Benjamins.

Lederer, M. (2003). *Translation: The Interpretive Model*. Manchester and Northampton, MA: St. Jerome.

Lee, J. (2016). A case study of the interpreter-mediated witness statement: Police interpreting in South Korea. *Police Practice and Research: An International Journal*.

Leggatt, T. (2010). Teaching as a profession. In J. A. Jackson (Ed.), *Professions and Professionalisation*: Vol. 3 (pp. 153–178). Cambridge, UK: Cambridge University Press.

Lieberman, M. (1956). *Education as a Profession*. Englewood Cliffs, NJ: Prentice-Hall.

Loader, I., & Walker, N. (2001). Policing as a public good: Reconstituting the connections between policing and the state. *Theoretical Criminology*, 5(1), 9–35.

Loewy, E. H. (1996). *Textbook of Healthcare Ethics.* New York: Plenum Press.
Longstaff, S. (1994). Some thoughts about how to make them work! In N. Preston (Ed.), *Ethics for the Public Sector: Education and Training* (pp. 237–246). Annandale, NSW: The Federation Press.
Lord Benson, H. (1992). "Criteria for a group to be considered a profession" as recorded in Hansard (Lords) 8 July, 1206–1207. Retrieved 20 June 2015 from: http://hansard.millbanksystems.com/lords/1992/jul/08/the-professions.
Loutan, L., Farinelli, T. & Pampallona, S. (1999). Medical interpreters have feelings too. *Sozial und Präventivmedizin, 44,* 280–282.
MacVean, A., & Neyroud, P. (2012). *Policing Matter: Police Ethics and Values.* London: SAGE.
Manning, P. K. (1997). *Police Work: The Social Organization of Policing.* Long Grove, Illinois: Waveland Press.
Marenin, O. (2004). Police training for democracy. *Police Practice and Research,* 5(2), 107–123.
McCoy, M. (2006). Teaching style and the application of adult learning principles by police instructors. *Policing: An International Journal of Police Strategies & Management,* 29(1), 77–91.
McGurk, B., Carr, J. & McGurk, D. (1993). *Investigative Interviewing Courses for Police Officers: An Evaluation.* (H. Office, Trans.). London: Home Office.
Megret, F. (2014). What is 'international impartiality'? In V. Popovski (Ed.), *International Rule of Law and Professional Ethics* (pp. 101–126). Surrey: Ashgate.
Metropolitan Police (2007). Working with interpreters & translators: Standard operating procedures. Retrieved 2 September 2015 from: http://www.met.police.uk/foi/pdfs/policies/interpreters_and_translators_sop.pdf.
Michultka, D. (2009). Mental health issues in new immigrant communities. In E. P. Congress & F. Chang-Muy (Eds.), *Social Work with Immigrants and Refugees: Legal Issues, Clinical Skills and Advocacy* (pp. 135–172). New York: Springer Publishing Company.
Mikkelson, H. (1998). Towards a redefinition of the role of the court interpreter. *Interpreting,* 3(1), 21–45.
Miller, S., Blackler, J. & Alexandra, A. (2006). *Police Ethics.* Melbourne: Allen & Unwin.
Ministry of Justice (2012). *The Registered Intermediary Procedural Guidance Manual.* Retrieved 5 September 2015 from: http://www.cps.gov.uk/publications/docs/ri_proceduralguidancemanual_2012.pdf.
Mizzoni, J. (2010). *Ethics: The basics.* Chichester, West Sussex, UK and Malden, MA: Wiley-Blackwell.
Moral Philosophy. (n.d.). Retrieved 1 September 2015 from: http://moralphilosophy.info/normative-ethics/.
Morris, R. (1999). The Gum Syndrome: Predicaments in court interpreting. *International Journal of Speech, Language and the Law,* 6(1), 6–29.
Morrissey, S. A., & Redd, P. (2006). *Ethics and Professional Practice for Psychologists.* Melbourne, Australia: Thomson/Social Science Press.
Mosk, R. M., & Ginsburg, T. (2012). Becoming an international arbitrator: Qualifications, disclosures, conduct and removal. In D. M. Kolkey, R. Chernick & B. R. Neal (Eds.), *Practitioner's Handbook on International Arbitration and Mediation,* 3rd ed. (pp. 367–423). New York: Juris Net, LLC.

References

Mulayim, S., Lai, M., & Norma, C. (2015). *Police Investigative Interviews and Interpreting: Contact, Challenges, and Strategies*. New York: CRC Press, Taylor & Francis Group.

Munday, J. (2008). *Introducing Translation Studies: Theories and Applications*. Abingdon and New York: Routledge.

Muraskin, R. (2001). Overview of morality and the law. In R. Muraskin & M. Muraskin (Eds.), *Morality and the Law* (pp. 1–6). Upper Saddle River, NJ: Prentice Hall.

Murphy, K., & Cherney, A. (2012). Understanding cooperation with police in a diverse society. *British Journal of Criminology*, 52, 181–201. DOI:10.1093/bjc/azr065.

Napier, J. (2005). What makes an ideal interpreter? *NEWSLI, Magazine for the Association of Signed Language Interpreters for England, Wales & Northern Ireland*, 54, 4–7.

NCIHC (National Council on Interpreting in Health Care). (2004a). National standards of practice for interpreters in health care. Retrieved 3 September 2015 from: http://www.ncihc.org/assets/documents/publications/NCIHC%20National%20Standards%20of%20Practice.pdf.

NCIHC (National Council on Interpreting in Health Care). (2004b). A national code of ethics for interpreters in health care. Retrieved 3 September 2015 from: http://www.ncihc.org/assets/documents/publications/NCIHC%20National%20Code%20of%20Ethics.pdf.

Neukrug, E., Lovell, C., & Parker, R. (1996). Employing ethical codes and decision-making models: A developmental process. *Counseling and Values*, 40(2), 98–106.

Neukrug, E., Milliken, T., & Walden, S. (2001). Ethical complaints made against credentialed counselors: An updated survey of State Licensing Boards. *Counselor Education and Supervision*, 41(1), 57–70.

Neyroud, P. (2003). Policing and ethics. In T. Newburn (Ed.), *Handbook of Policing* (pp. 578–602). Cullompton, UK: Willan.

NHS (National Health Service). (n.d.). National Health Service: Aphasia. Retrieved 21 September 2015 from: http://www.nhs.uk/Conditions/Aphasia/Pages/Introduction.aspx.

Nida, E., & Taber, C. R. (1974). *The Theory and Practice of Translation*. Leiden, the Netherlands: E. J. Brill.

Niska, H. (1990). A new breed of interpreter for immigrants: Contact interpretation in Sweden. In C. Picken (Ed.), *Proceedings of Institute of Translation and Interpretation Conference 4* (pp. 94–104). London: ASLIB.

North Adelaide – Recent Meeting of Electors. (1851, 3 March) South Australian Register (Adelaide, SA: 1839–1900), p. 3. Retrieved 12 September 2015 from: http://nla.gov.au/nla.news-article38446761.NRPSI (National Register of Public Service Interpreters). (2014). *NRPSI Annual Review of Public Service Interpreting in the UK 2013*. Retrieved 2 December 2015 from: http://www.nrpsi.org.uk/downloads/NRPSI_Annual_Review_of_Public_Service_Interpreting_in_the_UK_2013.pdf.

O'Day, R. (2000). *The Professions in Early Modern England, 1450–1800: Servants of the Commonwealth*. Harlow, England: Pearson Education.

O'Neill, M., & Milne, B. (2014). Success within criminal investigation: Is communication still a key component? In R. Bull (Ed.), *Investigative Interviewing* (pp. 123–146). London: Springer.

Ozolins, U. (2015). Ethics and the role of the interpreter. In H. Mikkelson & R. Jourdenais (Eds.), *The Routledge Handbook of Interpreting* (pp. 319–336). Abingdon, UK and New York: Routledge.

Parsons, R. D. (2001). *The Ethics of Professional Practice*. Needham Heights, MA: Allyn and Bacon.

Patten, B. (2003). *Professional Negligence in Construction*. London: Spon Press.

Pellegrino, E. D. (1991). Trust and distrust in professional ethics. In E. D. Pellegrino, R. M. Veatch & J. P. Langan (Eds.), *Ethics, Trust, and the Professions: Philosophical and Cultural Aspects* (pp. 69–89). Washington, DC: Georgetown University Press.

Pierscionek, B. K. (2008). *Law & Ethics for the Eye Care Professional*. Edinburgh: Butterworth Heinemann Elsevier.

Pöchhacker, F. (2007). Critical linking up: Kinship and convergence in interpreting studies. In C. Wadensjo, B. E. Dimitrova & N. A.-L. (Eds.), *The Critical Link 4* (pp. 11–26). Amsterdam and Philadelphia: John Benjamins.

Powell, M. (2002). Specialist training in investigative and evidential interviewing: Is it having any effect on the behaviour of professionals in the field? *Psychiatry, Psychology and Law*, 9, 44–55.

Preedy, A. (2009, 9 July). Rudd bamboozles Germans with 'programmatic specificity'. *Perth Sunday Times*. Retrieved 2 August 2015 from: http://www.perthnow.com.au/news/rudd-bamboozles-germans-with-programmatic-specificity/story-e6frg12c-1225747867748.

Preston, N. (2014). *Understanding Ethics*, 4th ed. Sydney: Federation Press.

Professionals Australia (n.d.). What is a profession? Retrieved 21 August 2015 from: http://www.professions.com.au/about-us/what-is-a-professional.

Queensland (2012). Oaths Act 1867. Retrieved 10 September 2015 from: https://www.legislation.qld.gov.au/LEGISLTN/CURRENT/O/OathsA1867.pdf.

Rachels, J. (1991). Subjectivism. In P. Singer (Ed.), *A Companion to Ethics* (pp. 432–441). Cambridge, MA: Blackwell.

Rachels, J. (1999). *The Elements of Moral Philosophy*. Boston: McGraw-Hill College.

Reid, H. L. (n.d.). The educational value of Plato's early socratic dialogues. Retrieved 16 April 2015 from: https://www.bu.edu/wcp/Papers/Teac/TeacReid.htm.

Rittel, H. W., & Webber, M. M. (1973). Dilemmas in a general theory of planning. *Policy Sciences*, 4, 155–169.

Roberts, R. P. (2002). Community interpreting: A profession in search of its identity. In E. Hung (Ed.), *Teaching Translation and Interpreting 4: Building Bridges* (pp. 157–175). Amsterdam and Philadelphia: Benjamins.

Roberts-Smith, L. (2009). Forensic interpreting: Trial and error. In S. B. Hale, U. Ozolins, & L. Stern (Eds.), *Critical Link 5: Quality in Interpreting – A Shared Responsibility* (pp. 13–36). Amsterdam and Philadelphia: John Benjamins.

Rotter, J. B. (1967). A new scale for the measurement of interpersonal trust. *Journal of Personality*, 35(4), 651–665.

Routman, R. (2014). *Read, Write, Lead: Breakthrough Strategies for Schoolwide Literacy Success*. Alexandria, VA: ASCD.

Roy, C. B. (2000). *Interpreting as a Discourse Process*. Oxford: Oxford University Press.

References

Rudvin, M. (2003). Negotiating linguistic and cultural identities in interpreter-mediated communication for public health services. In A. Pym, M. Shlesinger & Z. Jettmarová (Eds.), *Sociocultural Aspects of Translating and Interpreting* (pp. 173–190). Amsterdam and Philadelphia: John Benjamins.

Russell, S. (2002). 'Three's a Crowd': Shifting dynamics in the interpreted interview. In J. Cotterill (Ed.), *Language in the Legal Process* (pp. 111–126). Hampshire and New York: Palgrave Macmillan.

Ryan, K. (2001). Doing right, being good: The Socratic question and the criminal justice practitioner. In R. Muraskin & M. Muraskin (Eds.), *Morality and the Law*. Upper Saddle River, NJ: Prentice Hall.

Samovar, L., Porter, R., McDaniel, E. & Roy, C. (2015). *Intercultural Communication: A Reader*, 14th ed. Boston: Cengage Learning.

Sapir, E. (1956). *Culture, Language and Personality: Selected Essays*. Berkeley: University of California Press.

SBS. (2010). The Gaddafi interview. Retrieved 10 July 2015 from: http://www.sbs.com.au/news/dateline/story/gaddafi-interview.

Scanlon, L. (2011). Becoming a professional. In L. Scallon (Ed.), *Becoming a Professional* (pp. 13–32). Dordrecht: Springer Science+Business Media B.V.

Schweda-Nicholson, N. (1994). Professional ethics for court and community interpreters. In D. L. Hammond (Ed.), *Professional Issues for Translators and Interpreters. ATA Scholarly Monograph Series* (Vol. VII, pp. 79–97). Amsterdam and Philadelphia: John Benjamins.

Shackman, J. (1984). *The Right to Be Understood: A Handbook on Working with, Employing and Training Community Interpreters*. Cambridge, UK: National Extension College.

Shanahan, T., & Wang, R. (2003). *Reason and Insight: Western and Eastern Perspectives on the Pursuit of Moral Wisdom*. Belmont, CA: Wadsworth.

Shannon, C. E. (1948). A mathematical theory of communication. *The Bell System Technical Journal, 27* (July), 379–423.

Sharma, S. K. (1994). *Privacy Law: A Comparative Study*. New Delhi: Atlantic Publishers & Distributors.

Shepherd, E. (2007). *Investigative Interviewing: The Conversation Management Approach*. Oxford and New York: Oxford University Press.

Shlesinger, M., & Pöchhacker, F. (Eds.). (2010). *Doing Justice to Court Interpreting*. Amsterdam and Philadelphia: John Benjamins.

Shuttleworth, M., & Cowie, M. (1997). *Dictionary of Translation Studies*. Manchester, UK and Kinderhook, NY: St. Jerome Publishing.

Silvester, J. (2014). Police shootings aired on ABC TV, *The Age*. Retrieved 15 April 2015 from: http://www.theage.com.au/victoria/police-shootings-aired-on-abc-tv-20140606-39oka.html.

Simpson, P. (1997). Contemporary virtue ethics and Aristotle. In D. Statman (Ed.), *Virtue Ethics* (pp. 249–259). Edinburgh: Edinburgh University Press.

Smith, A. (1763). *Lectures on Justice, Police, Revenue and Arms, Delivered in the University of Glasgow by Adam Smith, Reported by a Student in 1763* (Glasgow, first published in 1776). E. Cannan (Ed.). London.

Smith, H. (1991). *The World's Religions: Our Great Wisdom Traditions*. New York: HarperCollins.

Snyder, N. (1994). The paradox of professionalism. In D. L. Hammond (Ed.), *Professional Issues for Translators and Interpreters* (pp. 13–22). Amsterdam and Philadelphia: John Benjamins.

Sokolowski, R. (1991). The fiduciary relationship and the nature of professions. In E. D. Pellegrino, R. M. Veatch & J. P. Pangan (Eds.), *Ethics, Trust, and the Professions: Philosophical and Cultural Aspects* (pp. 23–43). Washington, DC: Georgetown University Press.

Spada. (2009). British professions today; The state of the sector. Retrieved 3 August 2015 from: http://www.propertyweek.com/Journals/Builder_Group/Property_Week/10_July_2009/attachments/spada-british-professions-today.pdf.

Stanford Encyclopedia of Philosophy. (2012). Virtue ethics. Retrieved 20 September 2015 from: http://plato.stanford.edu/entries/ethics-virtue/.

Stanford Encyclopedia of Philosophy. (2014). The history of utilitarianism. Retrieved 20 September 2015 from: http://plato.stanford.edu/entries/utilitarianism-history/.

Steinberg, S. (2007). *An Introduction to Communication Studies*. Cape Town, South Africa: Juta & Co.

Sternberg, R. (2015). Epilogue: Why is ethical behaviour challenging? A Model of ethical reasoning. In R. J. Sternberg & S. T. Fiske (Eds.), *Ethical Challenges in the Behavioural and Brain Sciences, Case Studies and Commentaries* (pp. 219–226). Cambridge, UK: Cambridge University Press.

Strandberg, K. M. (2007). *Essentials of Law and Ethics for Pharmacy Technicians*, 2nd ed. New York: CRC Press.

Swanson, L.,Chamelin, C.R. & Territo, N. C. (2002). *Criminal Investigation*. Boston: McGraw-Hill Higher Education.

Tasmania Law Reform Institute (2006). Consolidation of arrest laws in Tasmania. Issues paper no. 10. Retrieved 10 July 2015 from: http://www.law.utas.edu.au/reform/docs/ArrestIP%209%20June%2006-A4%20final.pdf.

The New York State Unified Court System (n.d.). Working with interpreters in the courtroom: Benchcard for judges. Retrieved 22 September 2015 from: http://www.ncsc.org/~/media/Files/PDF/Services%20and%20Experts/Areas%20of%20expertise/Language%20Access/Resources%20for%20Program%20Managers/NY_JudBenchcard.ashx.

Thiroux, J. P., & Kraseman, K. W. (2007). *Ethics: Theory and Practice*, 9th ed. Upper Saddle River, NJ: Prentice Hall.

Thompson, A. K. (2011). *Religious Confession Privilege and the Common Law*. Leiden, the Netherlands: Koninklijke Brill NV.

Thompson, D. F. (n.d.). What is practical ethics? Retrieved 3 August 2015 from: http://ethics.harvard.edu/what-practical-ethics.

Thompson, I. E., Melia, K. M., Boyd, K. M. & Horsburgh, D. (2006). *Nursing Ethics*, 5th ed. Edinburgh: Churchill Livingston Elsevier.

Tyler Cassidy shooting: Police officer involved in teenager's death break their silence. (2014). Retrieved 2 August 2015 from: http://www.abc.net.au/news/2014-06-07/tyler-cassidy-shooting-police-officers-involved-break-silence/5506708.

UCS (Unified Court System). (2008). *Court Interpreter Manual and Code of Ethics*. Retrieved 20 September 2015 from: https://www.nycourts.gov/courtinterpreter/pdfs/CourtInterpreterManual.pdf.

References

United Nations (2004). *Human Rights Standards and Practice for the Police: Expanded Pocket Book on Human Rights for the Police*. Retrieved 25 August 2015 from: http://www.ohchr.org/Documents/Publications/training5Add3en.pdf.

VGSO (Victorian Government Solicitor's Office). (2007). *Understanding legal professional privilege*. Retrieved 10 September 2015 from: http://www.vgso.vic.gov.au/sites/default/files/Understanding%20Legal%20Professional%20Privilege.pdf.

Viaggio, S. (2000). Aptitude and simultaneous interpretation: A proposal for a testing methodology based on paraphrase. In G. V. Garzone & M. Viezzi (Eds.), *Interpreting in the 21st Century: Challenges and opportunities* (pp. 231–246). Amsterdam and Philadelphia: John Benjamins.

Victoria Police (n.d.). *Victoria Police Manual: Police Rules – Professional and Ethical Standards*. Retrieved 2 September 2015 from: https://www.policecareer.vic.gov.au/websites/victoriapolice/userdocuments/16714PMP_ProfStad.pdf.

Wadensjö, C. (1998). *Interpreting as Interaction*. Harlow: Longman.

Waldron, J. (1993). *Liberal Rights: Collected Papers 1981–1991*. Cambridge: Cambridge University Press.

Warren, S. D., & Brandeis, L. D. (1890). The right to privacy. *Harvard Law Review*, 4(5), 193–220.

Weiss, P. (1942). Morality and Ethics. *The Journal of Philosophy*, 39(14), 381–385. doi:10.2307/2018625.

West, R. (1997). *Caring for Justice*. New York: New York University Press.

Westermeyer, J. (1990). Working with an interpreter in psychiatric assessment and treatment. *Journal of Nervous and Mental Disease*, 178(12), 745–749.

What People Say. (1892, June 21). Barrier miner (Broken Hill, NSW: 1888–1954), p. 4. Retrieved 25 September 2015 from: http://nla.gov.au/nla.news-article44085214.

WMA (World Medical Association). (1948). Declaration of Geneva. Retrieved 20 July 2015 from: http://www.wma.net/en/30publications/10policies/g1/WMA_DECLARATION-OF-GENEVA_A4_EN.pdf.

Wueste, D. E. (Ed.). (1994). *Professional Ethics and Social Responsibilities*. Oxford: Rowan & Littlefield.

Yeschke, C. L. (2003). *The Art of Investigative Interviewing*, (2nd ed.). Boston: Butterworth-Heinemann.

Zaner, R. (1991). The fiduciary relationship and the nature of professions. In E. D. Pellegrino, R. M. Veatch & J. P. Langan (Eds.), *Ethics, Trust, and the Professions: Philosophical and Cultural Aspects* (pp. 23–44). Washington, DC: Georgetown University Press.

Index

Page numbers in italics refer to figures.

A

AAT (Administrative Appeals Tribunal), 105
Abbott, Andrew, 18, 22, 34
Aborigines, 25
Absolutism, xxxv–xxxvi
Accountants, 51
Accuracy, 67, 93
Administrative Appeals Tribunal (AAT), 105
AIIC, *see* International Association of Conference Interpreters (AIIC)
Alexandra, Andrew, xxxi, 3, 21, 62, 104
American Heritage Dictionary, 60
Anderson, R. Bruce W., 47
Antonetti, Jean-Claude, 99
Aphasia, 45
Applied ethics, 2, 10–11
Arbitration, 60
Aristotle, xxvii, 7
Arrest, 25
Attitudinal impartiality, 97–98
Audience, 36, *37*, *38*
Australian Institute of Translators and Interpreters (AUSIT), 66
Australian Law Dictionary, xxviii
Autonomy
　ethics of justice, 12
　exercise, 76
　moral, 114
　morality and, 11
　personal, 11, 57
　professional, 23
　professional activity, 28
　professional decision-making, 23
　respect for, 10

B

Background
　common, 37, 47
　ethnic, 95, 100
　non-English-speaking (NESB), 26, 40
Baier, Annette, 27
Banks, Cyndi, xxxiv, 2
Barber, Bernard, 16, 27, 117
Barnes, Dan, 33, 70
Barrier Miner, 83
Barsky, Allen, 53
Bauman, Zygmunt, 11
Beaton, George, 26, 27, 51
Beauchamp, Tom L., 10, 113
Beneficence, 11, 57
Benevolence, 7
Benn, Piers, 8, 62
Bennett, Christopher, 1
Benson, Baron (Henry Alexander Benson), 18
Bentham, Jeremy, xxvii, 4
Berk-Seligson, Susan, 102
Biomedical ethics, 10–11, 136
Black boxes, 32
Blackler, John, xxxi, 21, 104
Bloch, Sidney, xxix
The Bobby policeman, 19
Bokor, Gabe, 28
Botes, Annatjie, 12
Bot, Hanneke, xxxiii
Boyd, Kenneth M., 2
Brandeis, Louis, 61
Brook, Richard, 12
Brouwer, George, 21
Bryant, Martin, 86
Buddhism, 9
Buller, Sir Francis, 104
Bull, Ray, 25, 97–98

C

California Health Interpreting Association (CHIA), 32
Cambridge Dictionary, 16
Canale, Michael, 36, 38, 47
Candee, D., 5
Care, 12–13, 24, 57
Carr, Michael J., 71
Carr-Saunders, Sir Alexander Morris, 25
Carr vs. IRC, 17
Carson, William, 97
Case studies
  attitudinal impartiality, 97–98
  compliance, 108
  conflict of interest, 102
  giving information, 90–91, 92
  inaccuracies and distortions, 94
  interpreters prodding speakers, 87, 88
  intervention decision, 78–80
  Martin Bryant, 86
  Muammar Al-Gaddafi, 84
  road rage incident, 86–87
  South Korean murder case, 78
Categorical imperative principle, 6
Channel, communication, *37*, 38, *38*
Chartered Institute of Linguists (CIOL), 67, 137
Cheetham, Graham, 17
CHIA (California Health Interpreting Association), 32
Children, 25
Childress, James F., 10, 113
Chivers, Geoffrey E., 17
Chomsky, Noam, 38
Chun yung, 9
CIOL (Chartered Institute of Linguists), 67, 137
Cipher, 32
Civility, 7
Clergy, 17
Clients, *see* People (clients)
Coady, Margaret, xxix
Code of Ethics for Interpreters in Medical Settings, xxx
Codes of conduct, 58–63
  codes of ethics and, xxx; *see also* Codes of ethics
  common areas of concern, 59–62
    conflict of interest, 61
    impartiality, 59–60
    privacy and confidentiality, 61–62
  overview, 58–59

Codes of ethics, 51–58
  codes of conduct and, xxx; *see also* Codes of conduct
  compliance
    introduction, 107–112
    need of oath/affirmation, 119–122
    use of personality measures, 122–125
    value of moral self-understanding, 112–119
  ethical behaviour, xxxiii–xxxvi
  Hippocratic Oath, xxix, 52
  overview, 51–54
  purpose and scope, xxxi–xxxiii
  shortcomings, 54–58
  significance, xxix, 52
  UN Police, 21
Cognitive rationalisation, 114–115
Colby, A., 5
Collins Dictionary, 16
Collins, Gary G., 124
Collste, Göran, 10
Communication, 32, 36–40, 41–42
Communication facilitator, xxxii
Competence, 80–96
  content revision, 82–87
  giving advice, opinion or information, 88–93
  inaccuracies and distortions, 93–96
  interpreters prodding speakers, 87–88
  linguistic, 43, 67, 93
  overview, 80–82
  professional, 67
  as standard, 66, 67
  subject, 67
Compliance
  introduction, 107–112
  need of oath/affirmation, 119–122
  use of personality measures, 122–125
  value of moral self-understanding, 112–119
Comprehension, 46
Conduit model, xxxii, 74
Conduit of communication, 32
Confidentiality, 61–62, 66, 67, 103–105
Conflict of interest, 61, 67, 101–103
Confucianism, 9
Confucius (Kong, Fuzi), 9
Consequences, 4
Consequentialist ethics, 3
Cooperativeness, 7
Courage, 7
Courteousness, 7

Index

Cowie, Moira, 31
Craftsmen, 26
Credat emptor, 29, 48, 118, 131
Credence, 29, 48, 118, 131
Cruess, Richard, 19
Cruess, Sylvia R., 19
Cultural clarifiers, 32
Cultural mediators, 32
Cultural relativism, xxxv
Cultures
  common, 37, 39, 47
  languages and, 41

D

Dael, Ruud van, 31
Davids, Cindys, 61
Decision-making
  ethical, 2, 10, 12, 114, 116, 36
  moral force, 20
  professional, 22
Decisions, autonomous, 23, 42
Declaration of Geneva (1948), 52
Defining interest, xxxi, 20, 39, 114, 116–117
Demeanour, 67
Deontological ethics, 3–4
Deontology, 6–7
Dependability, 7
Detachment, professional, 66
Development, professional, 67
Dharma, 10
Die Hard, 42
Dignity, 67
Discretion, xxvi, 111–112
Distortions, 93–96
Distrust, ethics of, 117
Doctor–patient relationship, 20, 28
Doctors, 18, 26, 29, 51, 52
Dr. Death, *see* Shipman, Harold
Drew, Paul, 43, 129
Dual relationships, 101
Du Barré v. Livette (1791), 104
du Parcq, Baron (Herbert du Parcq), 17
Dyer, Allen, 53
Dynamic equivalence, 33

E

Elias-Bursać, Ellen, 96, 99
Elliot, Kevin A., 5, 114
Empathy, 13, 97–98

Engineers, 51
Entrusted person, 105
Equality, 12, 41
Ethical behaviour, xxxiii–xxxvi
Ethical decision making, 2, 10, 12, 114, 116, 36
Ethical dilemmas, 3, 8, 11, 20, 53
Ethical issues, xxv–xxvii, 3
Ethical theories
  contemporary, 10–13
  deontology, 6–7
  eastern approaches, 8–10
  normative, 3–8
  overview, 3–4
  traditional, 1–8
  utilitarianism, 3, 4–5
  virtue ethics, 4, 7–8
Ethics
  applied, 2, 10–11
  biomedical, 10–11
  cultural relativism, xxxv
  definition, xxxiv, 1
  deontological, 3–4
  of distrust, 117
  feelings and, xxxv
  meta-, 1–2
  morality and, 2–3
  normative, 2
  overarching frameworks, 56
  personal, 53–54
  professional, *see* Professional ethics
  theories, *see* Ethical theories
Ethics of distrust, 117
Ethics of justice, 12–13
Ethnic background, 95
European Association for Legal Interpreters and Translators (EULITA), 67
European Code of Police Ethics, 21
Euthanasia, xxvi–xxvii, 3, 6
Evidence Act (1995), 120
Evidence Act (2008), 120
Excellence, 66

F

Fair conduct, 67
Fairness, 7, 12, 60
Fédération Internationale de Football Association (FIFA), xxvi
Fidelity, 114, 118
Fiduciary, definition, 48
Fiduciary relationship, xxviii, 59, 118

FIFA (Fédération Internationale de Football Association), xxvi
Firefighters, 29
Fisher, Mary Alice, 60
Flanagan, Owen, 13
Freckelton, Ian, 51
Freidson, Eliot, 20
Friendliness, 7
Fullinwider, Robert, xxvii, xxxi, 19, 35, 114
Fullinwider's schema
   overview
      application to interpreters and translators, 35–36
      characteristics, 19–20
      people may be vulnerable during the practice of the profession, 25–27, 47–49
      possessing special knowledge and training, 22–25, 40–47
      serving the public good, 20–22, 36–40

G

Gaddafi, Muammar Al-, 84
Gaio vs. The Queen (1961), 40
Gamez, Ana M., 124
Gaukroger, Stephen, 96
Gautama, Siddhārtha, 9
Gentile, Adolfo, 76
Gerver, David, 32
GFK Verein, 29
Gibbons, John, 91
Gibbs, J., 5
Gift giving, xxxv–xxxvi
Gile, Daniel, 46
Gold Rush, 34
González, Roseann Dueñas, 33
Google Translate, 42
Groundwork for the Metaphysics of Morals (1785/1998), 6
Guðjónsson, Gísli, 72
Gum syndrome, 32

H

Hale, Sandra Beatriz, 35, 59
Haworth, Kate, 72
Heilbrun, Kirk, 60
Hendley, Kathryn, 60
Heydon, Georgina, 123
Hinduism, 10
Hippocratic Oath, xxix, 52

Honesty, 7, 57
Horsburgh, Dorothy, 2
Houser, Rick, 53, 54
Hughes, Everett C., 22
Hughes, Jonathan, xxvii, 48, 54

I

Identities, 115–116
Impartiality
   attitudinal, 97–98
   ethics of justice and, 12
   interactional, 99–101
   linguistic, 98–99
   preexisting relationship with police and, 96–101
      attitudinal, 97–98
      interactional, 99–101
      linguistic, 98–99
      overview, 96–97
   professional ethics, 59–60
   as standard characteristic, 67
Inaccuracies, 93–96
Industriousness, 7
Information transfer principle, 40, 70
Inghilleri, Moira, 113
Insurance agents, 29
Integrity, 68
Interactional impartiality, 99–101
Interest, defining, xxxi, 20, 39, 114, 116–117
International Association of Conference Interpreters (AIIC), xxx, 35
International Criminal Tribunal for the former Yugoslavia, 75, 99
Interpretation, 31, 32
Interpreters and translators
   attributes, 132
   Chinese, 83, 95
   clients' expectations, 117
   description, 32
   desirable skills, 41
   Fullinwider's schema; *see also* Fullinwider's schema
      overview, 35–36
      people may be vulnerable as a result of the practice of the professional, 47–49
      performance for the public good, 36–40
      possessing special knowledge and training, 40–47
   fundamental skill, 76

Index 153

gum syndrome, 32
introduction to professional ethics, 65–68
issues, 108–110, *110*, *111*, 112
as linguistic conduit, xxxii
medical settings, xxx
most effective, 76
need of oath/affirmation, 119–122
primary or preexisting relationship, 69–80
  between police and suspects/witnesses, 71–80
  overview, 69–71
  prodding speakers, 87–88
  role, xxxii, 31–35, 38
  service-oriented role, 76
Intervention, unjustified, 77
An Introduction to the Principles of Morals and Legislation (1789), 4

J

Jackson, Kathryn, 13
Jakobson, Roman, 42
Janzen, Terry, 118
Johnston, Sharon, 19
Judges, 60, 65, 68, 99, 108, 120
Judicial College (Australia), 65
Justice, 7, 11, 12–13, 57

K

Kant, Immanuel, xxvii, 6
Kaplan, Leslie S., 22
Kaufman, Irving R., 53
Keith-Spiegel, Patricia, 58
Kenyon, 1st Baron (Lloyd Kenyon), 104
Knowledge, 22–25, 40–47
Kohlberg, L., 5
Kong, Fuzi (Confucius), 9
Koocher, Gerald 58
Korpiniski, Donna, 118
Kuusela, Oskari, 10

L

Lai, Miranda, xxxvii, 123
Langer, Ellen, xxxv
Langford, Glenn, 18
Language
  assistance, 16, 39, 48, 72–77
  barriers, xxviii, 38

common, 37, 39, 47, 70, 72, 88, 115
in communication, 36–40, 37, *38*
machine, 32
source (SL), 33, 93
special knowledge and training, 41–47
speech features, 46, 73
target (TL), 33, 82, 118
Language assistance, 16, 39, 48, 72–77
Language barriers, xxviii, 38
Language machine, 32
Laster, K., xxx, xxxii, 41, 52, 54, 65, 72, 73, 80, 88, 95, 103, 108, 113, 119, 120
Latimer, Paul, 48
Latitude, discretionary, 73
Law, 16, 17, 23–24, 107, 128
Law Institute of Victoria (LIV), 56
Law of obligations, 23
Lawyers, 21, 26, 29, 59, 88–89
Lectures in Jurisprudence, 71
Legal professional privilege, breach of, 104
LEP (Limited English Proficiency), 83–84
Li, 9
Lieberman, Myron, 18
Limited English Proficiency (LEP), 83–84
Linguistic impartiality, 98–99
LIV (Law Institute of Victoria), 56
Longman Dictionary of Contemporary English, xxxiv
Longstaff, Simon, xxx

M

MacVean, Allyson, 19, 26
Magistrates, 65
The Maitland Daily Mercury Australia, 95
Maume, Philipp, 48
McGurk, Barry J., 71
McGurk, Debra, 71
Mediation, 60
Medicine, 17, 24, 107
Medium of communication, 32
Megret, Frédéric, 60
Melia, Kath M., 2
Merkel, Angella, 46
Merriam–Webster Dictionary, xxviii
Message, 36, *37*, *38*
Message clarifier, 32
Message converter, 32
Message language, *38*
Meta-ethics, 1–2
Metropolitan Police (London), 21, 59, 67, 69, 72, 89, 91, 102, 121

Metselaar, Carolein, 31
Mikkelson, Holly, 33
Miller, Seumas, xxxi, 3, 21, 23, 25, 62, 104
Mill, John Stuart, xxvii
Milne, Becky, 71
Minnesota Multiphanic Personality Inventory-Revised (MMPI-2), 124
Mizzoni, John, xxxvi, 4, 6
MMPI-2 (Minnesota Multiphanic Personality Inventory-Revised), 124
Moderation, 7
Moral autonomy, 114
Morality; *see also* Ethical theories
 ethics and, 2–3
 internal, 117
 personal, 122
Moral self-understanding, 112–119
Mulayim, Sedat, xxxvii, 123
Muraskin, Roslyn, 2

N

Napier, Jermina, 41, 47
National Council on Interpreting in Health Care (NCIHC), xxx, 32
National Register of Public Service Interpreters (NRPSI), 109, *110*, *111*
Nature, need-centered, 12
NCIHC, *see* National Council on Interpreting in Health Care (NCIHC)
Negligence, 23–24
NEO Personality Inventory-Revised (NEO-PI-R), 124
NESB (Non-English-speaking background), 26, 40
Neukrug, Edward S., 54
New Centurion police officer, 19
New Jersey Supreme Court Task Force, 108
New York State Unified Court System, 68, 120
Neyroud, Peter, 19, 26, 57
Nida, Eugene Albert, 33
Nirvana, 9
Niska, H., 40, 70
Noble Eightfold Path, 9
Noise, 37, 38
Non-consequentialist approach, 3, 4
Non-consequentialist ethics, 3–4
Non-English-speaking background (NESB), 26, 40
Nonmaleficence, 10, 57
Normative ethical theories, 3–8

Normative ethics, 2
NRPSI, *see* National Register of Public Service Interpreters (NRPSI)
Nurses, 29, 51

O

Oath/affirmation, 119–122
 Hippocratic Oath, xxix, 52
Oaths Act (1867), 120
Objectivity, 12, 66
Obligations, 9
O'Connor, Tom, 97
O'Day, Rosemary, 17
Office of Police Integrity (Australia), 21
O'Neill, Martin, 71
Overarching frameworks, 56
Owings, William A., 22
Oxford Dictionary, 27
Oxford English Dictionary, xxvi, 36, 93
Ozolins, Uldis, 66, 68

P

PAI (Personality Assessment Inventory), 124
Pane of glass, 33
Parker, Richard, 61
Parsons, Richard D., xxxiv, 62, 76, 81, 95, 101, 115
Patient advocate, 32
Patten, Ben, 17
Peel, Sir Robert (2nd Baronet), 21
Pellegrino, Edmund D., xxviii, 27, 28, 73, 117
People (clients)
 children, 25
 deaf, 47
 with disability, 26
 disordered, 26
 entrusted person, 105
 expectations from interpreters, 117
 issues with interpreters, 108–110, *110*, *111*, 112
 mentally ill, 26
 non-English-speaking background (NESB), 26, 40
 preexisting relationship with police, 71–80
  competence, 80–96
  conflict of interest, 101–103
  impartiality, 96–101
  intervention decision, 77–80

Index

language assistance, 72–77
overview, 71–72
privacy and confidentiality, 103–105
vulnerability during professional practice, 25–27, 47–49
young, 37
Personal ethics, 53–54
Personal identities, 115–116
Personality Assessment Inventory (PAI), 124
Personality measures, 122–125
Pharmacists, 29
Pittaro, Michael, 123
Plato, xxvii, 7
Police; *see also* Professionals
Bobby, 19
code of ethics, 21, 57
interviews, 43–45
New Centurion, 19
notion, 26, 71
policing styles, 19
preexisting relationship, 71–80
competence, 80–96
conflict of interest, 101–103
impartiality, 96–101
intervention decision, 77–80
language assistance, 72–77
overview, 71–72
privacy and confidentiality, 103–105
Professional, 19
trust ratings, 29
Uniform Carrier, 19
Politicians, xxv, 29
Pollock, Jocelyn A., 5, 114
Postmodern ethics, 11
Powell, Martine B., 25
Preston, Noel, xxxii, xxxiv, 18, 55, 61, 73, 102, 113, 114
Privacy, 62, 105
Professional activity, characteristics, 28
Professional autonomy, 23
Professional detachment, 66
Professional development, 67
Professional ethics
definition, xxxii, 53
fairness, 60
interpreters and translators; *see also* Interpreters and translators
introduction, 65–68
primary or preexisting relationship, 69–80
personal ethics and, 53–54

Professionalisation, xxix
Professionalism, 68
Professional judgement, 67
Professional police officer, 19
Professional privilege, legal, 104
Professionals, 19, 25–27, 47–49; *see also* Police
Professional trust, 29
Professional trustworthiness, 117
Profession of words, xxxii
Professions
characteristics
Barber's, 16
Cheetham and Chivers', 17–18
Fullinwider's, 19–27; *see also* Fullinwider's schema
Lieberman's, 18–19
defining, 16–27, 34
defining interest, 20, 116–117
interest, xxvii, xxviii
introduction, 15–16
learned, xxix
Middle Ages, 17
moral purpose, xxvii, xxviii, 20, 117
Preston's criteria, 18
primary, xxix
public perception, 17
trust and professionals, 27–29
Protocol, 67
Public good, 20–22, 36–40
Public identities, 116
Public perception, 17
Public servants, 51
Punishment, capital, 3, 4–5

R

Rachels, James, xxx, 74
Rationality, 12, 13
Reasonableness, 7
Receiver/decoder, 36, *37*, 38
Reiner, Robert, 19
Ren, 9
Respect, 67
Respectful regard, 29
Responsibility, 57
Responsibleness, xxx, 67
Rittel, Horst W. J., 111, 112
Roberts, Roda, 32
Rotter, Julian B., 28
Routman, Regie, 29
Roy, Cynthia, 43, 70, 73

Rudd, Kevin, 46
Rudvin, Mette, 115
Ryan, Kevin, 8

S

Sapir, Edward, 41
Schramm's model of communication, *37*
Schramm, Wilbur, 37, 39
Schweda-Nicholson, Nancy, 68, 70, 85, 99, 108
Screening tests, 124
Self-confidence, 7
Self-control, 7
Self-discipline, 7
Self-reliance, 7
Sender/encoder, 36, *37*, 38
Šešel, Vojislav, 99
Setzer, Valdemar W., xxxv
Shannon, Claude, 37, 39
Shepherd, Eric, 74, 89
Shipman, Harold, 57
Shuttleworth, Mark, 31
Simple identification, 101
SL (Source Language), 33, 93
Smith, Adam, 71
Smith, Huston, 9
Snyder, Nancy, 58
Socrates, xxvii
Sokolowski, Robert, 16, 28
Solidarity, 67
Source Language (SL), 33
South Australian Register, 34
Speakers, 36, *37*, 38
Specialised training, 22–25, 40–47
Special knowledge, 22–25, 40–47
Speech features, 46, 73
Speicher-Dubin, B., 5
Standard Operating Procedures (2007), 69, 72, 89, 91, 102, 121
Sternberg, Robert J., xxxiv, 108
Stewardship, 57
Suspects, preexisting relationship with police, 71–80
  competence, 80–96
  conflict of interest, 101–103
  impartiality, 96–101
  intervention decision, 77–80
  language assistance, 72–77
  overview, 71–72
  privacy and confidentiality, 103–105

T

Taber, Charles Russell, 33
Tao, 9
Taoism, 9
Target Language (TL), 33, 82, 118
Tasmania Law Reform Institute, 25
Taylor, V., xxx, xxxii, 41, 52, 54, 65, 72, 73, 81, 88, 95, 103, 108, 113, 119, 120
Teachers, 18, 29
Tein, Charles, 95
Thompson, Ian E., 2
TIPS (Translator Interpreter Personality Screening), 124
TL (Target Language), 33, 82, 118
Tolerance, 7
Tookie, *see* Williams, Stanley 'Tookie'
Torres Strait Islanders, 25
Tort law, 23–24
Tradesmen, 26
Training, specialised, 22–25, 40–47
Transference, 101
Translator Interpreter Personality Screening (TIPS), 124
Translators, *see* Interpreters and translators
Trust; *see also* Fullinwider's schema
  beginning, xix–xx, xxviii
  breach of, *see* Confidentiality
  credat emptor, 29, 48, 118, 131
  definition, 27
  fidelity, 114
  fiduciary relationship and, xxviii, xxxvi, 59, 118
  interpersonal, 28–29
  language assistance, 74–76
  professional, 29
  professional activity requirements, 28
  professionals and, 27–29
Trustworthiness, professional, 117

U

Uniform Carrier police officer, 19
UN Police code of ethics, 21
Utilitarianism, 3, 4–5
Utility principle, 4

V

Value of Moral Self-Understanding in Compliance, 112
Van Beek, Mick, xxvi

Index

Vásquez, Victoria F., 33
Viaggio, Sergio, 33
Victorian Criminal Proceedings Manual, 65
Virtue ethics, 4, 7–8
Virtues
    essential, 7
    profession-specific, xxxi

W

Wadensjö, Cecilia, 33
Waldron, Jeremy, 22
Warren, Samuel, 61
Webb, Beatrice, 16
Webber, Melvin M., 112
Webb, Sidney, 16
Weber, Melvin M., 111
Weiss, Paul, 3
West, Robin, 12
Why accuracy, 75
Wickedness concept, 111–112
Williams, Stanley 'Tookie,' 6–7
Wilson, Paul Alexander, 25

Witnesses, preexisting relationship
    with police, 71–80
    competence, 80–96
    conflict of interest, 101–103
    impartiality, 96–101
    intervention decision, 77–80
    language assistance, 72–77
    overview, 71–72
    privacy and confidentiality, 103–105
Working with Interpreters in the Courtroom, 68, 120
World Medical Association, 52
Wueste, Daniel E., 47, 53
Wu wei, 9

Y

Yeschke, Charles L., 72
Yin–yang, 9

Z

Zaner, Richard M., 29, 48, 117, 131